ROSE-TINTED SUMMER

The Dressing Room Diary

by Joe Sayers

**In the 150th Anniversary Year of
Yorkshire County Cricket Club**

Pictures by SWpix.com
Vaughn Ridley, Alex Whitehead and Simon Wilkinson
Yorkshire County Cricket Club
and Joe Sayers

GREAT N ORTHERN

Great Northern Books
PO Box 213, Ilkley, LS29 9WS
www.greatnorthernbooks.co.uk

© Joseph Sayers, 2013

ISBN: 978-0-9576399-5-9

Design and layout: David Burrill

Photography: SWpix.com
Vaughn Ridley, Alex Whitehead
and Simon Wilkinson
Yorkshire County Cricket Club
and Joe Sayers

CIP Data
A catalogue for this book is available
from the British Library

To my wife, Lisa

CONTENTS

PREFACE

International Perspectives of Yorkshire

The County of Yorkshire is embedded with the game of cricket. This was something I first realised when I arrived from over the Pennines as an eight year old boy. Immediately struck by the power and strength of the White Rose, I remember my excitement of the County Club playing a first class fixture at Abbeydale Park, the home of my local Club, Sheffield Collegiate CC. Walking into the dressing room and picking up the cap of Ian Botham, who was playing in the game, remains one of my most vivid cricketing memories.

From the time I represented Yorkshire schoolboys at the age of 11, the County and its people have been a central part of my life. There is a discipline about Yorkshire folk that I love, a certain smartness and, above all, a definite will to win.

As a Yorkshire player, you know where you stand. There is a straight talking nature about the Club, the captain, his team and the watching members. And every player knows he is the custodian of a Club steeped in history, a past that hits you square in the face on taking your first step inside the ground. Memories of past successes eek out of walls adorned with portraits of the County Club's greats.

But we should not be too focussed upon the past. The current crop of Yorkshire players promises a bright future for the Club, a future graced by home-grown talent developing into the Test arena and winning trophies for Club and Country. As it always has, the Club continues to produce cricketers of international quality and is perfectly capable of creating a Yorkshire team that can dominate the domestic game in the years to come.

Past and present Yorkshire players are spoken about more than any other County players around the country. They are representatives of a world-renowned cricket club, one with more tradition and heritage than any other, and invariably more talking points. They play in a stadium that must embrace the need to be ever-changing in its environment. And they must do the same, creating a cricketing legacy of which the County can be proud.

Congratulations to my former team mate Joe Sayers in producing Rose-tinted Summer: The Dressing Room Diary. It is, and forever will be, an insightful and valuable snapshot in history of the inner sanctum of the greatest club in the cricketing world. Enjoy your step inside the Yorkshire dressing room.

Best wishes,
Michael Vaughan OBE

It's a huge honour to be asked to put pen to paper and write something for Joe Sayers' excellent and thought-provoking book *Rose-Tinted Summer*. Joe gives an honest and detailed account of the 150th anniversary season of Yorkshire CCC which is a club that I owe a lot more to than I gave. Yorkshire would not be the great club that it has become over 150 years but for the loyalty shown by all who have served it in whatever form.

I loved my time up North and the Club instantly made it feel like a second home when I walked through the doors for the first time in 1997. I might add that I was sporting long hair and a beard and I was made to take that off very quickly!

The people involved in the Club throughout my playing days there, from Sir Lawrence Byford, to Colin Graves, are etched in my memory for ever and the times I shared on and off the field are fantastic memories for me and all of my family. I hope you all enjoyed the way we played and which culminated in the fantastic Championship success of 2001.

Who could ever forget the fall of that last Glamorgan wicket in Scarborough and for David Byas, on his home ground, to lift the trophy for the first time in 33 years?

It was a proud moment for all Yorkshire people and the support we have had over the years is unbelievable.

Yorkshire folk are passionate and friendly as well as being as close to the Aussie temperament as it is possible to get. I love the way all of the county get behind the players on and off the field, especially when battling against their arch rivals with the Red Rose (I won't mention them by name as I remember copping so much abuse from them over the years).

Thank-you also, Yorkshire, on behalf of my whole family, for looking after us so well during our time with you. You are all special people and I am indebted to you for the life

you gave me and the family along the way.

I even married a Yorkshire girl and have a brother-in-law from Yorkshire so I feel very much a part of the county.

The playing side for me was enjoyable to the nth degree with a lot of highlights. Apart from the trophies, some of the most treasured moments from a personal point of view would be my 255 against the Red Rose and the 339 against Durham at Headingley in my last innings.

To play with so many legends and to speak with so many greats throughout the years allowed me to grow as a person and play international cricket along the way.

Another huge honour was to captain the county and this remains one of the highlights of my career.

I hope all of you continue to have a great time and get the results you deserve under my great mate Dizzy! He loves being a part of the family and you have looked after him so well.

Congratulations once again, Joe, on the book and I hope it is the success that it deserves to be.

Best wishes,
Darren (Boof) Lehmann.

INTRODUCTION

A sense of perspective

Jogging around the boundary rope at the Stretford End, I knew something was wrong. There were two hours until the first over of the 2009 Roses Championship match at Old Trafford, and it was clear I was in no fit state to play. My legs felt heavy beyond familiar levels of training stiffness, my breathing was short and my chest wheezed with fatigue. A Pennine rambler would have overtaken me with comfort.

The ten months that followed were as surreal as they were concerning for my family, friends, teammates and doctors. Days and weeks were blurred into one by endless spells of the deepest sleep that offered no refreshment. Medical tests of various descriptions came and went, nudging me slowly towards that final diagnosis of Post Viral Fatigue by process of elimination. And in truth, the thought of once again being able to play cricket held little hope. At that time, a climb up the stairs at home without a pause for breath was challenge enough.

So on that sunny April day at Worcester, that most archetypal of English County grounds, it was with great relief and withheld emotion that I walked to the crease to begin Yorkshire's Championship season of 2010. My footwork was rusty, my concentration in need of practice, but I was back, with a newfound sense of perspective and utter appreciation of the enjoyment of being a professional sportsman.

And so it is through this lens that I write this book, the official account of the sesquicentennial year in the history of the world's most famous cricket club. A cricketing year attracting great hope and expectation like any other preceding it; a strengthening and very real romance in anticipation of what may be; but no guarantee. That simultaneous unpredictability and promise seduces us all from the bleak winter months and early morning Test match highlights from sunnier climes and leads us on a summer's journey of highs, lows and parts in between.

Rose-tinted Summer will chart this journey through my eyes as one of the County Club's players. And though the year ahead will test as much as it rewards, I intend to record the ride in its fullest. For Yorkshire County Cricket Club is rightly a club of renowned heritage and a celebrated past. But it is also going somewhere, a place it has not been before in so many ways, led by people with as much passion for its success as those custodians gone before us. One hundred and fifty years after its formation on the site of Sheffield's Crucible, this is the story of a Yorkshire team's endeavours to celebrate a glorious past by making the very best of its daily present.

Club President Geoffrey Boycott presents the Sesquicentennial Soiree at The Crucible Theatre.

CHAPTER ONE

Winter Tales

A Sheffield Soiree

On a dark, dismal January evening in Sheffield, last year's so-called summer of cricket seems a distant memory. The festive excesses have come and gone and though the early days of the new season are still some months away, for the hardened followers of Yorkshire County Cricket Club, you might say the cricketing year has begun.

And no ordinary cricketing year either. For the coming together of the County's members and most famous faces on this wintry south Yorkshire night marks the launch of the Club's Sesquicentennial Anniversary. To you and me, that is the commemoration of 150 long and eventful years of Yorkshire cricket since the County Club's inauguration in 1863. So on the very same site of that formation, today occupied by The Crucible Theatre of snooker fame, the great and good of White Rose cricket huddled into a darkened auditorium to mark the occasion.

The sight of a complimentary pie and pea supper on arrival could not have been more welcome after a coach trip lasting over two and half hours through the rush hour traffic. First XI coach Jason Gillespie, our physio Scot McAllister and I smiled knowingly as our delayed departure from Headingley prompted ironic cheers from the paying members near the front of the coach.

Harry Gration MC's a chat with Geoffrey Boycott, Michael Vaughan and Andrew Gale at the Sesquicentennial Soiree.

Suitably wined and dined, no sooner had I taken my seat than the lights had dropped and into the auditorium spotlight walked the unmistakable figure of Geoffrey Boycott. Even at the most challenging of times, followers of Yorkshire cricket know how Geoffrey maintains an irrepressible presence. But this evening, sporting a commemorative sesquicentennial blazer, pinstriped in Cambridge blue and gold, he stood that much taller, oozing the pride and confidence for which he is renowned.

The audience indulged in talk of the dominance of Yorkshire cricket and the modest resolve of its custodians. The feats of Bob Appleyard through extreme adversity and the consistent brilliance of George Hirst raised the eyebrows of Moin Ashraf, sat beside me in the stalls. "200 wickets in a season?!" he said with newfound perspective of his recent on-field successes.

Guest speakers came and went, and Geoffrey interjected with tales of his own, all strengthening the mood of common cause in the audience. How good it was to feel part of something, to give in to the romance of the evening, even if it was at times a little rose-tinted. Surely that is what a Club is really about?

I took my seat alongside Jack Brooks and Andrew Hodd, two relative newcomers to the playing staff. "What must they be making of proceedings?" I thought. With respect to their previous counties, surely neither Northampton nor Brighton played host to such orchestrated celebration of years gone by?

The soiree concluded, members left lifted by tales of Fred Trueman, Len Hutton and Brian Close and with appetites whetted for sunnier days and Yorkshire cricket on show. Unsurprisingly, talk of County Championship silverware in the anniversary year was not far away. If not optimistic, certainly premature on this dank January night. One thing was for sure, however; the cricketing year had begun.

Behind closed doors

With the ever-increasing congestion of domestic and International playing schedules, the off-season months for a County cricketer have become an important period of preparation, rehabilitation and planning. Long gone are the days of returning to a County ground when the daffodils begin to flower. Rather, the first day of November marks the start of a new campaign with one eye on the following spring and beyond. For those players not travelling to warmer climes for winter tours, it also signals the start of a training programme of indoor net practices and fitness sessions.

It is the last week of January and the car park at Headingley is white with snow. The winter weather put pay to Monday's training this week and stranded Adam 'Budgie' Lyth in his home town of Whitby for three days, much to the amusement, and certain scepticism, of some of his team mates. Poor old 'Budge' was left helpless with many of the roads from the East Coast closed, but seeing an opportunity for some early-morning banter to liven an otherwise mundane warm-up, Messrs Gale and Patterson are having none of it.

"You're telling me they were lettin' NO ONE outta' Whitby fo' THREEEE days Budge?" came the question from the skipper.

If Gale were the Police Inspector and Lyth the man in custody, Budgie's lawyer would by now be asking for "a moment with his client". There were holes aplenty in his tales of snowbound life by the East Coast. Joking aside, any temptation to look too far ahead to the County season is tempered with one look outside of the East Stand windows.

There is plenty of time for Lythy to perfect those signature off-drives before the season, methinks.

Having said that, the past month has seen the now typical build up towards pre-season mode as we know it. Those long and lean members we call the bowlers have begun their annual quota of deliveries with competitions of "Yorker Golf" – a simple target bowling drill, as the name suggests, in which a delivery successfully bowled at yorker length suitably scores a "birdie". Meanwhile, the whirring and coughing of the bowling machines has restarted for the batsmen as each revisits the technical basics under the coaches' supervision. Until we board the plane to Barbados for our pre-season tour in eight weeks' time, the white-washed indoor nets in the East Stand at Headingley will house our preparation for the coming summer.

And what a strange and somewhat surreal existence it is to be a County cricketer at this time of year. 'Working' days often begin after the commuters' rush-hour and end in time for a late lunch, and the training in between, though physically taxing to our respective limits at times, bears no comparison to the demands of a proper day's work. At this time of year, I cannot help but feel fortunate to make a living as a professional cricketer. Roll on summer, by all means, but the pleasures of working on my game, bat in hand, and feeling daily improvements, is something I have always enjoyed.

To be frank, an element of the job I have found less fulfilling is the fitness testing and training. The modern game is faster and more powerful than ever, requiring fitter and stronger athletes to showcase the skills required, so there is no denying that a disciplined approach to fitness training is vital for an attempt at summer silverware. However, the importance of pushing one's physical limits does not make the practice of it any more enjoyable or less painful.

So as some batsmen and bowlers go about their cricketing ways within netted corridors, others put down their bats and pick up dumbbells and medicine balls inside the mirrored walls of the East Stand gym. The batsmen outside the gym door could be forgiven for losing their concentration, for the iPod playlist from inside the gym could probably be heard, and not necessarily enjoyed, on St. Michael's Lane. Inside the gym, Strength and Conditioning Coach, Tom Summers, overlooks and instructs the players in exercises of increasing complexity. There is little doubt in the fact that this is a Yorkshire squad building new levels of fitness and training discipline.

The Wizard on Wheels

Today's net session prompted some thought about the latest addition to the laws of the one-day game, recently introduced into international matches overseas. Bowling to me in the East Stand indoor nets was our ever reliable and highly talented Merlyn. Not a new signing kept under wraps, you understand; rather, a programmable spin bowling machine capable of replicating "The Gatting Ball" on request.

With Merlyn in off-spin mode, Director of Professional Cricket Martyn Moxon presents me with a target run chase with field placings set to meet the game's newest law change. Namely, the requirement to have a further fielder within the inner fielding circle in the non-power play overs. For a spinner, having four fielders in the inner ring was previously seen as relatively comfortable, choosing to have five somewhat of a gamble or sign of confidence. On that basis, the new law may not appear to enforce much change. But today's practice is suggesting otherwise.

For Merlyn and his feeder, Martyn, bowling off-spin to my left-handed self, the obvious fifth inner ring fielder is mid-on, brought in from long-on, where he would previously have been when the laws required just four fielders in the inner ring. Stay with me here - I realise this is getting a bit technical. With the ball turning away from the bat, having mid-on up in the inner ring presents me with a question of chosen risk. Should I choose the traditional options of scoring areas, generally hitting with the spin or sweeping the ball of good length? Or should I take the carrot offered by the new laws and attempt a boundary against the spin over or past the mid-on fielder?

This analysis summarises a conundrum that may become commonplace for middle order batsmen this season. And the result may be higher average run rates from the success of batsmen taking advantage, and/or the rise in wickets taken by the better spinners tempting batsmen into higher risk options and coming out on top. "I love it", confirms the ever-competitive off-spinner Azeem Rafiq when asked about the law change. Whilst other bowlers curse a game moving the goalposts in the batsman's favour, this key figure in our one-day plans has a typically positive view. "If I keep spinning the ball, it's an opportunity for me to take more wickets".

It is certainly a scenario worth practising, particularly with such valuable equipment as the Merlyn machine at our disposal. Maybe today will come in handy in a key moment in our one-day season? And yes, against all MCC advice of playing with the spin, I pulled off a somewhat unsightly bunt over mid-on to win this imaginary contest. Sayers 1, Merlyn 0.

Bat versus Ball

With February comes a progression in training to our first taste of bat versus ball. Bowling workloads are managed and monitored to such an extent these days – and rightly so – that we batsmen do not get our first look at our battery of bowlers until this time of year. So today's net session was the closest simulation of the match play challenges to come in a number of weeks. Bowling machines placed aside and the distracting gym music conspicuous by its absence, I had the whiles of Patterson and Brooks with which to contend.

For me, the enjoyment in this transition to typical net practice lies in the opportunity to simulate the rhythms and mental routines of an over faced out in the middle, and to venture into that most important inner world of focus and concentration. Previous weeks' work had involved the repetition of technical grooving, the two-way conversation between batsman and coach, constant feedback, criticism and review. With that work banked, it is often refreshing to begin the practice of batting, not merely as an exercise in technical proficiency, but as a means of scoring runs, occupying the crease and neutralising attack. It is refreshing

to escape into that inner world no coach can touch, where one is alone in one's thoughts and in charge of one's approach. From my experience, batting is so much about that place in which you find yourself, the present moment, how you feel and how those feelings allow you to move. As my fellow opening partner for Yorkshire at the time, Michael Vaughan, once said, batting "...is about where your head is". Giving Vaughany credit where it is due, I think his was a reference to so much more than just technique.

So on this Monday morning in February, 40 minutes of batting against Steve Patterson and Jack Brooks is that refreshing escape and one step closer to walking to the middle to take guard on the first morning of a Championship match. It is also my first chance to see Brooks, our new signing from Northamptonshire, at close hand, at least since our only previous encounter – a floodlit T20 match at Northampton two years ago.

First impressions of Brooksy cannot ignore that signature Bjorg-like headband, a different colour by the day. (Surely those of a commercial mind behind the scenes should be planning the sale of replica headbands by the hundred this summer, aimed at energetic youths or tipsy students in the stands?). Joking aside, our new signing also appears to be a strong athlete – unbeaten in sprints tests so far – and a durable character, both essential qualities in tackling the summer's quota of overs. Bowlers are said to have a "decent wrist" if they can deliver the ball with an unwavering seam position, and Brooksy appears to have that. Fitness permitting, here's hoping Brooksy will prove a valuable addition to the Yorkshire attack.

Stood at the back of the East stand nets is another cricketer once known for flowing locks and headbands, our coach Jason "Dizzy" Gillespie. Now with a slightly greying short back and sides, he observes our net session, taking mental notes and offering compliment in his resonant tone.

During his time as our overseas player five years ago, Dizzy made the key adjustment as a

Clockwise from top left: Dizzy directs a squad training debrief; the essential coach's kit – baseball mitt and practice balls; second XI coach Paul Farbrace talks batting with Andrew Hodd; Iain Wardlaw equipped for an indoor net session

bowler from bowling slightly short of a good length, as is appropriate on flatter Australian wickets, to pitching the ball fuller on a length so as to hit the top of off stump, or the knee-roll of the batsman's pads. This adjustment proved predictably successful, and so it remains a key message to our bowlers and a measure of potential success.

Getting 20 opposition wickets on a regular basis can be the difference between challenging for Championship silverware and scrapping for top flight survival, particularly since the latest change in the points system rewards wins (16 points) and discourages draws (three points). So this ploy of bowling a fuller length gives an attack the greatest possible chance of dismissals, enticing higher-risk drives, giving the ball greater chance to swing and the batsmen less time to adjust. Leg-before and bowled are clear possibilities of dismissal, as well as the obvious others. Those exasperated members shouting from their seats "Bawl at the bloody wickeeets!" were certainly not wrong – bowling is a target-based sport, after all.

As I take stance to face my first delivery from Patto, out of the corner of my eye I see a square of white chalk dust drawn on the synthetic surface in front of me, marking the bowler's target. Surprisingly not much of a distraction for me as it turns out, but a valuable aid for our bowlers.

Fast and true indoor surfaces encourage the quicks to bowl a shorter length that flies through over the stumps, and we batsmen to drive through good length deliveries, such is our trust of the plastic under our feet. But in five weeks time, on our pre-season tour, we will have Caribbean soil under our feet with its natural variations in bounce. As one of the very few of the playing staff flirting with 30, this is a lesson years previous have taught me well. Bouncers and flashing drives may look pretty indoors in February, but preparation for the spring is about so much more than that.

Good morning Herbert

Arriving at Headingley this morning, I park in view of a collage of famous faces to have graced the turf beyond the East Stand in front of me. Behind the famous few is the Club museum, telling the story of cricketing years gone by. Vaughan, Gough and Boycott are accompanied in action by faces less recognisable to the young player of today. Through my windscreen is Herbert Sutcliffe, hands high in backswing and Brylcreemed head of hair moving towards the ball out of shot. His gaze is firmly set and his expression relaxed, exuding the graceful calm of his strokeplay. There is little doubt in the success of the ensuing cover drive.

One cannot help but feel part of something special here at Headingley, with such daily reminders of those custodians gone before. What greater inspiration must a player need on arrival at their "place of work"? And what would the likes of Bill Bowes, Herbert Sutcliffe and George Hirst make of this modern game? Recent developments to the game are clear to see but there is no coincidence that these images of Yorkshire's most successful names display excellence in those technical basics we current players aim to groom today. In so many ways, cricket and its practice is the same game it always was, and will continue to be so, perhaps just with the modern embellishments and commercial razzmatazz we have come to know.

An encouraging part of training for me this week has been the consistency of my bowling. These are early days, admittedly, but the feedback received points positively into pre-season, and opportunity to take the ball more often, perhaps adding another string to my cricketing bow, particularly in the shorter forms. Never have I been part of a Yorkshire squad at this time of year that could combine in so many different ways for the first match of the season in April. And with the prospect of up to four first XI players away with the Test or ODI squads, offering strong contributions with bat, ball and in the field will do my case no harm. Specialism in a single discipline is arguably no longer sufficient, unless it is one of match winning consistency. Players are now required to display skills in at least two disciplines and generally be more flexible. For me, anything that gives me a better chance to play first XI cricket is worth the effort - that is where I want to be.

With Thursday's training passed, my thoughts turn to tomorrow and the weather forecast, for Friday brings the lung-busting venture out of doors to round off the week. There must be some more snow on the way before winter's out..?

To our limits and beyond

It is a blustery Friday morning in February and today the summer's cricket feels some time away. The New Year novelty of squad training has faded somewhat and this morning's session was the toughest of the week. The sight of ten of the team spreadeagled on their backs gasping for breath was proof that this week's Friday blowout was no different from usual. Interval training on the nearby University AstroTurf pitch is never pretty, but needs to be done to attain those all-important fitness levels in four weeks time.

So the coming month will be a firm push towards personal bests in the gym and further efforts to make net sessions a better simulation of match play. In the not-too-distant past, fitness sessions of this morning's intensity would have attracted obvious indifference from senior players not convinced about the Strength and Conditioning revolution taking place. Now, in contrast, there seems to be buy-in not bitterness within a Yorkshire squad with a significantly lower average age. For there is no escaping the fact that the modern game is a faster, higher-impact version of its previous self, requiring strong athletes with cricketing skill, not cricketers sufficient in fitness. But, as a weary Steve Patterson reminded me this morning in one of his moments of pseudo-cynical wisdom, "...if I can't bowl straight in April, it doesn't matter how fast I can run!" I

suppose you can't argue with that.

February and March bring an enjoyable but somewhat false sense of squad unity, I have often thought. Training sessions are physically tough and require team mates to pull each other through, and indoor net practices can never accurately simulate the pressures of competition outdoors. So there is little to challenge the ties between players, to reveal potential conflicts or expose the group's default dynamic in key moments. I have heard it called a honeymoon period for a new set of players, a time when half-day fitness sessions and developmental skills work demands far less of the spirit than the months to follow. Camaraderie on the training field in February is a positive sign, do not miss my point, but equal spirit with our backs against the wall in August is worth so much more.

An unexpected arrival

By mid-February, the naturally repetitive nature of indoor practice begins to take the spring out of the step of a few members of the squad. Most players have by now found some form of rhythm with bat or ball and have one eye on the first chance to get the spikes back on and practice outdoors. Similarly, after four months of gym training for most, fitness programmes are an albeit important means to an end, namely the annual pre-season fitness testing in the first week of March. So any opportunity to break the repetition of routine or inject some energy to proceedings on a winter's morning is snapped up quickly by all.

Despite this, there is one event that excites most players at this time of year, regardless of age or experience: the arrival of the summer's job lot of kit from their respective suppliers. Heads turn as the latest brown box gets dumped in the middle of the dressing room for the expectant recipient. And every dressing room has its most eager individuals when it comes to shiny, unblemished kit straight from the wrapper. Young players and those recently on to the staff understandably enjoy the privilege of hundreds of pounds of bats, gloves and pads on request.

But in the Headingley dressing room, no one competes with Adam "Budgie" Lyth for sheer excitement when it is his name written on that box. Like a child under the Christmas tree, expectant to the point of mumbling his words, Budgie tears off the parcel tape to reveal his new gleaming blade in the middle of the dressing room. "Oooooo, look at this 'un lads, they've sent another belter". Surrounding half-dressed team mates are then treated to a montage of Lythy's signature shots as he tests out the pick-up of his new favourite toy. Eyebrows raise skywards with a smile – this is an annual event, after all.

Only this week, Budgie had a surprise for us. For not only did this magic box reveal what appeared to be a bat pushing the regulations of width, but another similarly long, yet slightly slimmer package that had onlookers perplexed. "What a beauty! They've done it again. Glad I ordered this one", Budgie cried as I turned around, expecting the usual highlights package of cover drives. No Gower-esque flourishes this time, for the mystery package was a brand-new snooker cue sent by his bat suppliers! "Might come in handy when the rain arrives Budge", said one of the lads as warm-up begun.

Pondering life beyond the game

After three months adhering to continuous training programmes, a week away from the nets and gym offers welcome relief and an opportunity to recharge before the run-in to pre-season. Personally, I feel confidence from the progress I have made with bat in hand in recent weeks and, like numerous others in the squad, have one eye firmly set on packing the bags for warmer climes in March. Nonetheless, a week without training has not been without noteworthy event.

With the County staff recuperating at home, Headingley's indoor cricket centre opens its doors to the hundreds of young wannabe professionals attending the Club's half-term coaching courses. So for team mate Rich Pyrah and I, the week has offered the chance to put on our coaching hats and police the tracksuited minions running off the half-term high. "RP" is a long-standing friend of mine and, like me, a cricketer new to fatherhood, so it was good to take time to catch up with his latest news during our lunchbreak between coaching sessions today.

RP's career has presented some life-changing challenges in recent years and a series of severe and unusual injuries that have kept him out of the first class game. The first of these came during a 40-over fixture at Canterbury in 2011, when Rich dislocated his right knee aiming for the boundary in the late overs of our batting innings. More recently, a seemingly innocuous landing whilst fielding in a Championship match last season led to the loss of feeling in his left forearm and fingers, something he was still recovering from as we spoke today. "I have no feeling in these two fingers" he said, holding onto the two outermost fingers on his hand. "And they're not sure I ever will". The grip of his fork is not what it should be.

To his credit, Rich has always been a battler, keen for a challenge and no stranger to adversity. In fact, I would go so far to say he thrives upon the underdog's status, quietly going about his business as the most professional of sportsmen. And over lunch, it was inspiring to listen to him talk with a perspective surely gained from the challenges of recent months. His expression is tired, not only from the pain of injury, but from the unavoidable sleep deprivation that comes with fathering twin daughters. But his outlook is positive and realistic. He knows full well that he has some hard yards ahead of him to reassert himself upon the first class circuit. "I know I can do it", he begins, "and I've got nothin' to lose. But I realise there's a chance this could be me last year in t'game".

Sobering thoughts indeed from a friend with whom I have played for almost 16 years. Rich continues with some weighty words. "If you'd 'av told me six months ago that I'd be 'ere, not far 'off gettin' back in t'first team, I'd 'av not believed you. I'm ahead of where I wanted t'be". And he is right – sportsmen less determined and committed than Rich would have thrown in the towel well before now. And despite his deep-rooted disappointment in the hand dealt to him by cricketing fate, he looks forward with optimism and gratitude for another crack at County cricket. "I'm just goin' t'make sure I enjoy m'self this season" he declares with a smile. "And whatever happens, happens. I've given m'self the best chance, after all".

As a long-standing friend and team mate, I can certainly vouch for those words. In fact, I would not be surprised if the months of frustration at being out of action propel this battler of a Yorkshire cricketer into some of his most eye-catching form, particularly with the ball in one-day cricket. This is one Yorkshireman who will not want to bow out quietly.

Talking of adversity and career change, peering through the netted wall of the indoor school this morning was the familiar face of another close friend and team mate looking ahead to new possibilities, Anthony McGrath. "Mags" had called in to approve a press release confirming his retirement from the game, forced upon him by a thumb injury that had been paining him for some time.

Whilst my class of cricketers loosened off, I had chance to spend time with the man who helped me through years of first class cricket, both from 22 yards away at the non-striking end, and up and down the M1, as travelling partners in the days before luxury coach travel.

I was relieved to see Mags upbeat about his future, if seemingly tired by the emotions of the day, but also saddened that a former Club captain and lifelong servant of Yorkshire cricket could retreat into retirement so quietly. And what a change the next few weeks and months will present for someone who has committed decades of his life to the game, touring the world and riding the emotional highs and lows of a career in professional sport. I do hope he's ok. Glancing at Facebook this afternoon, I noted Mags' status, "I'm going to miss everything about the game". Food for thought.

A quick glance at the TV today drew my attention to events in New Zealand, where team mate and one-time opening partner Joe Root has been raising eyebrows. "I see Rooty made runs again" has been a comment I have heard on a daily basis really, and it is no exaggeration. After a consistent season for us last year and a somewhat surprising selection for England's subsequent tour to India, Joe's composure has given him a start to an international career challenging the record books.

In hindsight, it should be no surprise that someone who, as a boy, displayed an insistent hunger to face hard new balls thrown from ten yards at his head has gone on to push boundaries at the highest level. Aside from being pleased for Rooty's deserved success, there is no ignoring the fact the knock-on effect his headline-making has on my situation for the coming year. For so long as Joe wears the three Lions this summer, there will be shoes to fill in Yorkshire's batting order, and I cannot help but be encouraged by the prospect. Good form and fitness assumed, there may well be just reward for my hard work on offer.

CHAPTER TWO

Pre-season Begins

Preparing to prepare

I arrived at Manchester's terminal two with stinging eyes and in growing need of my second breakfast of the day. For the final night at home before our much-awaited pre-season tour was a drawn out one spent taking shifts with my wife, Lisa, changing the nappies of Sebastian, our crying 15-month-old son.

It is that time of year again. A time when England's County cricketers meet in airport departure lounges and exchange tales of their respective winters, heading for warmer climes and the prospect of putting cricketing theory into practice. Caffeinated companion beside me, I write this from a café in said departure lounge looking out at airport runway clouded by flurries of Pennine snow.

"And this is why we fly away for pre-season!" had been Martyn Moxon's first words to me at Headingley this morning, pointing out of the pavilion window at the hallowed turf, blanketed white.

Joking aside, there have been occasions in my short career when efforts were made to begin outdoor net practice before the midpoint of March. (On one such occasion, I recall a shivering Mitchell Claydon – an Aussie by birth - approach the crease on his first day at Headingley squinting through the snow and northerly gale. Expletives aplenty, needless to say).

So no wonder those freshly tracksuited team mates in Manchester this morning have wide grins and a spring in their step. Slip catching drills in sub-zero temperatures can wait, at least for the next couple of weeks. What awaits is a fortnight spent in Caribbean idyll getting stuck in to some competitive cricket with the sun on our backs, after months restrained by artificially-lit indoor net sessions. And let's be honest; for some, the prospect of off-the-field Bajan hospitality and

that syrupy nightcap will be equally promising. How lucky we are.

The sun is going down on our first day in Barbados and I have exchanged the airport café for the balcony outside my room at the Barbados Beach Club Hotel to write this entry. Think Bajan Benidorm and you're not far off, a seven storey peach-coloured high-rise overlooking the turquoise sea and swinging to the reggae of the poolside bar.

Our first day took us half an hour's drive through the fields of sugar cane to the Franklyn Stephenson Academy for our first outdoor net session. The small and typically Caribbean cricket ground was a decent setting for our first experience of grass under spiked boots. Photos and newspaper articles on the walls of the tin roofed pavilion reminded us of the long-levered Stephenson and his dominance with bat and ball for his adopted Nottinghamshire. Martyn's eyebrows raised knowingly in memory of his 11-wicket haul on one such occasion. "He didn't half hit a long ball too", he said in reinforcement.

Stephenson was given the Wisden Cricketer of the Year award in 1989 for achieving the all-rounder's double of 1,000 runs and 100 wickets in a season. He completed the double in Yorkshire's last Championship match of the season, at Trent Bridge in September 1988, adding a century in each innings to his 11 victims with the ball. Coincidentally, it was the same season that his adopted County celebrated the 150th anniversary of their much-loved Test ground.

The two net pitches for this morning's practice appeared heavily grassed and heavily rolled, a notable change from the Caribbean norm of grassless slabs of rolled soil. Fortunately, the pitches played well and so did I on my first turnout, opening proceedings beside Phil Jaques in the neighbouring net and enjoying the feeling of grass under the feet.

Net practices are the most effective way to provide ample practice for a squad of players but, for me, there is no substitute for time spent in the middle in real-time competition. Net bowlers turn and deliver in quick repetition, often leaving me feeling rushed, and there is clearly no creation of that intangible we call pressure that drives the game in every form. Despite this, my first outdoor net went well, giving me the welcome confidence that my game is in good order and just enough of a reality check to highlight areas of my game I need to improve.

For me, and to plagiarise the M.C.C. coaching manual, I get into my best positions at the crease when my head leads towards the ball. And when I do this well, the rest follows, whether in defence, or hitting the ball for six, as I did on a couple of occasions today.

The truth is, as one gets better at a sport, one's understanding of it simplifies, or at least it should. Whilst a junior professional wrestles with the complicated mix of technical advice between his ears, the best in the world tweak the finest of details in pursuit of excellence in the basics of the game. So for me, that simple technical aim of moving the head towards the ball and transferring the weight helps everything else fall nicely into place.

An afternoon recovering at the hotel will provide a welcome chance to acclimatise to the heat and jet lag, and apply the first dose of aftersun to pinkish necks. It is certainly a case of us hitting the ground running in pre-season, as our first competitive match awaits tomorrow, a two-day fixture between two sides picked from our squad. If last year is anything to go by, such fixtures encourage more needle than you'd expect and are anything but friendly. As captain of the winning side last year, there may be chance to repeat the feat.

As I sign off for another day, a poolside team meeting is on this evening's agenda, presumably intended to put down some markers for the year ahead and announce tomorrow's teams. Though the first class season is still some weeks away, our familiar cricketing routines have begun; planning, travelling, training, playing and reflecting. The bleak winter months seem a world away.

Putting words into action

It is easy to form cricketing theory in team meetings – many of us have heard the buzzwords before – but today was our first opportunity to put yesterday's white board list into practice. The venue was the Desmond Haynes Oval and two teams were selected from the squad to contest a two-day fixture. Captain Azeem Rafiq chose to bat, much to the frustration of his rival skipper Lyth, and I was to open the innings with Phil Jaques.

Earlier in the morning, the Bajan "rush" hour (perhaps a tenuous description) had left us late to arrive and with just enough time to loosen off and assess conditions, which were more akin to what one might expect in the Caribbean. In the middle of a large, rough and sloping outfield was a hard but tacky surface of rolled Bajan soil drying fast in the morning heat. The only grass on this pitch was in the form of dry cuttings rolled into the surface. Not quite the northern sticky dog of pre-season at home.

Phil "Pro" Jaques, so called for his love of hitting an insurmountable number of balls in the nets, joined me to open the innings and take on the attack of Steve Patterson, Jack Brooks, Moin Ashraf and Co. And after half an hour's batting, we were both settling well, with boundaries to our name and a first wicket stand building nicely.

That was until Pro clipped a ball from Patterson to the left hand of square leg and set off running with a firm "Yeeeeeeesssss!" Trusting the call instinctively, I set off, head down, as fast as I could. A direct hit at the striker's end left me in no need of a third umpire to prove my dismissal. Run out by a distance. Oh dear. That familiar sinking feeling ensued.

There is nothing like that feeling of getting out, the realisation that your chance has come

The Yorkshire squad boards the team coach to the airport en route to the pre-season tour of Barbados.

It's a hard life: Views of Barbados from my hotel room.

and gone, that brutal finality that cannot be reversed. Commiseration came from all onlookers. This is the game we love, that rewards commitment to processes with bat and ball but with no guarantee of that outcome we most prefer.

Encouragingly, thirty-odd minutes at the crease gave me a great deal of confidence today, despite the obvious disappointment from my uncontrollable demise. My feet moved decisively, my head led my movements as intended and I lined up the bowlers well, feeling relaxed but sharp enough to react instinctively.

After months of indoor nets, I was pleased to adjust well on my first outing to the slower rhythms of matchplay, running through my pre-ball routines and watching the ball closely; a promising start in so many ways and something to build on. The emotional challenges of preparation for a game of cricket are impossible to simulate, so there is no substitute for taking the plunge into competition after a period of relatively pressure-less practice.

The "place" in which ones feels as a batsman is so important, and that "place" for me today was a peaceful and alert one. Runs come consistently to those who stay in that place that suits them best, whether it be one of peace of mind or outward aggression.

For the team as a whole, the day's cricket was a good exercise in familiarising ourselves with the tests four-innings cricket can produce. The quicks got some important overs in their legs, key batsmen spent some time at the crease and everyone benefited from time in the field. Tomorrow offers similar opportunity and another step closer to the fast-approaching season.

Miles in the legs

There's nothing like a long day in the dirt to keep you grounded and today delivered that sobering dose of pre-season reality. The Desmond Haynes Oval offered no shelter from the baking sun and 60 overs in the legs felt like quite a few more. Encouragingly, the majority of the squad gained useful time at the crease or with the ball in hand, notably Adil Rashid, who showed glimpses of the instinctive flair we wish we could see more often, during his unbeaten innings of fifty-odd before lunch. Each of our seamers could have been forgiven for dreaming of a new Dukes ball on a northern nibbler in English April, but to a man they equipped themselves well on an increasingly benign pitch.

And after an innings that promised much but was unnecessarily curtailed on day one, I had opportunity for an extended bat with thirty overs remaining in the day. Good practice it was too, not only from a technical point of view, but in tackling an opening batsman's familiar challenge; that of switching into fast-footed gear after a wearying stint in the field. Here lies another good reason for gaining outdoor match practice before the first class season. For if we were at home, the chance of a grassed net pitch would be a tough ask of the groundstaff, let alone a centre wicket.

In continuation from yesterday morning, my feet moved well from the start of my innings, despite the unavoidable heaviness of legs and I walked off the ground unbeaten at the close with over two hours valuable practice under my belt. With the pavilion sat square of the wicket at Carlton, Farby could monitor my head position and weight transfer into the ball from the comfort of his chair, and it was good to hear of his satisfaction with both.

It is always a boost to receive such feedback from a coach you trust – no player is secure enough not to require compliment – but in truth, I knew it myself. Contact on the ball was clean and my hitting areas straight and getting straighter, a sure sign of that head position and commitment I had been practising under the striplights of the indoor school.

Above all, the most rewarding part of my batting today was that I enjoyed it and really wanted to be out there for as long as possible. The batting crease can be a powerful and peaceful place to be on such days, when the mind is focussed on the ball but nowhere in particular, embracing the surroundings with the freedom of relaxed concentration. For me, that concentration is a detachment from any one thing, including the perception of pressure that fielding sides look to create. And aside from the encouraging signs of technical proficiency felt in the past two days, my most valuable progress has been in this regard.

Our evening, or part of it anyway, was spent in the company of greats. Greats of West Indian cricket, present and proud for the launch of the T20 tournament that awaits us this weekend. Six squads of sunburnt cricketers mingled and exchanged tales of their pre-season escapades as the line of honorary guests took turns to take to the microphone. Many were oblivious to the dulcit tones of the speakers and the accompanying black and white highlights reel reflecting on a golden age for Caribbean cricket.

A man with a West Indian drawl interrupted my conversation with new Warwickshire Director of Cricket Dougie Brown. "Where's that glass of wine, Dougie? Have you still not been served?" Realising his interruption, he continued, "Sorry, I'm Jeffrey Dujon. Pleased to meet you". Pro and I introduced ourselves to the famous West Indian wicketkeeper of the eighties.

"The one time I opened the batting for West Indies was at Headingley," he reminisced. "Gordon (Greenidge) didn't fancy facing the new ball there. I made 15 and 46". Dougie quipped "…and still you don't get served!" One can understand why so many continue to be seduced by the memories of the fearsome side of which Jeffrey was a part and the era of world cricket domination that ensued.

Supping his beer some time later, Dizzy recalled taking on an attack of Curtly Ambrose, Courtney Walsh, Winston Benjamin and Ian Bishop years after the time of Dujon and Greenidge. At the forefront of his memory was the image of Benjamin approaching the crease, gold chains jangling around his neck, en route to delivering one of many throat-high bouncers. Another soothing sip of beer required.

Each time I visit the Caribbean, I cannot help but get the sense of a cricketing culture divided by two equally enthusiastic sides; the open-minded youth attracted by modern change and the romantic purists with at least one eye on that formidable past. Frequent reminders of the achievements of famous ex-players surround developing cricketers in these parts on a daily basis. Cricket grounds, the stands that form them, and even roundabouts are dedicated to the memories created by Garry Sobers, Desmond Haynes, Walsh and their peers. But future success on these shores must surely depend on a truce between past and present, celebrating rose-tinted memories with a simultaneous excitement for what lies ahead. I'm sure I've heard that said somewhere before closer to home…

The Three Ws

Though our training and match practice has had the necessary edge thus far, the intensity of our first taste of competitive matchplay today could not be simulated. In a repeat of August's Twenty20 final, Hampshire were our opposition for our first match in the T20 tournament which forms the commercial focus of the trip, at least in the eyes of the local tourism board.

And as captain Gale made clear in his pre-match pep talk, today was about winning for us, and in doing so forming the foundations of a winning habit for the season ahead. In hindsight, the momentum gained from winning the same tournament last season proved a vital first step towards our subsequent success.

The venue was the 3 Ws Oval, a custom built and well-manicured ground on high land looking out to sea. Yesterday, the best of intentions to prepare for today's match were scuppered by an oversight by hosting officials, leaving us without a surface on the square on which to practice and just two net pitches that crumbled with every ball bowled on them.

Any touring side to the Caribbean will have

The Franklyn Stephenson Oval, the venue of our first squad training session.

similar tales of poor organisation or a lack of facilities – tours to the islands have become renowned for such mishaps – but it is no less frustrating for coaches having to reorganise at late notice.

Frustrations were lifted momentarily as Martyn asked selected players for the names of the three W's as we stretched on the outfield. Needless to say, there were a few laughs as many suggestions other than Messrs Worrell, Weekes, and Walcott were splurted out under pressure. And no, Warburton of bread-making fame did certainly not play for West Indies!

The beauty of our approach in the shortest form of the game over the past 12 months could be summed up in the two words written clearly on the dressing room white board today. Clarity. Enjoyment. And both were successfully put into practice in a seven-wicket

win over Hampshire that never looked in doubt. Having lost the toss on a slow, dry surface and made to field against our wishes, we applied the pressure with the ball and in the field that had proved so successful in last year's competition.

The shortest form of the game is often a tough one to get right at the first attempt, so a clinical victory putting us through to the semi-final was encouraging for all involved.

When Twenty20 cricket first appeared on the County cricket calendar, players approached it with a laissez-faire philosophy more likely seen during a testimonial match. The game was such an unknown to many that inconsistencies in performance were quickly forgiven. In time, however, the competitive juices of the Counties and the much-publicised financial incentives created a more

First team coach Jason Gillespie writes the schedule for our first net session of the tour.

Phil Jaques and I acclimatise to conditions with a net session at The Franklyn Stephenson Academy Ground.

serious and deliberate approach.

Players quickly started to realise that they had entered a race to develop skills not previously valued, whether they liked it or not. And year by year, Counties and their strategic minds set out increasingly objective methods to reach Finals Day and entice more spectators through the turnstiles to the County Ground bar. So what we see today is a domestic competition highly valued by the Counties, players who have carved out a niche for themselves with specialised skills and fixtures hard-fought by teams hungry for Twenty20 silverware.

Back to The Oval

Our victory over Hampshire took us back to the Kensington Oval, the venue of last year's Twenty20 final win under lights. For me, the ground is the source of fond memories of not only the team's pre-season success, but of a half-century in the final that ranks as one of my best limited-overs innings in a Yorkshire shirt.

Unfortunately, there was no repeat of such success in this year's semi-final. A Nottinghamshire side boasting the international experience of Alex Hales, Michael Lumb, James Taylor and Chris Read, were predictably strong, but the result was as much down to a Yorkshire performance not sufficiently polished as it was the opposition's skill.

Two days earlier, the Oval had been host to a nine-wicket win by West Indies over the Zimbabwean tourists that was sealed just two hours into the third morning. And frustratingly, the Twenty20 tournament organisers had arranged for the same pitch to be used for the four matches scheduled within the day. The surface was predictably unpredictable, offering turn for the spinners from ball one and inconsistent bounce for the quicks. Far from ideal for any t20 fixture, let alone the tournament semi-final.

Our score of 128 was evidence of a decent, if at times unsightly, scrap for a competitive total. The scorers were not troubled by my innings, lasting a matter of four balls and ended by a turning off-spinner in the middle overs. And as the pitch deteriorated further, so our belief of an improbable win increased. But a fielding performance short of yesterday's high standards could not defend the total, and the winning runs were struck with six balls remaining.

A disappointing result but a timely reminder of the need for fielding excellence in Twenty20 cricket and an unwavering will to force a win. In this form of the game, you are really not out of the contest until that final deathblow but a lack of belief with bat, ball or in the field at any one moment can have fatal consequences.

Pre-season silverware would have been an encouraging boost ahead of the season but in truth, the lessons of today may lead us down a more successful path. The week ahead offers key preparation for the start of the Championship, with two two-day fixtures against County opposition and the opportunity to build confidence in four-innings cricket before our return. As I sign off for another day, room mate 'Budgie' informs me the Headingley turf is under two inches of snow. A sobering thought.

Whilst the snow continued to fall at home, the remaining cricket provided useful opportunity to refocus on the skills that will bring about Championship success. For captain and coach, the two two-day fixtures against County opposition, above all else, were a useful experiment in testing different combinations of our seam attack, with one eye on four-innings cricket at Headingley around the corner.

In tough conditions for the quicks, the bustling spells of Jack Brooks came as notable encouragement, despite signs of the Achilles stiffness that had curtailed his progress at Northampton last year. Challenging for Division One silverware demands an ability to take 20 opposition wickets on a regular basis, so we will need every element of our new-found bowling depth come the first class season. As any captain would wish for, our attack offers important variety, with the consistency of Patterson, the swing of Ryan Sidebottom, the pace and unpredictability of Liam Plunkett and the aggression of Brooks. Not forgetting the fast developing skills of Ashraf in all forms and the stamina of Iain Wardlaw, Galey and Dizzy may well be spoilt for choice, assuming a clean bill of health and fitness.

A principled path

With that all-important first XI selection days away, all indications suggest there may be two possible avenues for me into the line-up; my familiar role opening the batting, presumably with Adam Lyth in the absence of Joe Root on international duty; or at number six in the order, providing the batting depth required to compile first innings scores to set up the game. In truth, I would bat anywhere to get into the first XI and have opportunity to firm-up a place.

This week's two-day match against Northamptonshire presented a useful dress-rehearsal for the middle-order role, sitting as I was for hours with the pads on before taking on the second new ball with an hour's play remaining in the day. Waiting to bat is a skill I have rarely had chance to practice, but the relaxed novelty was actually quite enjoyable. Different batsmen will have their own respective methods to while away the hours waiting to go in. Some thrive on watching each ball, clapping and punching the air with each boundary or milestone; others, like Jonny Bairstow, prefer an impromptu nap or alternative escape from the action.

During a wicketless afternoon session for our opposition this week, my waiting to bat led me into conversation with Adil Rashid, one place above me in the order. Conversations with "Dilo" can often be short-lived and straight to the point but on this occasion, he was keen to talk. And talk he did, for the best part of an hour, about his return to a rewarding path in his life: that of Islam, and prayer.

Almost seven years ago, Rashid, then a wiry teenager, was thrown the ball shortly before the lunch break at Scarborough, in speculation of breaking a strengthening Warwickshire partnership. Hours later, the debutant picked for a string of eye-catching hundreds in the second XI, had taken six Warwickshire wickets with eye-catching bounce and turn and led us towards victory. At short leg for that spell, I could see from a yard away that the Warwickshire batsmen were as surprised and dumbfounded as anyone on that day at North Marine Road.

Subsequent seasons brought spells of similar success and international recognition, but perhaps not with the regularity that many expected. At times enigmatic and often impulsive, with varying degrees of success, Adil has ridden a cricketing rollercoaster that has tested his resolve and his ways.

So there we were, pads on waiting to bat, looking back and looking forward, me mostly listening and Dilo describing the place in which he found himself. By his description, that place is one of early morning prayer, reflection and a commitment to a way extending beyond googlies and cover drives. Where previously I had seen someone searching and confused, on that afternoon there was a peacefulness and a philosophy in his words.

"Are you a religious person, Joe lad?" he would ask. The questions came thick and fast. "Do you believe in God, or Jesus? Do you go to church?"

The answers and conversation that ensued are not for these pages, but raise a point of real importance for the future of the County Club. The marriage of cultural and religious differences amongst players is a delicate but powerful part of any team's way in the modern day, but increasingly so for the Yorkshire team of the future.

The likes of Rashid and Ashraf are not only priceless cogs in the Yorkshire wheel, but role models for the County's Asian population that exudes a deep passion for the game. During a quick glance at Facebook yesterday, I noticed

Phil Jaques and Andrew Gale prepare for action at The Kensington Oval.

photographs of large groups of young cricketers of Asian descent learning the game in coaching sessions run by the Adil Rashid Academy in Bradford – just one very simple sign of such enthusiasm and grass roots potential in large numbers. As with any member of a team, it requires a certain strength to uphold one's values and beliefs, particularly if they differ in any way from the majority. And in the case of Adil and Moin, I am eased by the knowledge that they perform in an environment that will at once respect their path and challenge their development as members of a team.

Whether the Club's 150th year is one of statistical brilliance for Adil I cannot say but, based upon his words on that sunny afternoon, I have a sense it may be one of his most fulfilling.

Galey looks forward

If you needed any indication of the growing gulf in the standards of Championship cricket in Divisions One and Two, you need not have looked further than our two-day match against Nottinghamshire this week, the final competitive cricket of the tour. In our previous fixture, Northamptonshire threatened only temporarily with the pace of Steven Crook, signed from Division One Middlesex, and with glimpses of batting experience. Once such threats had passed, there was little in batting or bowling depth to maintain any significant pressure for periods of play. In contrast, behind a new-ball attack of Ben Philips and Andrew Carter followed Luke Fletcher and former Tyke Ajmal Shazhad. Not the strongest County attack by any means but certainly a step up in quality. With the bat, any side that includes Chris Read at no. 7 boasts more than sufficient quality higher up the order.

No sun cream required: Headingley on our return from Barbados.

So with the deepest snow of the winter still falling at home, two long, hot days wrestling with such opposition was the best possible preparation for the coming season.

In answer to a question posed by Farby before the tour at Headingley, I said that, above all, what I wanted to achieve during the fortnight in Barbados was a peace of mind at the crease. And two hours spent batting against Nottinghamshire's new ball near enough confirmed that I had done that. Of course, there are no guarantees of early-season selection or success, but the relaxed, positive, watchful state of mind I have cultivated over the past two weeks in the Caribbean will certainly give me the best possible chance.

During the afternoon session in the field, I stood beside skipper Gale at first slip. Captaincy has developed in Galey a pensive and introspective way rarely seen during the years of our playing together for Yorkshire Schools. Leading a County side is a challenging role that can consume all thought, particularly whilst on the field. But on this occasion, his brow was less furrowed and his demeanour more relaxed than usual.

"You know what Squirrel", he said, "I'm bloody excited by this year. We've got a right attack, avn't we?" Before I go on, a certain Anthony McGrath named me Squirrel after a long search for a suitable nickname in 2007. I still cannot work out why, but the nickname stuck.

Galey was right. Our bowling attack for the summer ahead was and is looking as strong as I have witnessed as a Yorkshire player. And undoubtedly, any side serious about winning Championship silverware must have a conveyor belt of such bowlers. Though I am reluctant to include this before the season opener, Galey's comment sparked a reminder of the bowling strength of Yorkshire's 2001 side, and we all know how they did. It would be naïve and presumptuous to get ahead of oneself at this time of year, but the quality and consistency of Messrs Sidebottom, Plunkett, Patterson and Brooks, to name a few, is worth getting excited about. You cannot win a Championship match without taking 20 wickets, after all.

Back to Blighty

It is the morning after the night before and our heads are fuzzy and sore from a little too much local liquor. In the traditional way, the tour was underlined last night with a well-lubricated team event bringing us all together before today's departure for home. Whilst the effects of last night's excesses fade away, a quiet and cricketless day allows time for some natural reflection on an eventful fortnight.

Our flight home this afternoon brings to an end a successful tour and a winter's preparation that, for me at least, began almost five months ago. The ten-mile runs, the indoor nets, the fitness testing – now a fairly distant memory but each important in bringing us to this point.

And this point is a pivotal one in the cricketing year, a threshold between months of preparation and the season, when looking long into the future becomes focussing on the shortest of terms. The first glimpse of that "one game at a time" cliché so much overused, you might say. Pre-season is a wonderful time of year to be a sportsman. "Working" days are completed in time for lunch, tours provide a sunny break from the frost and snow, and the levels of perceived pressure are very low. It is a time for development of skill, of social camaraderie and of energy levels, when players can experiment and become absorbed in creative play, in its truest sense.

But change lies around the corner, a return from sunnier climes to the frosty freshness of April and the start of a challenging campaign. Thoughts begin to turn towards the uncontrollables of selection, external judgment and results, to winning and losing, and the emotional fallout that accompanies each. Playful experimentation in training becomes the fine-tuning of a method refined over the winter and the mind begins to plan for the pressures of the competition to come. The more experienced amongst us dilute the hope and optimism of pre-season with a sense of reality and a respect for the challenges ahead, whilst those new on the scene get seduced by the perfection of dreams and goals.

And what are our goals for the year ahead?

The question every journalist likes to ask and most sportspeople like to avoid, or at least side-step, at this time of year. The magic numbers are never far away from mention for individual players – 1,000 runs, 50 wickets – those markers for success.

Teams talk of silverware, or at least challenging, or competing with the best. Spectators entice the cricketer's mind into the future when all he wants to do is deal fully with what lies in front of him. But a few enjoy the setting of targets and objective measures, to motivate the mind and break down a long summer into manageable parts. The "How?" of daily processes lead to the "What?" of desired outcomes in smooth and perfect theory.

For the time being, the effects of the evening's Bajan brew stands in the way of such planning.

Trust over tinkering

The days preceding our opening first class fixture of the season provided useful time to acclimatise to the unseasonal cold and adjust to outdoor conditions at Headingley. Against our wishes, however, preparations were forced indoors for our first day back after the Barbados tour, allowing the shivering groundstaff to continue their snow shovelling outside. After the progress made in practice on grass wickets over the past fortnight, this was certainly not ideal, but rain delays and unfit outdoor net pitches are likely to be a predictable part of the coming weeks. In small doses at this time of year, indoor practice is better than no practice at all.

Personally, a return indoors enabled me to address part of my game that had been on my mind since our last practice in the Caribbean. After my innings in the two-day match against Nottinghamshire last week, I returned to the dressing room boosted by what I felt was an encouraging period at the crease. I felt organised, in a positive and calm state of mind, and generally pleased with my game against a decent attack and a new ball. Curiously, however, Jacquesy and Martyn separately offered opinions that, on occasion, I was transferring my weight slightly slower into the ball than I should, particularly facing bowlers with pace. Though surprised by the comments, I promised to look further into a possible cause in later practice sessions. And our first day back gave me this opportunity to return to practice after the instinctive nature of matchplay.

Usefully, during our final practice session in Barbados, I had asked Danny Reuben, our travelling manager of all things Communication and PR at the Club, to film my net session with his portable camera, intended mainly for his video tour diaries and interviews. The footage showed a possible cause of the technical observations relating to my pre-delivery movements. Without getting too technical, pre-delivery movements, as the term suggests, are those movements made by a batsman just before the ball is released, and are intended to bring a fluid and quick-footed response to the delivery. Some occur naturally, others are adopted consciously out of choice.

In an ideal world, batsmen would stand still and move only after release of the ball – see Sachin Tendulkar and Matthew Hayden for world-class examples of such simplicity – but the right movements at the appropriate time can work nicely for lesser mortals.

Cricket is a side-on game, so the manual rightly says, and in my case, a slight rotation in my left foot in pre-delivery had occasionally made it more difficult for me to "get into the ball", or transfer my weight. Relieved to have identified this without too much analysis, I ironed out this habit with time spent facing the bowling machine and left feeling settled and confident once again.

At this time of year, with days before we begin the season's campaign, one must be guarded against over-analysis or questioning of one's ways with bat and ball. It is all about trust not tinkering. Trust in the months of fitness training and technical work, in the winter's preparation, and in oneself.

Easter weekend, the last before the season, brought that much-awaited event in the Yorkshire members' calendar, the Club's Annual General Meeting. No event in the cricketing year could be said to divide opinion to such extent as the AGM. In all honesty, all players wait with fingers crossed as Director Moxon reads out the names of those to draw the shortest straws and attend. Organisers and Board members are nervously on their toes and poised to deal with the advance of democracy amongst the membership.

And in contrast, it appears the attending members await the formal opening with great anticipation. Shortly before the meeting, many of them walk purposefully into the Headingley Long Room with queries and intended comments at the forefront of their minds. Balance sheets and minutes folded neatly under their arms, they look forward to their chance to make their voice, or at least their vote, heard. And rightly so, for many of the attendees have been devoted supporters of the Club for decades, through both the thick and the thin. With every query, comment and vote, the eyelids of team mate Adil appeared to weigh heavier.

"Naaaaaaaame!!!!" was the firm chorus of instruction from the members as someone from the back row stood up to make their point without announcing their title and locality. A certain anonymous member is renowned amongst the players for his list of lengthy and somewhat pedantic questions, but thankfully he is not here. With promotion, Twenty20 success and a reduced financial deficit to boast about, few questions were as pointed as in the past and all in attendance seemed intent on keeping the status quo. It is the anniversary year, after all.

CHAPTER THREE

April

A sobering cold snap

The car thermometer read zero degrees as I arrived for training on Monday. After two weeks of Caribbean heat, much of the talk in the week leading up to our first match has been about the cold. Unseasonal cold at that. At lunchtime, the dining room television showed a shivering Lancashire squad lining up for their official squad photograph at Old Trafford and veteran Glen Chapple talking about the cold sweats and stiff back he was expecting when the season gets underway. Meanwhile, physio Scott McAllister took delivery of extra handwarmers with sensible caution.

Despite the wintry wind, the standard of training at Headingley has been impressive this week, a sure sign of each player's eagerness to make a strong bid for a place in the starting line-up for our first Championship match next week.

This is invariably a challenging week of the cricketing year for the majority of players. Monday morning began with a team meeting to announce the squad to take part in our first first-class fixture of the summer, a three-day encounter against the Leeds-Bradford MCCU, starting on Friday. For the chosen 13, this provided useful advanced notice and the opportunity to tailor preparations accordingly. For others, it was perhaps the first indication of their respective whereabouts in the coming weeks as the Championship season gets underway. And understandably, therefore, the pleasantries of pre-season unity come under pressure as players in either camp become a little more introspective and focussed on the job in hand.

Next week, with the selection for the opening Championship match due, the splitting of the squad will be much more pronounced. For some players, news of their expected selection will come as no surprise, whilst others exude the excitement of gaining that first team place upon which they have focussed their winter's work. An unfortunate few will face time spent in the second XI, waiting in the wings for an opportunity or actively staking a claim. My career has led me down each of these paths, giving me an appreciation of the importance of this time of year for many players and its potential effect on the months to come.

Thankfully, the alphabetical list of 13 chosen names included Sayers very late in the order. Having spent many years as an opening batsman, I have come to expect my name first or second in the team announcement but Dizzy's way keeps his strategist's cards close to his chest and we players guessing as to the balance of the team.

Two elements of the 13 selected stood out to all listening in. Firstly, the inclusion of Jonny Bairstow after his recent return home from a dispiriting winter with the England team and secondly, the teaming up of an exciting battery of quicks: Sidebottom, Patterson, Brooks and Plunkett, sure to give the students a decent examination with the ball.

Jonny has proved a match-winning asset for us in his short career so far, so his return further boosts the confidence of the team and our chances of early season success. Whilst his glovework provides priceless balance to the XI, his ability to quickly change the pace of an innings with the bat threatens any opposition attack. Having said that, his demeanour currently seems subdued and his spoken summaries of the winter seem well rehearsed, almost in tiredness of answering the same old questions.

Months of net sessions, gym work and drink-mixing, waiting on the sidelines for selection, can be a sapping experience. Home comforts and some early-season runs should do the trick, methinks.

For me, the week's work has been focussed on acclimatising to typically English conditions: marking my guard on a muddy crease, playing a seaming ball and adjusting to the slowness of grass-covered pitches. Furthermore, I have made an asserted effort to take on the advice of the coaching staff and show a greater intent to score at all times. It is very easy at this time of year to become hesitant and non-committal in the face of tough conditions, but a positive state of mind and an eye for scoring opportunity invariably gets a batsman into his best technical position, whether in defence or attack. Above all, like impatient students waiting outside the exam hall, we exude a sense of wanting to get underway with the season, and stuck in to our encounter.

Sat beside my kit bag on the Headingley turf, unstrapping pads and packing away gloves, I am in a familiar state of absorbed reflection. Passers-by may notice a glazed and somewhat pensive look on my face and could be forgiven for assuming that something is wrong. The truth is I have just walked out of a net practice against Sidebottom and Brooks and need some time to return to the real world. Ryan and Jack had their new Dukes balls seaming considerably off the green practice pitch and the majority of my 20 minutes at the crease was spent playing and missing or nodding with approval as I picked up the ball from the net behind me. Time and time again, I would line up the ball as intended, only to see it jag past the outside edge of my bat or thud into my thigh.

Years ago, I would have wasted time analysing my struggle and talking myself out of the state of confidence I have built. The self-criticism would have been easy to find at the forefront of my mind. And now I catch myself following a similar path, punishing myself for a disappointing net, but leading the inner conversation to a constructive and less judgmental conclusion. Dizzy was right when he said "That's as tough as it's going to get, Squiz" as I walked out of the net. Yes, at times

Welcome to the Yorkshire CCC inner sanctum. Need I say more?

putting bat on ball seemed an impossible task and yes, the quality of bowling and the difficulty of conditions left me feeling a little stupid for a moment, but I survived and persisted with the plan that is most likely to succeed, over time. The analytical heaviness of my mood will pass and I will take key lessons forward.

Net sessions that do not go to plan provide a cerebral challenge in the lead up to a match. A ten-minute working over on a net pitch can rock the boat of mental preparation and lead a player into an unnecessary questioning of his ability. Equally, such practices can act as a timely reality check and a reminder of the need to return to executing the key technical basics of the game. To this end, the success or otherwise of one's net practice can go only so far in predicting one's performance under pressure in the middle.

I am back out in the middle at Headingley and in a powerful and peaceful state of mind. This is our final net session before tomorrow's start to the first-class season, our last dress rehearsal. With the first XI bowlers easing their aches with a morning swim nearby, I have Moin Ashraf and the enthusiastic Academy bowlers to contend with. It feels good to be back in the middle, feeling the space, the familiar slope down from the Kirkstall Lane and the background of blue seats and advertising hoarding. And my net is going well, showing real signs of progress in my efforts to show more intent to score with cleaner, more decisive movements. Committing my top half into the ball with my hands close and beneath my head is attracting compliment from everyone around me. I would enjoy nothing more than doing this all day.

There is little better as a batsman than the feeling of a job well done at the crease, of the coming together of the technical jigsaw puzzle that had been taken to pieces and reassembled over the winter. When the movements rehearsed for hours become habits, the feeling of effortless grace is what professional sport is all about. After a net session such as this, that reflective state of introspection has a somewhat lighter feel, in which the mind revisits the good feelings felt in the middle. But a practice gone exactly to plan is not necessarily better preparation than that struggle through training.

Whether practice was "good" or "bad", it comes and goes very quickly, and the exact conditions of today cannot be recreated. There is a Zen-like paradox in sporting performance, one that makes our ideals impossible to grasp and our failures impossible to avoid. Tomorrow will bring a fresh challenge and a new opportunity, to be approached with the respect it deserves. But today felt good, there is no question, and I left the ground this morning feeling prepared for the challenges ahead. My winter's work had brought me to this point and I felt as ready as I was ever going to be.

The summer's prelude

"You're in, Squiz" comes the shout from Galey as I collect my helmet and gloves and begin the walk down the pavilion steps to the middle. Budge has just clipped a ball into the waiting hands of square leg in the third over of the day and I am on my way to the crease. On arrival, 11 energetic students are chirping in anticipation of a top-order collapse. I instinctively recall time spent in the other camp, an enthusiastic student chomping at the bit to claim whatever first-class scalps we could over three days at The Parks, and smile in understanding. "Watch the ball, it's ok". Each delivery leaves a bright green bruise on a surface that is cold to the touch – a sure sign of moisture in the Headingley pitch. A few balls later, I turn an inswinger off my pads to the left hand of square leg and open my account of runs for the summer. I feel calm and alert, relaxed in my movements and pleased that the summer's cricket has begun.

A short while later, the scoreboard on the Western Terrace read 14-4 and many of the day's small crowd were yet to walk through the turnstiles to watch our first innings against Leeds and Bradford Universities. Walking back to the pavilion after a brief stay at the crease, I had time to reflect on an eventful start to our first class season that went anything but to plan. Former Tyke Jimmy Lee had taken three top order wickets with his full-pitched, medium-paced seamers and the Yorkshire dressing room was in a startled state of surprise.

The pitch was predictably green and the students' attack perfectly suited to its slow pace. This was a batting challenge far different from facing the pace of County attacks on drying Caribbean pitches. As Lythy and I joked over a consoling cup of tea from the pavilion, it was a test akin to a Premiership side taking on non-league opposition away from home in the FA Cup. Clearly an exaggeration of the difference in style between the two sides, for this was a Universities attack deserving respect after last year's early-season scare, but you get my point.

After a night interrupted by a teething baby, my journey to the ground had been made all the more interesting by a car that stuttered and stalled on at least two occasions. It was a relief to make it to the ground without the help of the RAC, but the first morning of the season had begun in a way far from ideal. After edging a ball to the cordon of students just a few deliveries into my innings, I could have been forgiven for cursing the day's misfortune and generally being a grumpy presence in the dressing room.

Encouragingly, I reflected on a morning for which I was well prepared and a stay at the crease, albeit a short one, with some promising signs. My technical basics appeared in good order under the pressure of matchplay and my mind was clear – a non-negotiable for aspiring run-makers. Of course, a cricket season is so much about the match-winning hundreds and five-fors, but of equal importance is the ability to deal with the days that do not go to plan.

Taking away the lessons from a disappointing day is a cliched but vital part of any cricketer's life. If taken home, the lowlights of the day can haunt and tire the mind, compromising confidence and slowing any kind of mental refreshment. Seeing the cup half full when reflecting on a day, innings or indeed a single delivery is of paramount importance in order to build upon experience and progress. And today I did that, without force or self-kidology, and it felt good.

As is often the case at Headingley, the afternoon session went in the favour of the batting side, and 65-7 became a fast-improving position of strength centred around a partnership between Gary Ballance, fresh from England Lions duty, and Ryan Sidebottom, whose batting skill too often goes unnoticed. The first century of the first-class summer was just reward for Gary's patience and ability to play the seaming ball late, and led us to an above par total of 244 with an hour's play remaining in the day.

With the evening temperature dropping at a pace, brief spells of speed and aggression from new boys Brooks and Plunkett were the promising highlights of the final hour, whetting the appetite of the hardiest of spectators who remained to the close.

Referencing Dizzy's straight-to-the-point team talk the following morning, the word of day two was Discipline, and our much talked about arsenal of quicks put that into practice perfectly in the morning session. The eight remaining Universities wickets were claimed by lunch and shared amongst an attack doing exactly as the boss requested. In games such as these, carrying the perception of more to lose than gain, such no nonsense displays with the ball are exactly what is required. Brooks bowled with far more pace than his run-up length would suggest, Patterson and Sidebottom were reliable as ever, and Plunkett found rhythm and carry during his spell up the hill from the Rugby Stand End. To paraphrase our antipodean coach, "Job done".

Timely tweaking

Earlier that morning, before play, I had begun to put into practice a slight change to my game in the nets. During the lunch break on day one, I had taken the time to watch the video replays of my innings, recorded by cameras behind the bowler's arm at each end, and fed into a software programme by our resident analysts. The programme provides all the statistics you could reasonably think of, and a few more, as well as the aforementioned replays of each ball of the day, which can be slowed down, paused and compared with split screens. For ten minutes of the lunch break, my focus was on my pre-delivery movement and the timing of it relative to the release of the ball. On some occasions, the pre-delivery movement of my left foot was as intended, back and across towards the off-side, flat footed and early enough to have finished moving before release. In other cases, it was not as planned, moving back but not far enough across, weight on my toes and sometimes too late. Batting is a tough enough exercise when you are still and ready to move when the bowler lets go, but far more difficult and unnecessarily so if you are moving.

So, although this time of year is so much about trusting the work done before in off-season practice, the pressures of matchplay can introduce or exacerbate unwanted habits, and there is place for fine-tuning in search of consistency. That was this place and my resolution was to make my pre-delivery movement slightly earlier so as to be still on release, hopefully buying me a split second longer to make my judgement.

The net session went well, justifying my fine-tuning and giving me confidence going into the day. Tim Bresnan, progressing well through his rehabilitation from an elbow operation, ran in with a new ball at not far off full pace, providing a stern test of my theory and a useful workout for my footwork. And an earlier movement, albeit a conscious one in the nets, gave me more time after release, or at least the all-important feeling of having it.

This self-coaching process is a key part of a batsman's, or indeed bowler's, way. After improvements are made consciously in a practice environment, it is essential that the instinct is allowed to take over in matchplay, uninhibited by cognitive thought, theory or review. So that would be my next step, taking the confidence from successful practice to go and just play in the middle, in its truest sense.

Batting at three carries some similarities with walking out to face the first ball. When the opposition's final wicket falls, the same purposeful walk to the pavilion is required to pad-up within the ten minutes between innings. After all, a walk back to the middle may be required if the first ball does not go to plan for number one. And there I was, padded-up and tuned-in to the action, ready when required. Four hours later, I was still there, or rather taking off my pads after an unbeaten opening stand between openers Lyth and Alex Lees in our second innings, leaving us in a commanding position going into the final day. Both were in touching distance of centuries, their partnership nearing the 200 mark and underlining a day that could not really have got better.

After bringing up his century with a signature cover-drive late in the first hour of the third day, Lythy lofted a delivery from the Universities' off-spinner into the hands of the very relieved mid-off, and my chance had finally come. With four overs until the second new ball, at least there would be challenge enough ahead of me to prepare me for the Championship cricket to come.

Soon after my arrival at the crease, I was pleased to share in a special moment for Leesy – his maiden first-class century for Yorkshire – brought up with a lofted sweep over the head of square leg. He has worked hard over recent years to earn his chance in first XI cricket and overcome unspeakable personal challenges off the field at a young age. Every batsman to have reached the milestone remembers the shot to bring up his maiden century (I can still recall clipping an Otis Gibson delivery off the hip for four against Leicestershire at North Marine Road to bring up my first century years ago), and Alex will remember his, and the applause that followed.

Encouragingly, I had no difficulty letting my instinct take over after the self-coaching of the previous day. My timing and consistency of movements suggested an earlier movement before release and the success of my mid-game visit to the drawing board. Though the student attack was tired and approaching the point of crying "Mercy!" in the field, I took a great deal from an unbeaten two hours at the crease grooving the refined version of my game.

When Captain Gale relieved the student attack of its heavy legs and declared shortly after lunch, we had just over 50 overs remaining in the match to bowl out our opposition and force a three-day win. And the overs remaining were not required, thanks notably to two spells of truly fast bowling downhill from the Kirkstall Lane End by "Pudsey" Plunkett. Onlookers would have done well to recall a few bowling faster than this in recent years from a Yorkshire bowler. The top order came and went within overs, offering no answers to the unsympathetic barrage of throat high bouncers. And with half an hour remaining, the game was suitably wrapped up by the new recruit's sixth wicket, a top-edged bouncer held reliably by Siddy at long leg.

Though our opposition was relatively weak, much was gained from the first three days of the first-class summer. A number of our batsmen gained valuable time in the middle and three albeit cold days without stoppages for rain were a welcome surprise. Above all, it was the success of our seam attack that left players and coaches most excited. The strength in depth of our bowling department has been much discussed in recent weeks, leaving expectations high, but the performances of each of the bowlers could not be ignored.

Clearly, a thin Universities top six offered little challenge and wickets came far easier than they will in future matches, but the balance and variety of the attack would leave any County captain envious at mid-off. The displays of Brooks and Plunkett were particularly encouraging, as they showcased a pace and bounce that may prove useful when conditions are far less favourable for the seamers. Finally, the ability to win is a skill to be practised, and all followers of sport know how soon it can become a habit. The resistance from the visiting Sussex side for next week's opening Championship match will be far greater, but this was an encouraging start to the cricketing summer.

Digesting more than just tea

At tea on the third day and I have just watched Spurs equalise with minutes to go in their match against Everton at White Hart Lane, much to the relief of our jumping and screaming physio, Scot McAllister. As the son of a former Spurs physio himself, "Phys" prides himself on following the north Londoners, and takes his fair share of stick for his commitment.

Cup of tea in hand, I am walking back into the dressing room to put my spikes back on for the final session, when Dizzy directs me into the coaches' dressing room. "Can I have a minute, Squiz?" he says. I think I know what is coming. I have been here before. An announcement of team selection for Wednesday's game against Sussex is due.

"Squiz…We've selected the team for the Sussex match…and, unfortunately, you're not in it". A sip of tea disguises an unavoidable sinking feeling I have felt before. As Dizzy explains the reasoning for his decision, and the timing of his telling me, an inner dialogue is working out how I am going to respond.

The ensuing conversation remains confidential, as it should, but I took to the field digesting the news I had been given minutes earlier. As the game's final session panned out, I caught myself switching between modes with each delivery. A hustling fielder keen to do his part to edge his side towards victory was replaced by a quieter me, reflecting on my leaving out of the side and what that meant for the coming days and weeks.

At times such as this, a cricketer's ego demands a voice and a means of expelling its anger, bruised as it is by the critical judgment. The ego talks over the voice of reason, ranting and raving about the injustice and possible conspiracy. "Why me?" it shouts. "I don't deserve this". The inner voice continues its monologue until its impassioned reaction fades with time. All sportsmen are competitive creatures, each displaying such tendencies in different ways, but each has an inner ego to be tamed.

The drive home gave me a natural window to make sense of the news, both through quiet reflection and a conversation with Lisa over the phone. I could see the reasoning behind the decision - selecting Leesy on the back of his second innings hundred and the runs he scored in Barbados – but did not and could not agree with it. I was ready to play and eager to make an early statement with the bat. But as Dizzy said, I had done all I could to make the first XI of the Championship summer and my game was in excellent order. There was nothing I could do, other than accept the call and decide upon a way forward out of the disappointment.

As I walked through the front door, an excitable Sebastian ran straight to me to welcome Daddy home. Life was pretty good, after all. How consumed we become in the world of cricket and the ride it provides.

A season's eve controversy

It is the evening before our first match of the season and I am pushing a trolley around the aisles of our Morrison's beside my wife, Lisa, and son, Sebastian. En route to the fish counter, I double-take at a headline on the nearby newspaper rack. "Adil Rashid Exclusive" it reads, "Treat me better, or I'm Off". The shopping list can wait. I rarely read newspapers these days, particularly the sports sections, but this is an article I need to read. It does not sound good.

On the eve of the season, the centre spread of The Cricket Paper divulges the detail of an interview with Adil. There are damaging quotes aplenty, leaving no doubt over the deep unhappiness felt by our enigmatic legspinner. Apparently, Adil wants to "draw the line" over what he believes to be his own mismanagement and look forward to first-team cricket at a Club that values his contributions. There are no grey areas in this no-nonsense view of the conflict between the player and his coaches, and Captain Gale is a main target of the criticism. According to the article in front of me, he "doesn't get the art of leg spin". Ouch.

This picture of a tormented and unhappy player does not fit with the man I have seen on a daily basis exuding a peace of mind he has worked hard to achieve. The words I am reading do not paint a true representation of Dilo's view of his place within the Yorkshire squad, or at least I hope not. "Perhaps he's been misquoted," Lisa says in an attempt to explain this washing of dirty laundry in public. Either way, after the hard yards of the off-season and a successful overseas tour, this is not what Adil, the team, or the Club needs on the verge of the season opener.

Controversies and exclusives in the press and media are nothing new. You could reasonably argue they are becoming more commonplace in this age of social media and freedom of expression. But clearly, the content and timing of this article is potentially damaging for a squad intent on building some solid foundations of team spirit. If there were truths in the criticism quoted, I would expect Adil to be sorry for their publication. Any team faces its challenges and the political dynamics within a group of competitive and aspirational characters are often difficult to manage, but successful teams communicate their issues directly and find a common ground behind closed doors. Perhaps this is the constructive message to come out of this controversy?

Back down to earth

The expectant members are sat around me in near-silence. "There goes another one" someone murmurs as an inswinger from Chris Jordan cannons into Siddy's off-stump. The scoreboard is a sorry read. 96-9. From almost 50 overs. By three o'clock, Steve Patterson is running from the field to change his batting spikes for bowling boots, after Rafiq became our tenth and final wicket to fall.

After all the hype, the expectation, the getting ahead of ourselves and the dreaming of Championship silverware in our anniversary year, the first day of the Championship summer has delivered a sobering slap around the face.

From my seat in the terraces, the Headingley pitch shines in the April sun, the lightest of green stripes on a pristine, unblemished square, covered evenly in live grass. By all accounts, it is a slow surface that has provided seam movement for the Sussex attack, as they hoped in taking to the field after winning this morning's toss. But is it by no means a pitch as difficult to bat on as the Yorkshire score suggests.

Unless we strike early with the new ball, the Sussex top order will be poised to prove this point before the close. "Let's 'ope it gets better, ey Joe?" one disappointed member says as he shakes the last drops of tea from the cup of his flask. Let's hope, indeed.

As wickets tumbled in the middle, I am marking my guard in the nets a short walk from the turnstiles. Within earshot of events up the road, the sound of each successful appeal from the Sussex cordon gives us an idea of the score, or at least who is walking to the crease. Lining up against the eager and energetic squad of Academy bowlers, I have opportunity to refine the technical improvements I had made during the Universities match and dilute my disappointment of non-selection with some enjoyable time hitting balls.

But this morning I feel old. It did not seem long ago that I was that fifteen-year-old Academy lad mixing it with the likes of Darren Gough, Chris Silverwood, Craig White and Michael Vaughan. Watching the list of internationals and capped professionals going about their work is a memory still vivid in my mind. And now, 14 years on, the shoe is on the other foot, so to speak, as I watch an impressive bunch of future Yorkshire players learning their way. Is it me or is County cricket becoming a younger man's game? Anyway, an hour in the nets is the ideal use of my morning today, allowing me to enjoy retreating into my inner world at the crease. The net pitches favour the bowlers and the proud seams of the new balls in their hands, but it is a useful test and good preparation for similar conditions out in the middle.

The visitors ended the first day eight runs ahead of the Yorkshire score with seven first innings wickets remaining. Chris Nash gave a lesson in batting on this slow, seaming surface, racing to a half century at near a run a ball with an intent to score and a decisiveness in defence and attack. The Headingley surface is unforgiving of a batsman hesitant in his shot selection and mindful of any potential demons in the pitch, and today's play was a classic example of this. With conditions firmly in the bowler's favour at this time of year, it is key to make one's presence felt at the crease and place any pressure possible back on the seam attack. The lessons of the day struck a chord with me, though watching on from the stands.

The overcast conditions did little to stem the flow of Sussex runs on the second day. Nash continued briefly in the same vein, setting the example for his team mates to follow suit, scoring as they did at well over four runs per over. With three of the Sussex order falling just short of centuries in a total of 356, this was a clear indication of the batting depth prevalent in Division One cricket. When the final Sussex wicket fell in the afternoon session, a conceded lead of 260 was a near mountain to climb in the context of the game and our first innings. The Yorkshire attack had conceded runs at a pace, but two bowlers stood out in particular; the ever-reliable and economical Sidebottom, and debutant Brooks, who claimed four Sussex wickets after an expensive first spell.

Now at home, I checked the live score online between feeding mouthfuls of mashed potato to an impatient Sebastian. Bad light had brought play to a premature end in the evening session, but not before the loss of Lees, caught at slip off the bowling of Steve Magoffin. Having pipped me in the race for selection, Leesy had been dismissed early in both innings on his Championship debut, no doubt to his disappointment in the dressing room. Should I feel his disappointment and empathise with his situation or feel relieved that the man in my position in the team had failed to make a notable score?

Cricket challenges the mind and person in these ways, even when you are watching from afar. Few sports simultaneously demand the selflessness of a team player and the single-mindedness of individual success. Dominant cricket sides include those generous enough to enjoy the success of their colleagues and give themselves up to the common cause. But they also include those with a mind more for their own path, not necessarily pleased to see their dressing room rivals fall short, but perhaps less aware of their struggle. And with each spoonful of mash, I found two voices coming to mind, one in empathy for a young left-handed batsman finding his way in early-season conditions, and another looking forward to the possibility of future opportunity and the potential reward for my work.

Morning fog and drizzle prevented any further play before lunch on the third day, much to the relief of Captain Gale and his men, who had one hopeful eye on the forecast and one on the deficit of runs facing them when the game restarted. A weather-assisted draw would be the best result possible for Yorkshire fans from this point, excluding something Bothamesque with the bat.

A rain-affected morning gives me chance to meet up for a coffee with a good friend and former teammate, Anthony McGrath. How we could have done with his skill and experience this week, on and off the field. The venue is the Carnegie Café, a short walk behind the padded seats of the Taverner's Suite and into the neighbouring Carnegie Stand of the Rugby Ground.

"Mags" is here in his newfound capacity as a radio commentator after his enforced retirement from the game this winter. Looking admittedly tired from a week of guest appearances at local cricket Clubs, he talks about a new chapter in his career and his life.

"I still think about batting, y'know…", he says in reply to a little prompting. "…and I've been waking up thinking I'm late for training for weeks".

Of course, there is no training for Mags anymore, or at least not as he once knew. For this former player, the slightly milder weather, lighter evenings and the unavoidable talk of the new season in the media has evoked emotional responses that will have become habitual over the decades of his career.

"It all feels a bit surreal, Squiz", he continues. Understandably so, for the life of a player of Mags' longevity can so easily become consumed and defined by the game and its daily routines. One of the things he misses most, he says, is the daily contact with his team mates and friends, the energy of camaraderie and the sense of belonging. After years of intimate friendship with his peers, during the quieter days of this new chapter, his phone rarely rings. One begins to get a sense of the challenges posed by retirement from professional sport, regardless of material wealth or prospects.

Notably, a number of the current Yorkshire side have stayed in frequent touch with this character of the dressing room who is conspicuous by his absence. Many of the team have already mentioned how they miss the humour for which he was renowned and his commitment to upholding many of the Club's unwritten traditions.

Yorkshire cricket was at the heart of this former Club captain, and his qualities with the bat shone through until the final days of his playing career. There has been talk of his future involvement with the Club, but he is not so sure. "We'll see", he says, sitting comfortably on the fence.

Either way, I count myself as one of a number of the team who will continue to seek Mags' views of a cricketing nature in the future. Talking cricket with someone of a like mind cannot be underestimated as a means of learning the game and one's interpretation of it, and today's brief chat over coffee was no exception.

When play got under way in the unseasonal gloom, "Budgie" Lyth and Jaques followed the positive example of their opponents with a promising partnership full of intent. But when Lythy feathered an edge to wicketkeeper Ben Brown shortly after, Galey soon followed, leaving the middle order exposed and just seven wickets remaining with much of the day still to play. And so was the pattern of the remainder of the day, partnerships of promise and will cut short by dismissals at regular intervals. The wicket of "Pro" Jaques was a key one, ending almost all hope of a rearguard and starting the countdown to an inevitable loss, so long as the rain stayed away.

With each wicket to fall, the Sussex fielders would have been forgiven for discussing plans for their local night of celebration to follow. But to their frustration, Siddy followed his innings of 38 against the Universities with a resolute effort in support of Ballance, their partnership adding 80 runs in 29 overs for the eighth wicket. The embarrassment of a loss inside three days had been avoided but with 32 runs still needed to make the visitors bat again, only a fourth day washout would prevent a Sussex victory by an innings.

The rain came too late on the final day, and the Sussex bowlers made light work of wrapping up our second innings and the match. The remaining two wickets came in just 37 deliveries and the game was lost by an innings and 12 runs. Mother Cricket had offered a painful reality check and disposed of any remnants of that romantic vision of sesquicentennial silverware. At least for the time being.

According to the Press, the "sack the lot" faction was starting its vocal warm-up and newly-promoted Yorkshire had been given an early reminder of the growing gulf between the two Divisions of County cricket. Of course, this was not the start to the cricketing summer we were hoping for, but our first four-day defeat in 19 matches was by no means something to be blown out of proportion.

Without ignoring all disappointment, a resounding first-round win may well have produced excesses of fanciful foresight and a view too far ahead into the summer. In a year quite rightly full of hope, optimism and concerted effort to make it memorable, a heavy loss washing away any complacency could well be a blessing in disguise.

At home with family on Sunday afternoon, my phone vibrates on the kitchen worktop. A text from Dizzy. Part way through, it reads "…We will not allow one result to define our season". Prefacing his summary of a disappointing week of first-eleven cricket, his message confirms the team for next week's match, a three-day "friendly" against our Roses rivals over the Pennines. I am not one of the chosen thirteen, as Joe Root has returned to the side to replace Alex Lees and begin his preparations for a return to the Test squad. Lisa senses my disappointment – she has seen my expression before. But I was expecting this scenario and I know the season is still very young. The disappointment I feel is simply a sign of my determination and confidence to get back in the side, I tell myself. The week ahead will be spent in sunny Hartlepool taking on Durham's second string. I better pack the thermals.

The first swallow of summer

After the stark wake-up call of the Championship season opener, the second week of the summer promised a somewhat quieter return to the cricketing drawing board. Two three-day friendly matches occupied all members of the professional staff: the first a first-XI Roses fixture filling a natural break in the Championship fixture card, the second the opening match of the second XI summer

Academy Director Ian Dews revealing his reward for a lack of footballing skill – the second XI's infamous "Free Transfer" bib. During a repetitive fixture schedule, there is often nothing more effective in raising morale than a game of warm-up football.

against our north-eastern neighbours, Durham, in Hartlepool.

Dizzy's text on Saturday afternoon had confirmed my whereabouts for the coming week of cricket, so early on Tuesday morning, with my first XI team mates still to wake up to preparations in Leeds, I squeezed the usual luggage into my impractical Mini en route to three days with the second team beside the east coast.

The world of second XI cricket can be a strange and challenging place for a player of experience. The dressing room contains a unique mix of cricketers heading in differing directions in their careers, on occasion motivated by very different things, and certainly in contrasting states of mind.

At the foot of the food chain, academy players brim with hesitant excitement with their first taste of County cricket beyond youth level. Junior professionals enjoy their stepping up a rung and finding their way as full-time paid sportsmen. Regular second-teamers go day-to-day as journeymen, waiting in the wings for an improbable opportunity in the firsts. And senior players, either recovering from injury or fighting for form, use their experience to find motivation in the absence of any kind of adrenaline rush. Managing this unfortunate cocktail of ill-placed players, therefore, can be a tough job. But a highly important job it is, for the intermediate level of County cricket can, at any one time, incorporate the Club's most senior player and a 15-year-old debutant. Arguably, therefore, the success of the second team, in a developmental sense anyway, is the most accurate indication of the chance of future first-class consistency.

Since the management restructuring in 2011, the job of managing the second XI has fallen to Paul Farbrace. And an excellent choice he is, exuding an obvious love and deep knowledge of the game to the players under his management. In the short time he has been at the Club, Farby has become renowned for his "go get 'em" approach and his long list of superlatives projected with the utmost enthusiasm.

"That's world claars!" he often exclaims with his southern accent as another young lad throws himself into a full-blooded challenge in the pre-match football game. And at the archetypal second XI venue, a quiet, uninspiring league cricket ground somewhere in English suburbia, this extroverted energy rubs off on everyone involved, particularly the sleepy teenagers in need of sharpening up.

Farby's impassioned praise continued into the morning session of the first day at Hartlepool, the first opportunity for many of the squad to get their teeth into competitive cricket since the pre-season tour. Predictably, the surface was soft underfoot and green with thick grass, sure to present a challenge to the top order of both sides. But the sternest test for both sets of players was to be provided by the gale force wind howling from the South West, strong enough in gusts to blow the weighty sightscreens on to the field on numerous occasions. The heavy bails were simply not heavy enough.

The cold wind seemed to strengthen as the week progressed, leaving bowlers stiff in the back and all fielders relieved to leave the field at the close of play. As is typical of three-day second XI fixtures, the game progressed in a somewhat artificial way with intent to manufacture a competitive run chase in the final session of the third day.

For senior players accustomed to hard-fought contests in the first-class arena, it is often frustrating to see a game drifting towards a negotiated deal without edge or drama. But as was the case in the first XI Championship in years gone by, a significant part of productive three-day cricket is the cooperation between competing captains to find a common ground from which both sets of players have chance to take the spoils with deserving performance.

Furthermore, team results are not the only parameter of second team success. Rather, the declarations and deals that tinker with the game's flow create opportunity for the development of individuals, the most telling measure of the team's progress.

Hence our first innings declaration 74 runs adrift of the home side's total of 303, leaving four sessions remaining in the game, to be split between opposing batting orders to create a fair second innings chase, at least in Farby's theory.

The first XI fixture in Leeds was following a similar pattern of negotiation, suggesting a friendly alliance between coaches Gillespie and Peter Moores, no doubt to the frustration of some onlookers starved of Roses rivalry in the Championship this summer. But, by all accounts, the cricket was hard-fought and a productive filler of an untimely gap in the first-class season.

With a checked-drive piercing the gap between extra cover and mid-off and an insistent "Yeeeeeessss!", I set off towards the non-striker's end and make it comfortably, bringing up my century. I can count the spectators with one hand,

I'm convinced the odd old-timer is snoozing behind the pavilion windows, and the freezing wind still howls, but I don't care. There is no better feeling for a batsman than bringing up a hard-earned century and after a near-five hour spell at the crease in challenging conditions, I raise my bat to the changing room with satisfaction and relief in equal measure. Captain Dan Hodgson immediately signals our declaration, leaving me with an unbeaten three figures to my name. After the disappointment of my non-selection last week, I was determined to send a defiant message from the crease at my first opportunity, and this was exactly that.

The length of my five-hour innings was an indication of the style in which my century was compiled, steadily in third gear, you might say, until opportunities to score came more freely. As is typical on such surfaces, playing well through the tough periods of disciplined bowling is vital in building an innings and ensuring one remains out there when bowlers tire and conditions ease in the late afternoon.

Aside from the satisfaction of a relatively large number next to my name, what pleased me most in my first innings century was the clarity of my mind. A long innings is simply the act of facing a single ball time after time and when I focus fully on the ball to be delivered, and not the one gone before or others to come later, I know my focus is in good order.

Furthermore, I could feel progress in my working out of an effective game plan on seaming pitches such as this. Over a beer after play, opposition bowler and former team mate Mitch Claydon spoke about the methods of two of Durham's top order in recent years and their success on bowler-friendly wickets at The Riverside. The two concerned were Dale Benkenstein and Michael DiVenuto, the backbone of their team's batting order in their years of Championship domination.

As Mitch rightly said, both found consistent success when the ball seamed by scoring from deliveries short of a full length and being sound in defence against the full pitched ball. And I could feel that working at the crease at

Hartlepool. Front foot drives brought about a number of dismissals whilst the slowness of the pitch allowed batsmen to adjust to seaming deliveries short of a length.

By the time I had reached the 100 mark in Hartlepool, two of the first XI middle-order had done the same at Headingley in Yorkshire's first innings. Bairstow gained much sought-after confidence from a typically bullish knock whilst Adil, perhaps relieved by the passing of his revelations in the press, staked a claim for Championship inclusion with a century of his own full of characteristic flair. Though individual struggles continued at the top of the order, the batting success of two of Yorkshire's potential match-winners was a valuable highlight of the week.

A further positive from the three days of friendly Roses competition was the return of Tim Bresnan after an enforced lay-off for elbow surgery. Rarely do we see "Bres" in a Yorkshire shirt these days, after a spell of international success coming as no surprise, but Championship overs for his County will form a key part of Tim's return to the Test match fold. As with England's line-up, an all-rounder of such quality brings priceless balance and impressive batting depth to the Yorkshire side at a time when runs will be sorely needed.

Aside from both sets of players and their support staff, the only spectators witnessing my century at blustery Hartlepool were the handful of old-timers sat in their regular seats beside the bar, each with a half of ale. Yet within minutes of our declaration, news of the team and my score had been sent to almost 24,000 followers of the Club, courtesy of the weird and wonderful world of Twitter.

In the words of ECB Managing Director Hugh Morris, the use of the online social network by cricketers is "like giving a machine gun to a monkey", but the present day County Club uses it effectively to communicate with a mass of remote spectators. How surreal to think that events at a near-deserted league cricket Club somewhere in the country could be followed within moments by so many across the world.

The early-season return to the cricketing

A world away from Headingley: views of the Club cricket leagues... ...A sunny day at Skelmanthorpe CC...

Scrapping my way to a half-century on a sticky wicket at Thongsbridge CC

drawing board had been a very productive one for the majority concerned. Returning internationals had enjoyed success with bat and ball and lessons of a disappointing start to the Championship season had been put into practice by members of both Yorkshire sides taking to the field. For me, bruised thighs and windburnt cheeks were signs of useful time in the middle compiling a statement of a score, and I could rest with the quiet and peaceful satisfaction of a job well done. Just as the disappointments of an innings loss against Sussex would not define the Club's season, a century at the first opportunity would not guarantee further success in mine, but it was a step in a very enjoyable direction.

... Exposed to the elements at Hall Bower CC.

When Saturday comes

With County professionals into their well-rehearsed routines of the season, Saturday April 20 marked the start of the cricketing summer for the thousands of Club cricketers in the County. After months of waiting, it was time to bring the trusty kit bag down from the attic and dust it off ready for action. Time too to rub an oily rag over the favourite piece of willow in the hope it will last the summer and whiten the boots still soiled from last summer's finale.

And it is not only the players for whom Saturday marked the start of something. A quick glance at Facebook on Friday evening led me to a comment made by a friend widowed by weekend cricket, looking ahead with knowing. "And so it begins. Six hours each Saturday taking the boy to cricket to watch the old boy play. At least it's sunny. And there's a bar".

So late on Saturday morning, I set off from home wearing Club colours of a different kind, heading for the home ground of my adopted Club, Hoylandswaine C.C., an hour or so's journey south on the M1 into the South Yorkshire hills.

"Sorry Joe, it's a bit sticky" is my welcome from the Club groundsman on my arrival. Mopping his brow in a rush to prepare the first pitch of the summer, he sighs in reflection upon weeks of battling with the elements and April snow drifts to set the stage for the season's opener.

Arriving at the ground, a small and undulating patch of green high on the valley side, I park in my usual spot on the side of the road, a good 50 yards from the Club gates. The car park is empty, but experience tells me to keep my distance – the sound of leather on bonnet is a regular occurrence with sixes bludgeoned frequently out of the Club grounds over wide long on.

With kit bag in tow, my route to the dressing room takes me into the bar, where the bar man is laying out the bar mats in anticipation of a busy afternoon, then past the kitchen, where the tea lady is buttering dozens of slices of white bread, laid out on the kitchen surface. "Oooo, 'ello. 'Av you wintered well?" she says as I pass.

At the dressing room door, there is the usual problem. Not quite half the team have arrived, but the few that have are jostling for room as though in a busy nightclub, searching for bats and jockstraps amidst the floor covering of cricket bags.

Hoylandswaine's dressing rooms are comfortably the smallest I have ever witnessed at a cricket ground anywhere in the world. Comparable in size to a hotel bathroom, they offer just about enough space for five players to change without unintentional shoulder barges and apologies. Two players change in the showers, risking a kit bag full of soapy suds and others simply leave their batting kit in the car until the game requires. As usual, my spot is in the corridor, two yards from the gents toilet, with cricket bag hoisted up onto three adjacent bar stools to allow the bar regulars to pass.

"Eh up, Joe lad!" our resident number eleven shouts on seeing my arrival, dripping pork pie in both hand and mouth. "Get any runs in t'week, mate?"

So with the stumps brought out from the groundsman's shed and the white paint of the boundary line still drying in the late morning sun, the league cricket season gets underway. "Up the Swaine!" someone shouts from the pavilion as we take to the field. Our opposition is the newly-promoted Barkisland. I have no idea what to expect, but they appear to come in all shapes and sizes.

The field at Hoylandswaine is a curious sight. In its centre is a level and well-manicured square of four or five pitches. Walking from the square in any direction of choice, the outfield slopes like the turf of the crown green bowls club behind the sightscreen at one end. Bowling from the Village Hall end, square leg stands a considerable height above the pitch, looking down upon play, whilst the cover fielders have a steep incline to ascend to stop an early quick single. Behind square on the off side, the slope is so severe that the bowler can see his third man fielder only from the waist up. An alerting cry and wave is required to warn the unfortunate man stood down the slope as the ball quickens in his direction. So stood at slip for the first over of the day, my feet stand comfortably below those of the batsman, who stands awaiting each delivery on the raised plateau of the square. Bizarrely, even a nick from the bat on its way to ground could easily carry above waist height.

Along the boundary at the foot of the slope, a wall of netting hoisted 30 foot up a line of poles guards the neighbouring houses from the inevitable onslaught of heaves to leg in the late overs. At deep backward point, an opening in the row of Yorkshire stone buildings reveals a beautiful view down the valley side and into the distance. The eye follows the green expanses of the valley into the suburbs of Barnsley and beyond to the silhouettes of South Yorkshire power stations in the distance.

Our performance in the field is ordinary at best. The 50-yard boundaries are simply not big enough for a bowling display covered in early season cobwebs and rust. And the five catches dropped have not helped the cause. Club captain John Sadler would be pulling out his hair if he had any remaining on his capped bald head.

In reply to an above par score of 235, I walk out to bat full of confidence after my midweek hundred and keen to groove good habits with a match-winning innings. Pushing forward to my third ball – a slow medium seamer from a teenager trotting in from the Village Hall end – I see it seam away as it pitches and catch the edge of my bat. The nick just makes it to the wicketkeeper, who catches it above his bootlaces. Oh dear. What a funny game this is, I think, and with a wry smile, return to the dressing room corridor. Time to pack up the kit bag, put it back in the car, and make some room for the middle order.

Wickets fell at regular intervals throughout our reply, which ended 30 or so runs short of an improbable and undeserved victory. The after-match post-mortem was straight to the point and pulled no punches. Eleven players, the scorer and the Club Chairman squeezed into the dressing room box to draw a line under a rusty start and pledge their attendance at the midweek evening net practice. Even at the amateur level, cricket delivers a rollercoaster ride, and for other visiting professionals and I, an interesting perspective on how the game captures the hearts and minds of everyone concerned when Saturday comes.

The Opening Lunch

"One of my offies did for you, Geoffrey", comes the claim from the stage. "Do you remember?" Sat on the table behind Jonny Bairstow and I, Geoffrey Boycott looks skyward with a knowing intake of breath. The voice behind the microphone is that of Johnny Barclay, of Sussex CCC and MCC reputation, but on stage today in his capacity as raconteur and speaker for the opening lunch of the 150th year of Yorkshire County Cricket Club.

With the great man biting his lip, Barclay proceeds with a detailed account of an ordinary off-spinner which, having left his hand, found turn and bounce from a "flatty" at Hove, only to catch the glove of Geoffrey mid-sweep. An admirably brave anecdote with which to start one's speech as a visitor to Boycott's home County. For his sake, I hope he treads the fine line carefully.

A total of 391 guests and paying members were in attendance for this opening lunch with a difference. There were sesquicentennial pinstripes aplenty around the East Stand Long Room for a Sunday lunch of, naturally, roast beef and Yorkshire pudding, and vases of white roses in bloom on each of the many tables. In a repeat of the gesture at the retirement dinner of Lord Hawke, the Club's captain in 1883 and person responsible for the creation of the 11-petal emblem, guests were invited to take home a rose from their table.

Barclay continued off script, surveying the room for familiar faces. "Phil Sharpe, oh, Phil Sharpe, how great to see you! The ball used to melt into your hands! It really did!" Gesturing to the current players he could not find in the room, he went on candidly. "Lads, you probably don't know who Phil Sharpe is, do you?" Cue an awkward chuckle from the room.

At the best of times, cricket lunches can be dry affairs. The menu is often predictably unadventurous for the hundreds of guests, the running order occupied by familiar faces from the after-dinner circuit, and the feel of the event generally lacking any kind of energy. But today is slightly different, no doubt due to the extra effort made in anniversary celebrations, and the sense of occasion, therefore. Aside from that, the presence of a self-confessed "toff" from Sussex enticing reaction with stirring lines of the Queen's English seems to have lightened the mood.

The spotlight of attention was shone on the attending greats of Yorkshire's past as Barclay continued to survey the room and ignore his notes. "Illy, Dickie, Closey, how are you? Great to see you all! Are you still with us Closey or are you nodding off?" Each of the probing one-liners was taken in good humour and in the spirit of an entertaining afternoon. Siddy won some Wensleydale cheese in the raffle and Henry Blofeld turned up to introduce his guests William Hague, Alec Ferguson and David Beckham, courtesy of impressionist Kevin Connelly.

Thoughts of a disastrous start to the 150th Championship season were far from mind until you-know-who referred to his notes. "Andrew", he said, pointing directly to the Club captain on the table in front of him. "I was captain of Sussex for six long years and do you know what I would tell my men on the eve of our first match of the summer?" Galey did not know what to expect. "Don't peak too early, that's what I told them! Don't peak too early! And peak we did not. We always lost at the

A familiar view: Day One of the Championship match at Chester-le-Street, as seen from the players' balcony.

first attempt". Such words from a man from Sussex were of no consolation to Captain or his players.

Once again, a celebration of the Club's anniversary had been a resounding success, officially opening the summer of cricket and, at least momentarily, finding refuge from the stark reality of a first team itching for its first victory of the season. Pleasantries complete, the week ahead promised a putting aside of the romance of past and future, and a quick return to the stark reality of now.

Rooty grabs the headlines

In front of a capacity crowd on a sticky evening in Raipur, Mahela Jayawardene has just checked a delivery from Pune Warriors seamer Asoka Dinda into the hands of a waiting Luke Wright at short extra cover. The dancers are doing their thing on stage beside the boundary rope and the Pune fans are hysterical. This is Indian razzmatazz at its garish best.

The view out of the window behind me is a sorry one. A gale force wind continues to blow the persistent rain sideways across an increasingly boggy and uncovered pitch and the prospects of play are dwindling at a pace. It is teatime at Hall Bower Cricket Club and whilst the rain falls outside, I have live televised action from the IPL and a paper plate of triangular sandwiches to occupy my time.

I was 50-odd not out when the freezing rain became too much for the surprisingly resilient umpires. Up to that point, I can safely say I have never played through such persistent rain on a cricket field than I had for the previous 24 overs. High on the hills of Huddersfield, we are exposed to whatever the elements throw at us from above.

With conditions worsening, the home side turned to their overseas spinner, who had been practising all kinds of mystery deliveries from mid-off the over before his captain's call. Unsure of what to expect, I queried my opening partner Alex Morris. "Who's this lad, Almo?" I said. "Oh, I recognise him" he said immediately. "You know who he is – he played at that Club where the sheep shit on the field and the 'keeper talks a load of bollocks as he runs in". Needless to say, Championship cricket at Headingley seemed a world away.

The first three days of the Championship match at Chester-le-Street had produced first Division cricket that kept the travelling members on the edge of their seats. The lion's share of the first day went in our favour, with Bresnan continuing his promising return from injury with four key Durham wickets. With the home side 122-7, thoughts of the first-round disappointment were far from mind. However, a typically bullish riposte of 70 from 107 balls from "Colonel" Phil Mustard, aided by some faltering Yorkshire bowling, led Durham to a more than respectable 237 all out.

After a second day rain delay, Yorkshire's first innings reply stuttered from 57-3 overnight to a disappointing 177 all out, thanks in part to another member of England's squad of seamers, Graham Onions, who took 5-63 from his 19 overs of typically skiddy pace and aggression. After the collapse at Headingley two weeks earlier, only Rooty showed significant resistance and bucked the trend of ill discipline with the bat.

A 60-run deficit on first innings was considerable in such conditions, making victory unlikely. But further salt to the wound was added by a resilient display from Durham's top order in the second innings, leading them to almost certain safety, over 250 runs ahead with seven second-innings wickets in hand. Surely there were only two results possible in the remaining four sessions of the game?

"Root's out for 182" came the shout from the drinkers outside the pavilion bar. Our opponents, Skelmanthorpe, still needed 40-odd to win and I was at backward-point, doing all I could to prevent the single. On taking to the field two hours earlier, 'Swaine teammate Amar Rashid – brother of Adil – informed me of the score at The Riverside, where Yorkshire were closing in on an historic fourth innings run chase against Durham. Brother Adil was at the wicket and going well, at least so it seemed according to the frequently refreshing online scorecard.

"I knew they'd do it", I thought to myself as another 'Swaine delivery got dispatched to the short leg-side boundary. The previous evening, my text to Galey had proved close to the mark. "Go well tomorrow mate. Seems like a gettable total with a decent start?" With a game to win in front of me, I could not help but wish to be out in the middle at Chester-le-Street, or at least sharing the excitement on the changing room balcony.

But what a knock it must have been from the man keeping me out of first-XI recognition. A Championship century is hard to come by for the best of players, but particularly so against a new ball at The Riverside, where the pitch is renowned for its seam movement. Comparisons with another Sheffield-reared opening batsman were easy to make and not necessarily inaccurate. "An exhibition of technical artistry" was Chris Waters' summary in The Yorkshire Post, "the finest of Root's fledgling career". The statistics could not suggest otherwise – 182 from 283 balls carrying the team to within touching distance of an improbable victory. We got over the victory line with 6.1 overs remaining in the match and four wickets in hand.

A day earlier, at the close on day three, Durham captain Paul Collingwood had surprised some travelling Yorkshire members with a declaration without the typical half-an-hour-long swing of the willow that precedes such a decision. Though sporting to some onlookers, the declaration, leaving us needing 336 for victory, was sensible in so many ways. Graham Onions and Co. would have two spells with the first new ball, split by a restful third evening; the Yorkshire openers would have a spell of seven overs to face before the day three close that was nothing more than a hiding to nothing; a second new ball would be available at a key time in the final session of the game; and, above all, a tempting carrot had been dangled for a fourth innings chase. The declaration had all the textbook elements for which a captain could wish. And you could say it was another example of a commonplace trend in County Championship cricket these days, a captain in no doubt about risking loss in search of victory and a points tally to climb up the table.

So through their disappointment, the Durham players would be wrong to reflect on an overly generous offering from their captain. Rather, they may look back on a bowling performance lacking penetration, a day four pitch quickly losing its first innings pace, or simply a standout innings from a 22-year-old that was worthy of the spoils and just too good when it mattered.

Whilst Durham came to terms with a second successive defeat, the Yorkshire side would have left the North East with a contrasting view forward to the next four-day match. After a disastrous opening round and a week staring in the cricketing mirror, we could sigh with the relief of a victory snatched from the jaws of defeat. For the first innings batting display, deemed "unacceptable" by coach Gillespie, had echoes of the first-day collapse against Sussex. "Mindset" was the key, according to Director Moxon, who knows all there is to know about compiling an innings in trying English conditions. And there is certainly truth in his words, for when the Yorkshire line-up shows a somewhat old-fashioned stubbornness to balance its carefree aggression, there are few bowling attacks capable of breaking through.

As I left Skelmanthorpe for home, the disappointment of 'Swaines second successive defeat were quickly overcome by thoughts of what might be for me in the coming weeks. Runs for Root made his Test recall all the more likely, opening the door for a possible recall of my own back where I wanted to be, in Yorkshire's chosen first XI. Three days in competition with our friends over the Pennines promised another opportunity to knock on the door.

Clark joins an exclusive Club

Ask past and present Yorkshire cricketers where they most love to play, and you will get a variety of answers. Lord's would be the obvious choice for the fortunate few to have taken to the pristine slope. But chances are there will be another ground that gets a mention more often than most, an alternative Home of Cricket. A modest ground with no airs and graces, the source of many a Yorkshire win and the most famous of all in our last Championship-winning year, thanks to that catch from captain David Byas. A ground oozing with history and the memories of the greats to have taken to their stage. Described by David Hopps as "the finest amphitheatre in the land", that place is North Marine Road, Scarborough. And for the next three days, it would host a three-day friendly against our second-XI rivals from over the Pennines.

Yorkshire cricketers love to play at North Marine Road. "Who've we got at Scarborough this year?" is a question not far from the players' lips on that mid-winter release of the County fixtures. Stories are written during the annual cricketing pilgrimage to the East Coast, both on and off the field. People remember whole seasons by the events of Festival Week, whether they be good or otherwise. The weather, the toss, the quality of the fish and chips, all add to another year's chapter by the sea.

Even the two-hour drive towards the East

Coast kick starts the thoughts of what might be. And though the cricketing summer has brought me to Scarborough far earlier than usual on this occasion, this morning's journey was no different. My travelling partner for the week, young Ben Coad, was yet to appreciate the childlike excitement of those longer-in-the-tooth than him. In time, he would be seduced by the romance of our destination.

As expected during these early days of summer, Scarborough was quiet when we arrived, near-deserted in fact, as if waiting for the sun to break through and attract the travelling tourists in their droves. Much was unchanged from my last visit here over a year ago – the chippies, the cafes and the grand hotels all as they were, surviving the battering from the salty on shore wind.

And the ground was as silent as the streets when I drove the impractical Mini through the gates. No queue of expectant members lengthening quickly around the corner, no security presence at the turnstiles or sense of last-minute preparations within the ground. Just groundsman John Dodds, alone on his square, pushing stumps into the earth, and the familiar squawk of the hungry gulls circling overhead.

As is often the case at this special place, the week of cricket would be remembered by many for a piece of cricketing history. Approaching lunch on the second day, Yorkshire left-arm spinner Gurman Randhawa was settling comfortably into a bowling rhythm, with 2-15 from his overs to date. At the close of his 12th, middle-order batsman Jordan Clark appeared restless, rehearsing a slog-sweep as umpire Rob Bailey called "Over". No one could have predicted what was to follow.

Clark has decided to put his slog-sweep into action. The first ball of Gurman's 13th over, a perfectly respectable off-spinner of good length and line, has been despatched over the midwicket boundary for six, aided by a strengthening wind towards the terraces. Moments later, a repeat. 12 from two balls. From slip, I expect a change of plan from our young spinner – a change in the field, in pace of delivery, or simply in line or

length. But no change comes, just the rhythmical approach and delivery similar to the last. The ball bounces off the concrete terraces and back onto the field. Three from three.

Gurman fires his fourth delivery fuller and straighter, but Clark is equal to the task and helps it on its way, not out of the middle this time, but with enough willow for it to clear the ropes, square on the leg side. The Lancashire dressing room snaps out of its sleepy state and senses something special. Poor Gurman becomes quickly aware of the headline-writers waking up to the unthinkable. Five balls, five slog-swept sixes, all similar in style and equally effective. Clark turns to 'keeper Andrew Hodd behind the stumps. "Might as well 'av a pop 'ere" he says matter-of-factly. And have a pop he does, swinging the sixth and final ball of the over high and well beyond the leg-side boundary. This would have been six on any ground and possibly into a headwind.

Arms aloft as though reaching his century, Clark salutes the applause of his teammates and the hardy handful of spectators dotted around the ground.

Clark had become the first Englishman in the history of professional cricket and only the fifth batsman of any nationality to hit six maximums in an over, joining an elite club occupied by Sobers, Ravi Shastri, Herschelle Gibbs and Yuvraj Singh. Within minutes, though so few witnessed the feat live in the blustery cold, the news was online and common knowledge to anyone with an ear to the ground. The middle-order Lancastrian had given our promising left-arm spinner a record any bowler must dread, and he now stooped under the weight of his infamy.

A day earlier, the world of cricket had seen another record broken by carefree striking of the ball. Appearing for the Bangalore Royal Challengers in an IPL contest against the Pune Warriors, West Indian Chris Gayle had taken just 30 balls to reach his century and 66 to reach his unbeaten total of 175. His devastating assault broke the record for the fastest century in the history of the game and led his side to the highest team total of 263-5 in the shortest form.

A special place: the home dressing room at North Marine Road.

Though not devoid of six-hitting, my innings of 91 on the first day at Scarborough delivered another enjoyable knock on the first-XI door. With comments like "That's as close to perfect as you're going to get" coming from coach Farbrace at lunch, I must say it gave me an intense feeling of peaceful confidence. The pitch was hard and fast in pace, as good as any first-class surface at any time of year, delivering the signature bounce and *carry for which North Marine Road has become renowned. As umpire Rob Bailey remarked, it was a "good cricket wicket" – a well-used cricketing term suggesting equal reward for skilful performance with bat and ball.*

And it is this pace in the surface that makes the entertaining cricket we see so often at Scarborough all the more likely. Hit the pitch hard with wrist behind an upright seam and you will be duly rewarded. Meet full pitched deliveries late with a straight bat and you will be granted equal reward.

The honours boards, high on the walls of both home and away dressing rooms, list those with centuries and/or five-wicket hauls to their name in Championship matches involving Yorkshire at North Marine Road. From the moment they walk through the dressing room door, a player's gaze is drawn to the names, the scores, the records and the history. Hedley Verity, Fred Trueman, Geoffrey Boycott and Andrew Gale. And on two occasions, a certain J.J. Sayers, first a centurion in 2005 and again a year later.

Sipping my teatime cuppa on the second day, I am caught in a confused wonder. "2005? Was it really that long ago? Where have those eight years gone?" I could remember the clip off the hip from that Otis Gibson delivery that brought up my maiden Championship hundred, and the noise that followed. I could remember walking into the dressing room the next day to see my name in shiny gold transfer at the bottom of the list on the dressing room board, the most recent batsman to mark a place in Scarborough cricket history. And I could remember carrying my bat for an unbeaten 122 against Middlesex on a rainy day in 2006, with former teammate Chris Silverwood using all his guile down the hill from the Trafalgar Square End. "'Av a nibble!" he would shout as I left another ball wide of off stump. "It's time I got up on that board again", I said to myself, in private determination. And with that thought, I took to the field for the evening session.

Back to the present game and the pace and bounce of the Scarborough pitch had got the better of our inexperienced side with bat and ball. Our batsmen, trained from a young age on the slow, soft surfaces of the leagues, found few answers to the ball seaming at pace towards the cordon,

whilst our bowlers were left exposed by a much smaller margin for error. Taking the chance to quiz groundsman John Dodds as he passed the dressing room door, I could not help but ask for his secret recipe for pace in his pitches. "Well…", he said with humble reluctance, "…my ol' boss always told me I 'ad the knack for 'nowin when to get off t'roller". There it was. The simple method for preparing such a surface.

A first innings deficit of near 200 was a stark indication of the difference in quality between white and red rose in their respective first innings. So when the seasonal rain and coastal fret set in on the third afternoon and brought the game to a premature end, it gave us welcome relief from our efforts to save the game. The covers did not come out in time to prevent Alex Lees from bringing up a well-deserved century after his first innings disappointment. Scoring freely around the wicket, and showing glimpses of new-found options against spin developed during his pre-season tour to Sri Lanka, the knock was just deserts for his hard work over recent weeks. And I was pleased for him, even if he did run me out in the 20s. Our rivalry-cum-alliance was a healthy motivator for us both, setting a strong foundation for the second XI's batting and pushing us both to find new levels of performance.

Three days at Scarborough had produced the exciting and unpredictable cricket we have come to know by the seaside, and to our surprise, a piece of cricketing history. For me, it had taken me one step further to that return to first-class cricket I so wanted and solidified the confidence I had found during the windy week further north. Packing the car for home, I said farewell to the alternative Home of Yorkshire Cricket, hoping I would return as one of the XI for the Championship match in the not too distant future.

CHAPTER FOUR

April into May

A week full of promise

Peering over the screen of my laptop, I look down at a wearying Yorkshire fielding display against Derbyshire. If you had just walked into the ground, you would know the visitors were on top without a glance at the scoreboard. High on the third floor of the Carnegie Pavilion, in one of the quiet dual-purpose University study rooms, the students on neighbouring tables are oblivious to the struggle of the Yorkshire bowlers. The score is 240-1, 230 runs on since Bresnan chalked up our first wicket of the day, Billy Godleman caught at third slip whilst the ball was new. Ominously, reluctant opener Chesney Hughes is 140 not out and keen to open his arms. Though there is nothing more I would like than to be back in the first team, it seems this one is not a bad one to miss.

Half an hour later, the second XI players and I are loading our kit bags into the team minibus outside the indoor school. Destination North Wales for three more days cricket against Lancashire. Typically, players would be required to pair up with a willing travelling partner and find their way to the team hotel, assisted by Sat Nav and mobile internet. But in these recessional times, a minibus and kit van saves the pounds and pence of travelling expenses.

As we leave, there is a cheer from the crowd. A wicket at last? A twitter update aboard the minibus confirms our assumptions. Shivnarine Chanderpaul caught Lyth bowled Rashid for four. Good news.

Aside from the obvious heartache of our much-talked-about attack, the theme of the first day's cricket at Headingley was nothing other than the pitch. A week earlier, captain Paul Collingwood fell victim to his home surface at The Riverside, underestimating the extent to which it would lose pace in the second innings and open the door for an improbable fourth innings chase. And today, after openly celebrating his first successful toss of the coin and opportunity to insert the visitors, captain Gale was ruing his decision and searching for answers. By all accounts, his decision to fire up his bowlers on winning the toss was quite understandable. The surface was cold and damp after early-morning rain, and the skies were overcast: traditional signs of Headingley conditions favouring the seamers. And when Godleman fended a delivery that bounced and left him to slip, the decision at the toss appeared justifiable.

Little did Galey know that the man at the other end when the first wicket fell would remain unbeaten, just four short of his Club's record individual score, leading the visitors to a first innings total of 475. From the Holiday Inn in North Wales, I felt sympathy for our skipper. There had been more experienced heads than his deceived by the Headingley surface, but that would be no consolation for him. Home advantage in First Division cricket is of paramount importance and that starts with preparing a pitch to suit your strengths over those of the opposition. As Collingwood and Gale found out within a fortnight, striving for points without this inside knowledge is a difficult and tiring task.

The Headingley surface was clearly flat, but our bowling was falling short of expectation. The statistics from our resident analyst told the story. In the afternoon session on day one, only 24% of deliveries pitched in "Dizzy's box", the area on the pitch from which a ball goes on to hit the top of off stump, or the knee-roll of the batsman's pads. And out of the 155 runs scored between lunch and tea, only eight were scored from that percentage. The statistics did not lie, and confirmed the theory of consistently hitting the "box" to build pressure with the ball.

The second day at Headingley coincided with the first for the second XI in their three-day match at Northop Hall Cricket Club. A Union Jack and a Welsh dragon both flew on the pavilion flagpole, but our opponents were certainly not from Wales' only County Club. It seemed everyone was confused as to our whereabouts.

Our Director of Cricket and Kit Van Driver for the week, Mr. Moxon, felt it appropriate to clear up the confusion and ask one of the players to look up the answer. Always keen to challenge a player when possible, Martyn trusted the research of Gurman Randhawa, perhaps not the keenest fact-seeker of our select few, but willing nonetheless. The second day warm-up was preceded by the much-awaited announcement. "Lads…", Gurman began with confidence, "…after much research I can confirm that the County we are in…is… er…". His mind went blank and the heckling began. "Er,…Flint…er…Flintwick! That's it! Flintwick! No, not Flintwick,…er… Flintstone!" Those listening in needed no further fuel for their heckling fire. It later emerged that Flintshire was our location. Good effort, Gurman, nonetheless.

Much like the equivalent at Headingley, the pitch in Flintshire raised more than a few eyebrows on the first morning. Dry, bare and almost white in appearance, it was not what you would come to expect at a Club ground in April. "It reminds me of the pitch in Gauhati in India in '84" remarked kit van man Moxon. "You don't often hear that in Lancashire" I replied.

The three-day fixture would be the second of three such matches against Lancashire for the second team. Deliberately close in succession, the fixtures provided a decent quality of second XI cricket for two large and local squads. As in Scarborough, the Lancashire top order would provide a tough challenge for our developing attack, whilst Oliver Newby, Tom Smith and Wayne White would ask sufficiently testing questions of myself and partner Lees with the new ball.

The close on the penultimate day in both Yorkshire matches left the respective home sides planning an attacking hour of batting on the final day before an inevitable declaration. Lancashire had twisted the knife in Flintshire with quick second innings runs adding to their sizeable first innings lead. Meanwhile, Yorkshire's first XI had bounced back from a first innings disappointment with incredible results. Root had followed his headline grabbing at Chester-le-Street with the second double century of his fledgling career, whilst Bairstow rattled to a belligerent 186 at near a run-a-ball. The pair added 231 for the fourth wicket in just over four hours and by the close, Yorkshire led by 122 with a day to play.

On the minibus home to the Holiday Inn, Martyn made his predictions for Headingley from the seat beside me. "Another hour's batting in the morning, Squiz, then stick 'em in for a tricky third innings. Funny things happen in the third innings, you know?"

In North Wales, the Lancashire middle order proceeded as predicted on the final morning, scoring freely for an hour before making their declaration. With the pitch fast becoming the slow paced turner we expected, a victory target of 353 seemed beyond reach, particularly with our first innings collapse in mind. Nonetheless, a solid and steady start from Alex Lees and myself took us into the lunch break without loss and within comfortable reach of closing out the game as a draw.

The first ten overs of the final day at Headingley produced a further 80 runs for the White Rose, leaving Derbyshire needing 202 to make the home side bat again and the prospect of a tricky third innings. And with the key wickets of Hughes and Chanderpaul taken by Plunkett within the first hour of the innings, leaving Derbyshire 47-3, the improbable began to seem possible.

The afternoon session ticked along quietly at Northop Hall, suggesting nothing other than an early handshake between captains accepting the stalemate of a draw. At tea, the Lancashire fielders had one eye on an early close and drive home along the M56. With eight second innings wickets remaining, not

Jonny Bairstow and Joe Root take to the field in the Championship match against Derbyshire at Headingley.

even a repeat of our first innings collapse would bring about defeat before the close.

In Leeds, a partnership of 92 between Wayne Madsen and Wes Durston seemed to be leading the Championship match to a similar stalemate, and many a wise head was accepting the predictable draw. But then a piece of paper was placed in captain Gale's hand. A scrap sent from the dressing room, detailed with a plan to break the deadlock, an experimental field setting, and it worked. Within moments, Durston had chipped Brooks to Jaques at midwicket and Madsen had fallen leg before to a reverse-swinging delivery from the same man. The abrasive nature of the dry, grassless pitch was creating ideal conditions for reverse swing, and at 150-5, still requiring 52 to avoid an innings defeat, the visitors were beginning to wobble.

With the Lancashire bowlers devoid of the intensity they showed when pushing for victory, Yorkshire seconds' middle order scored freely after tea. Hodd and Hodgson made particularly pugnacious contributions, pricking up the ears of coach Farbrace, who began to sniff an opportunity to push on. Within half an hour's cricket, and with the Lancashire fielders slowly waking up to a fast-changing game situation, Farby gave orders to go for the win, made all the more likely by an explosive 42 off 27 balls from skipper Pyrah. Having conceded a first innings deficit of over 180, could we really steal a win in the last hour of the match?

The tea break could not stop the momentum of the home side at Headingley. Brooks took two wickets in two balls after tea and the reverse swing was proving too much to handle

Onwards and upwards: Joe Root celebrates his double century against Derbyshire.

for the Derbyshire lower order. Derbyshire facing the unthinkable at 157-8. News quickly spread to Northop Hall, where Ashraf alerted everyone to the latest from his twitter feed in the dressing room. "Brooksy's got another, lads!"

The second-teamers now had eyes on two matches at once. A run chase going to the wire outside the pavilion window and an all-out push for victory with the ball at Headingley. "I'm pleased for Brooksy", Moin continued. "There were a few groans at Headingley when he went for those boundaries against Sussex, but he's come back well".

Moments later, young Lewis Stabler stood up out of seat. "Rashid's got another! 162 for 9! We've done it. It's over now!"

"Never say that!" said Moin, correcting his teammate. "It's not over yet. Palladino can bat". The injured Palladino took strike as the visitor's last chance of avoiding defeat, but fell shortly after, trapped leg before by the reverse swing of Brooks. Cue the Tino Best-like celebrations of new signing Brooks, sprinting to the midwicket wicket boundary, arms pumping, fists punching the air. Think Drogba at Stamford Bridge and you are not far off. We had done it, pulled off the most improbable of victories from nowhere, thanks in part to the polished aggression of our first innings batting, and clearly to the destructive skill of new-boy Brooks, who finished with figures of 5-40 from his 14 overs of reverse swinging pace. The self-confessed "so-called foreigner from down south" had quietened any remaining doubters and brought about our second four-day surge to victory in as many weeks. After the anti-climax of the innings loss to Sussex, who would have thought the following fortnight of Championship cricket would produce such a change?

At Northop Hall, Moin confirmed the result as his twitter feed refreshed. "Lads, 163 all out! Brooksy got a five-for!" Outside, the body language of the Lancashire fielders said it all. From within reach of an accepted draw, we were getting quickly closer to an improbable win. Hodgson fell for a fine 87 and the finishing task was left to two younger members of the team, "Wilfred" Rhodes and Jack Leaning.

The experienced White did his best to unsettle their composure with a procession of aggressive short balls but the young pair was equal to the task. With two needed for victory, White tried one too many short balls to Leaning, who hooked the ball over the ropes for six. Two wins out of two for the Club on the same day, victories on which few would have bet. As a voice from the second team dressing room said, "We've pulled two out of the bag. [They were] two games we never looked like winning. That's a good sign". Understandably, coaches Moxon and Farbrace could not have been happier drivers of their respective minibuses on the route home to Leeds.

Stuck in the M62 traffic on the way home that evening, I could reflect on three weeks of second XI cricket that had gone nicely to plan. I had built upon an encouraging pre-season with time in the middle, a century and a 90-odd to my name, and further trust in the technical improvements I had made during the winter. But I now hungered for more, for a proper contest with the bat, cricket with higher stakes and the opportunity to make a match-winning contribution when it mattered most. The second XI environment had been a cosy introduction to the summer, and a valuable nursery for my game, but without the crowds and the cameras, the adrenaline kick of cricket with consequence and the common drive for Championship points. Root and Bairstow would soon be leaving us for well-deserved duties with the Lions, and the time was right for my return to the first-class arena. Would the text I so wished for come in the coming days? Was my case for selection strong enough to earn a recall to the senior team?

Back where I belong

It is a sleepy Bank Holiday morning and the roads to Headingley are empty of the usual rush-hour traffic. The sounds of Norah Jones occasionally distract my thoughts, which are with my return to the first XI dressing room and the start of tomorrow's Championship match against visitors Somerset. A year ago to the day, a call from Dizzy disrupted my chat with Lisa in our local village café in Harrogate. The tone of his voice and his slow, considered start to our short conversation gave it all away. "We've decided to give Lythy a crack" I remember him saying. I had lost my place in the first team and a return to the second XI was the salt in my wound. But this morning, a day before the start of tomorrow's match, I can feel the tingle of nervous excitement for which I have hungered. With many of tomorrow's team sleeping off the effects of a late return home from the one-dayer at Colwyn Bay, this morning promises a short and sharp net session for the rested few.

The text came on Friday afternoon. Pushing Sebastian and buggy around the parks of Harrogate, I was relieved by the slowness of a day free from cricket. Lisa lost my attention for a few moments. "I knew it was something important," she admitted, later. The message from Dizz listed the 12-man squad for the fourth Championship match of the summer and there I was, second on the list. I had done it. The opportunity I so wanted had apparently come and my first significant goal of the season had been reached. I was back where I wanted to be in the first-class arena, the place where I felt at once challenged and alive, and in the Club's flagship team, pushing for every possible success. The long, quiet days on the nursery slopes of the second XI had been worth it. I could have punched the air and sighed with relief.

"Where should I sit?" I thought as I walked into the Carnegie Stand dressing rooms. Siddy had been the first to arrive, sat in just his pink boxers in the corner. My internal conversation continued. "Rooty's off with the Lions but he's left all sorts of kit in his spot, Jonny much the same. Richy might not play but moving him from his usual corner could be a little awkward. And everyone else appears well set in their dressing room ways. Mmmm…Jonny's spot it is. He won't mind me cleaning up his 'keeping stuff and piles of unopened letters". I look forward to the day when someone can say: "You can't sit there. That's where Squiz sits". Bressie follows Brooksy into the room, suitably dressed in preparation for a Bank Holiday barbecue. It is good to be back.

My pre-match net session was exactly what I was hoping for in preparation for tomorrow. A challenging 20-minute workout against Brooks and Bresnan on a lively surface was a sharpening reminder of the need for excellent technical basics and the step-up in quality from the second tier of County cricket. Each ball was a testing question, seaming one way or the other, sometimes bouncing more than expected, and every time hitting the willow hard. Only on one occasion did opportunity for a boundary present itself – a short ball from Brooks I gladly cut away.

The key tomorrow was going to be committing my top half towards the ball, thereby playing the moving ball more easily under my eyes, and above all trusting in the ways that had brought me success in the early days of the season. I could rest assured that my movements were decisive and consistent and my usual game plan as steadily productive as it had been previously against the opening attack.

Ballance walks into the dressing room as I unstrap my pads. He is sleepy-eyed from last night's late return from Wales. "We didn't bowl well," he says in summary of Yorkshire's loss to Glamorgan in the season's opening 40-over contest at Colwyn Bay. "The ground was small, the pitch decent, but they should never have got that many. Losing two wickets early didn't help either. We were always behind the chase from there".

Our first outing of the one-day season, an away fixture against Glamorgan at Colwyn Bay, did not quite go to plan. The game had some

Jack "The Headband Warrior" Brooks celebrates the important wicket of Wes Durston on the final day against Derbyshire.

Brooks receives his teammates' approval after taking his fifth Derbyshire victim.

An improbable victory: Brooksy takes the applause of his home crowd with five wickets in the second innings.

notable firsts - the start of our commercially-minded existence as the "Yorkshire Vikings"; a List 'A' debut for a somewhat surprised Will Rhodes after some eye-catching pre-season performances; and our first taste of the new rules of fielding restrictions, stipulating one extra man to be inside the inner circle.

That first taste was somewhat bitter sweet. Bitter for the bowlers, who naturally conceded significantly more runs through field settings made more attacking by regulations than they previously were. And equally sweet for the batsmen, who benefitted from an extra scoring option, gifted to them by the new laws. Never one to be verbose, Patto summed up the challenge. "You just had to compromise with your field settings somewhere, and take a risk with the extra man in the ring. You were left wishing for one more defensive position outside the circle".

Unsurprisingly, Rich Pyrah was the pick of the attack, using all his limited overs experience and new-found determination to take 4-43 from his allotted overs. But the home side's total of 285-7 was a big score from 40 overs and, despite the relatively short outground boundaries, clearly above par.

The target score was made all the more difficult to achieve after the loss of two top order wickets in the early stages of our reply, Jaques and Root both dismissed by the easily underestimated Graham Wagg. The most encouraging sign of our reply was welcome success with the bat for Galey, who perhaps benefitted from having to throw caution to the wind and make amends for our stuttering start.

In recent weeks, an instinctive pre-delivery movement across to the off-side had left our captain struggling to transfer his weight into the ball towards his target. But as is so often the case, it appeared that the pressing need to score quickly in one-day cricket and create opportunity to free the arms had refined his movements and encouraged him to transfer his weight towards the bowler. 65 from 67 balls brought some respectability to the early stages of our chase and broke a developing pattern of early dismissals in his season.

Where the captain led, Bairstow followed, racing to his half-century from just 34 balls in typically bullish style. After his dismissal, Adil did all he could to edge us towards the target, but his 42 from just 28 balls could do little about the far-too-frequent loss of his partners at the other end. As most spectators could have predicted at the halfway point, the home side's total was beyond our reach, confirmed by our dismissal for an insufficient 257.

With respect to our opposition, one look at the fixture card before the season would have given every Yorkshire cricketer the confidence that our one-day season would start in winning ways. Glamorgan were certainly not to be underestimated, but neither were they to be feared, and anything close to a satisfactory performance would have been expected to be enough for victory. But we had fallen significantly short with both bat and ball, and the slowness of our reaction to the new fielding regulations was no excuse. Progression through the group stages of the 40-over competition would only come with significant improvements.

"You never know, lads"

A ball from Peter Trego has found the edge of my bat and my first innings back in the first team is over. Showered, changed and with a polystyrene cup of therapeutic tea, the feelings of disappointment are raw in my mind. Replays of the delivery have played repeatedly between my ears, interrupted only by a deep and heavy feeling in my gut and the odd mumbled expletive. "What did I do wrong? Could I have done anything different? If only I had…" The 'coulds' and 'woulds' change nothing. I am out and have the prospect of a long day watching from the pavilion. Oh shit.

For 45 minutes at the crease, I felt reservedly confident and at home. With a blue sky above and an unblemished pitch beneath my feet, any first game nerves were tempered by a calm enjoyment of the stage. Former teammate Steve Kirby was full of his usual wide-eyed aggression down the hill from the Kirkstall Lane End, but I was equal to his attack, moving decisively and watching well.

"Watch the ball. Late and straight. You're playing well. Keep going."

Trego swung the first ball of the day back into the pads of my opening partner, Lyth. "Bit of shape, Squiz" he confirmed, strolling down the pitch. Three balls later, he pushed one across to the cordon, and "Budge" edged to 'keeper Jos Buttler. Good bowling.

"That'll be his plan. Swing it back and push it across. Just as expected."

The opening half an hour was tough going. Kirby and Trego hardly strayed from their intended line or length, and partner Jaques and I had little option but to sit and wait. "Moving well, Squiz", "Pro" would say with his Aussie twang between overs. "Good positions". This is what it was about, scoring runs against bowling of such quality and consistency, and riding the spells of perceived pressure that drive the game one way then the other.

"Keep trusting. Runs will come. One ball at a time."

It was over so quickly. In a moment, a ball from Trego bounced slightly and left my defensive blade, and I heard the click of leather on edge and the thud of ball into 'keeper's gloves. Bollocks.

With overs still remaining before lunch on the first day, a score of 75-4 left our captain in danger of appearing to have made the wrong decision at the toss for the second time in as many weeks. As it so often does, the new ball had proved a stern test at Headingley, holding in the tufty grass covering and offering just enough seam movement for the visitor's attack. The sun was out, the pitch certainly better than our score suggested, and conditions for batting were likely to improve.

The lunch break offered welcome relief from an eventful morning, and not only on the field of play. Hours earlier, walking into the dressing room at nine o'clock, the first face I saw was that of our captain, pacing hastily around the room. My pleasantries were met with an unexpected response. "I'm a bit stressed to be honest, Squiz", Galey confirmed. "How are those offies coming out? You might be bowling before lunch if I lose the toss!" Not the line I was expecting minutes after my return to the first XI dressing room. "Siddy's gone down with food poisoning over night, Brooksy's touch-and-go with his back and achilles, and now Bressie's pulled up stiff! Moin's on his way up from the two's game at Canterbury". With 90 minutes to the scheduled start, we had two seamers fit enough to play. An early spell of those offies to Marcus Trescothick was looking increasingly likely.

Thankfully, Moin's trip from Canterbury to Headingley was cut short and Brooks and Bresnan declared themselves fit for the start. Even so, considering our fragile lunchtime position, both quicks would have been relieved by the day's rest granted to them by the batting efforts of our middle order on the first day.

Thanks to the skill and persistence of Ballance and Rashid, the afternoon and evening sessions followed a path so often seen on a sunny day at Headingley. The new ball softened with time, the Somerset bowlers gradually lost the patience they had so clearly shown through the morning, and Gary and Adil were adept in taking their opportunity. A partnership of 207 was a record fifth wicket

stand for Yorkshire at the ground in first class matches and quickly justified the decision at the toss to bat first. In his typical way, Gary played the seaming ball wonderfully late and took any opportunity to score square of the wicket through the off side. A similar plan was put into practice at the other end by Adil, who saved his wristy flicks and flamboyant drives for later in the evening session.

"Were you there on Saturday, Dickie?" Martyn shouts as he pauses from his usual pre-match role on day two, offering catching practice to the waiting cordon of Ballance, Lyth and I. The reference is to Barnsley's relegation decider against local rivals Huddersfield Town last weekend, ending in a two-all draw. Dickie Bird continues his stroll around the outfield in his knee-length University of Huddersfield coat.. "Aye, I was lad. Good result for us. But we'll be back down there battling again next year".

"You're probably right, Dickie" Martyn admits as he nicks another one to Ballance at first slip. "We could do with you buying two players for us. I hear QPR have got some going cheap". Dickie nods, chuckles and continues his pre-match lap, hands firmly in his pockets.

Months earlier, on a sunny day in Barbados, Adil filled his time waiting to bat by giving me a glimpse into his return to a fulfilling path in his life, centred around his Faith. He exuded a quiet calm and a perspective unseen throughout recent years spent searching for consistency with bat and ball. And 25 minutes before tea on the second day, saluting a standing ovation from the Yorkshire members as he left the field, that intangible calm was there again. A relaxed, settled calm offering no suggestion of the personal best he had just achieved with the bat or the 4,000 first class runs now to his name. Adil moved from an unbeaten 120 overnight to 180, shepherding the lower middle order towards a total of 505-9 and a declaration. He greeted the dressing room congratulations with the matter-of-factness of a person detached from the outcomes of the game and seemingly less bothered about his achievements than those

"Did you play at that one, Marcus?"
Tim Bresnan delivers the ball on day
two of the Championship match
against Somerset at Headingley.

"Catch it!" (From left to right): Tim Bresnan, me, Adam Lyth and Gary Ballance track the ball from the bat in the Somerset second innings.

patting him on the back. Paradoxically, this apparent lack of concern and letting go of control may be exactly what brings about his continued success.

"Did you play at that one, Marcus?" Bres asks as he completes his follow through. Trescothick smiles and shakes his head as he strolls towards square leg. The Headingley gloom has returned and our opening attack is posing some testing questions for the visitors' first wicket partnership of Trescothick and Nick Compton. As is so often the case, as the cloud descends, the pitch livens up and offers seam and bounce from a moistened surface. But as the ball seams, Trescothick withdraws his blade inside the line and lets it pass to wicketkeeper Hodd. "I'll give you that one" Bres concedes after another good length delivery jags away off the seam. "Another crowd-pleasing

leave!"

Now and again, the form of England-hopeful Bresnan is too good for Trescothick, and he is beaten outside his off stump. "Played at that one, I reckon". In between such occasions, 'Tres' appears to have all the time in the world. At the other end, partner Compton is finding conditions much more difficult and showing signs of his internal battle.

After our first innings declaration, two hours and 20 minutes in the field produced the best bowling performance I have witnessed from a set of four Yorkshire seamers in a single innings. Admittedly in favourable conditions, but against the skill and poise of two players with considerable international experience, this was bowling of the highest quality. Though Trescothick looked assured and decisive in the main, restricting his scoring to 39 from 33 overs was an achievement in itself. On another day, the score at the close would have told the story of the five or six Somerset wickets we deserved.

"That's the toughest two hours batting I've ever had" Compton admitted as he walked from the field at the close, unbeaten but bruised by his mental ordeal at the crease. "I'm not playing that badly, am I?" Such concessions from England's Test match opener were an accurate measure of our bowling quality and our misfortune not to close the second day in a more favourable position.

The early weeks of the season had been relatively dry and the rain was "overdue", according to some. And they were right, as 120 of the remaining overs in a game heading naturally for a positive result were lost to drizzle and gloom. Two hours play on the third day left the game near enough as it was on the second, and over two hours rain on the fourth morning left another four-day win beyond improbable. But after last week's Headingley heroics against Derbyshire, "You never know" quickly became the quote of a showery final day.

Talking Test cricket with Compo

Rain breaks send cricketers in many differing directions, some straight to the gym, others more likely to the kettle, newspaper or online deck of cards. On this occasion, the persistent rain gave me opportunity to catch up with Compton, a good friend of mine from our England Under 19 days and subsequent overseas tours. It had been sometime since we last spoke in person, so we were not short of topics for conversation. And our chat was my first opportunity to get a glimpse into "Compo's" whirlwind year - including his marathon season at Taunton last year and his subsequent success at the top of the order in Test cricket. So, over a bowl of peach crumble and custard in the players' dining room, we talked cricket, and batting. "There's just so

many distractions in the Test cricket environment", he said reflecting on his winter in New Zealand. For him, his experience as a batsman was increasingly about just him and the ball, "…being in the moment and respecting each delivery in turn". He had failed to do that on the second ball of the third day, so he said, leaving a nip-backer from Bres and falling leg before without adding to his overnight score.

But he was right, the professional game was becoming filled with non-essential "stuff" with the potential to distract the player's mind from what really matters. Even at County level, it can be a daily effort for a player to strip away the distractions and enter that internal world of relaxed focus.

Valuable time to prepare, practise or switch off from it all can be subtly eaten up by the autograph-hunters, the ticket-requesters, the pitch inspectors and national selectors, all keen for a minute or two. Players more traditional in their ways would be equally mindful of the "in-house" distractions produced by Sports Science and media-based obligations, though this is a sensitive subject. Nonetheless, the core simplicity of a game of bat and ball can often be difficult to find amidst the chaos of non-essentials.

Two headline-makers from our victory over Derbyshire were conspicuous by their absence as the rain fell at Headingley. Selected as part of an England Lions team to take on the touring New Zealanders at Leicester, Rooty and Jonny were turning their minds to the potential for a summer wearing an England shirt, the former as captain of his side. And both fared well during a rain-affected week, continuing their County form with key contributions against a strong New Zealand attack. Runs at the top of the order before the Lord's Test could certainly do his chances of Test selection no harm.

After a winter's talk of Joe's promotion to the opening slot in Test cricket, I wondered how Compo was viewing events at Grace Road from the Headingley gloom. Would Rooty's runs have compounded the bruise to his confidence inflicted by a torrid two hours at the crease?

Whilst Compo could have been forgiven for being wary of Joe's runs, I was feeling rather differently. Aside from being pleased for a good friend and fellow Yorkshire opener making his way at the top level, I felt relieved not to be forecasting his imminent return to the Yorkshire side, probably at my expense. Runs for Rooty made his Test selection and my breathing space a little more likely.

Contrary to the forecast, play on the final day at Headingley failed to get under way until half an hour after lunch, leaving just 50-odd overs in the game and the visitors only part-way through their first innings of the match. Even after last week's heroics against Derbyshire, a positive result in this game would surely be beyond reach.

"You never know" was Dizzy's parting call as we walked down the dressing room steps and on to the field.

Between the afternoon showers, wickets continued to fall at regular intervals, thanks both to a moistened pitch from its overnight cover and the indecision of the Somerset lower order batsmen. Their attacking instinct, honed on the trustworthy pitches of the south-west, presented many a risk on an increasingly unpredictable fourth-day surface, and we could sense the dressing room panic from the middle. Within two balls, the ninth and tenth wickets fell, the former awarding us an all important third bowling point, and the latter wrapping up the innings. Just 25 overs were left in the day, leaving a win surely beyond possibility.

"You never know".

"What we doin' skip?" Lythy asks Galey at the close of the Somerset innings. "We'll bowl again" he confirms to both Budge and umpire George Sharp, signalling the follow-on for the visitors. A win was highly unlikely, but there was opportunity to inflict further blows to the Somerset confidence and little use in our batsmen tackling testing conditions with such little time left in the game.

"You never know lads".

Four overs bowled, four wickets down, and all four to Brooks, attacking the crease with apparent freshness down the hill from the Kirkstall Lane End. Compton and Alviro Petersen caught by Budge at second slip, the former for a duck, then James Hildreth and Arul Suppiah both caught on the crease, losing their off stump.

"You never know".

In Brooks' fifth over, more drama. Batting for the second time in the day, Buttler bunted a good length ball back down the wicket. Following through, Jack stuck out a hand, stopped the straight drive of the Somerset man, and curled up instantly on the pitch, clenching his thumb. Physio McAllister led him from the field on first look and we feared the worst.

Two wickets for just four runs from replacement Patterson left the visitors 48-6 from 18 overs. "You never know". Could we really do it again?

Time was running out and the ever-dependable Trescothick remained at the other end, watchful of the worsening conditions but rarely unsettled. Chances appeared probable with every over bowled, particularly when Trescothick was given the single to expose his more vulnerable partners.

But with three balls remaining and four wickets still required, captains Gale and Trescothick shook hands in acceptance of a draw. Though a repeat of last week's headlines had been prevented by the elements, a message of equal strength had been sent out to those looking on.

Brief celebrations of our moral victory were tempered by news from Leeds Infirmary, where Jack sat waiting for the x-ray that would reveal the almost certain break in his left thumb. A six-week break for the "headband warrior" seemed inevitable.

"They'll come out swinging tomorrow", said Patto during his post-match shower, looking forward to the following day's 40-over fixture against our Championship opponents, also at Headingley.

'Patto' was spot on. Batting first after losing the toss, Somerset showed none of the previous

A winning beer tastes good: views of our victory celebrations at Edgbaston.

day's indecision and raced to a formidable total of 338 from the allotted overs. The pitch, whiter in colour than its Championship equivalent, offered little of the sideways movement that caused such problems for the visitors in the four-day match, and our mainly medium-paced attack found no answers to the all-out aggression of the Somerset order. Unsurprisingly, a required rate of over eight an over proved too great an ask in our reply, and our tenth and final wicket fell with ten overs remaining, 132 runs short of the target.

As our Championship season continued its resolute recovery, our one-day season was yet to stutter out of the starting blocks. The first two fixtures of the summer had followed a similar losing trend and in both cases our opponents had scored insurmountable totals batting first. A return to red-ball cricket would hopefully give our bowlers the confidence boost they needed before our next 40-over fixture eight days later.

Taking on the Champions

It is lunch on the second day at Edgbaston and I have made a late appearance in the players' dining room, still emerging from my post-dismissal daze. Having scrapped our way to a first wicket partnership of 77 in testing conditions, Lythy and I have fallen in quick succession just before the break, 48 runs shy of Warwickshire's first innings total.

Reflecting on our morning's work over lunch, Budge and I are joined by former Yorkshire player John Hampshire, a familiar face at first team fixtures in his capacity as a monitor of umpires' performance. In front of his bowl of fruit and jelly, John is complimentary of our morning's efforts, assuring us that our hard work against the new ball will pay dividends for our lower order in the evening session.

Somehow, conversation turns to John's memories of his playing days, and his comparisons with the modern game. "So many players seem to miss out on scoring opportunity through the leg side these days", he observes. "Particularly on

uncovered pitches, anything through here [he puts down his spoon and signals to his rib cage] would be bread and butter to rotate the strike".

Budge takes the opportunity to pick the ex-player's brains. "How did ya' look to score on uncovered pitches, John? An' 'ow quick was the bowlin' you faced?" "It were quick enough" John replied with a nod "but 160 or 170 could often be a winning score in those days. You'd look for the single to get down the other end, and if you scored three an over you were doin' all right. But if it lifted on you, you'd 'av to just do this and let it hit you". Spoon back in his bowl of jelly, John shoulders both arms above his head, allowing the imaginary ball to cannon into his ribs.

Budgie's eyebrows raise in a sympathetic grimace. In agreement with another prompt from Budge, John continues. "Aye, I 'ad a towel for a thigh pad, and didn't wear a cap". "Did you get 'it on the 'ed?" asks Budge. "Mmmm, a few times…" Our morning's graft suddenly seemed less of an ordeal.

The first three sessions of our Championship match against defending Champions Warwickshire had gone exactly to plan. A pre-match rain delay did nothing to prevent another impressive Yorkshire bowling display after inserting the home team on a surface tacky from hours undercover, and by the close we had begun our first innings reply. Conditions were similar to those found at a cloud-covered Headingley, with the ball consistently seaming just enough to find the edge and expose indifferent batting.

Though each of our battery of four bowled with miserly discipline, the returning Plunkett was the pick of the bunch, completing his first Championship five-wicket haul for his adopted County with the final wicket to fall. Rarely does a bowling performance go so smoothly to plan after inserting the opposition, and Captain Gale would have been relieved to see his decision at the toss so quickly justified.

In line with the first day trend, the remaining sessions of the game went very much in our favour, leading us to an extraordinary victory just under two hours before the close on the third day. Our slow but steady first-wicket platform proved to be a key part of a first innings total of 407, blunting the home side's hopes of a day two counter-punch with the new ball.

For the second time in as many weeks, the standout performer with the bat was Adil, chaperoning our lower order of significant depth to great effect on his way to an unbeaten 110.

Heavy-legged from near four sessions in the field, the Warwickshire top order had no answers to our second innings bowling, which persisted with deliveries of a fuller length, in "Dizzy's box". Victory was sealed shortly after tea, with the home side still 139 runs shy of making Budge and I don the pads and the local members voicing their frustrations.

We had defeated the defending Champions inside three days, less than two months since our arrival back in the top flight, with ruthlessly simple and disciplined cricket. A few weeks ago, there was talk of our struggle to adjust to the growing gap in standards between Divisions; now we were reflecting on the Champions' first defeat in 14 Championship matches, decisively at our hands. Where to from here?

There are few better experiences in the world of professional sport than the taste of a cold, winning beer. Sat in the concrete box that is the visitors' dressing room at Edgbaston, strewn with open kit bags and grass-stained whites, I have that very taste. "It just tastes that little bit better when you win, lads", confirms Dizzy, concluding his post-match team-talk. "We won every session" says 'Pudsey' Plunkett, "…with simple, effective cricket" adds the skipper.

Beside their respective lockers, each of the team nods in agreement, some looking down to the floor in reflection upon a memorable win and the key moments that took us there. As the sheer ruthlessness of this victory begins to sink in, there is a sense that the team's visions for the summer ahead are changing, or at least becoming clearer.

Fading away is the concession that our return to Division One would be a six-month struggle for survival; in its place a growing belief that we can beat anyone on such form, and that such

success leads only to one place.

Hang on a minute, no one wins anything in May. This is an hour to be savoured; a time spent toasting the rewards of three days cricketing work, in the company of team mates. And it feels good.

Through no fault of his own, day one at Edgbaston was the first and final in this Championship game for Rich Pyrah. For the remainder of the match, he would be sat watching two games of cricket – the one he would take no further part in, and the televised Lord's Test, from which his former housemate Bresnan would travel, having fallen short of selection in England's final XI.

The arrival of our "super-sub" was an example of a peculiarity of modern County cricket - the substitution of a player part-way through a four-day contest with one of England's Test squad, obliged to be in attendance at the Test until the team announcement at the toss, and thereafter required to 'tick over' in the nursery ground of the County circuit. After a first-innings performance with the ball deserving no criticism, Rich was unfortunate in being handed the shortest of straws, but who could argue with such a cricketing no-brainer giving captain Gale an embarrassment of riches? "Not a bad second-innings sub to throw the ball to, 'ey?" he remarked from mid-off before Tim's first delivery on that third morning in Birmingham.

Whilst 'Bres' was helping Sidebottom to remove the Warwickshire top order within a matter of overs at Edgbaston, the teammates he left behind at Lord's were under no illusion as to the difficulty of the struggle in which they found themselves with the touring Kiwis. Including 'Bres', three Yorkshiremen featured in England's 12 for the first Test of the summer, and no prizes for guessing the other two.

Riding high after passing 300 Test wickets in his career, Jimmy Anderson bowled to Neil Wagner of the Kiwi tail, and Aggers and Geoffrey told the story in their definitive style from the TMS commentary box.

"Just a thought, Geoffrey" Aggers disgresses between Anderson deliveries. "The Kiwis have

Wagner, pronounced "Vargner", England had Strauss, of course, and I hear there's a South African by the name of Elgar out there". A quip from the back of the box. "Yes, he was known to have many variations".

Geoffrey interrupts as Wagner survives an Anderson away swinger. "I don't know much about that sort of muuusic, Jonathan. I'm a Nessun Dorma man". "Oh I see" Aggers replies, sensing a colourful story to supplement his commentary. Geoffrey's subsequent tale of his meeting Pavarotti on a Bajan beach was classic summertime Test Match Special.

"Just like I 'ad to train my talent with t'bat, heee'd 'av to train 'is voice, rehearsin' his scales whilst hee were paddlin' in t'sea". "Not a Speedos man, I expect, Geoff?" Back to the cricket: "Anderson, in, bowls to Varg-ner…"

In early-season conditions seen more often north of the Midlands, Root and Bairstow showed composure and skill with the bat in a low scoring game, Joe following up his first innings 40 with a vital second innings 71 to set the visitors a tempting fourth day chase to win the game. As it happened, a destructive 11-over spell from Stuart Broad brought about a New Zealand collapse 170 runs short of the target, but both Tykes had stood up to their task and played valuable parts in setting up England's win. Onwards to home ground Headingley for the second Test in which all three representative Yorkshiremen would be desperate to figure.

The morning after the night before in Birmingham, the team bus and I went our separate ways, the former transporting the remaining "Vikings" to Chesterfield for Sunday's one-dayer, whilst I hitched a lift home with Bres in his customary England Jaguar. "It might be a squeeze, mate", Bres said before opening the boot to throw in my bags. Inside, the contents of this shiny white sportscar told the story of this cricketer's week. Bags of various descriptions, most branded with Three Lions and associated sponsors, and all with a purpose.

Seventeen years ago, I played my first game for Yorkshire Schools Under 12s at Ampleforth College, and shared the new ball with a ten-

year old Bresnan. This morning, I am enjoying getting up to pace with the life of that new ball partner, the life of an international sportsman that takes him around the world and only occasionally across my path in County cricket.

So much of Bres is lovingly normal – awaiting him at home is a pile of flat-packed kitchen furniture to assemble on a rare day off – but there is no ignoring the world away that is his existence as a regular in England's Test, one-day and T20 squads. International cricketers, like my driver this morning, live a somewhat surreal life of wealth, celebrity and public responsibility, rarely able to undress themselves of their public persona.

So, without prompting, our en-route conversations touch upon the complications – and blessings – of a life of apparent privilege. The club of cricket's elite performers play the very same game as their less able counterparts in the domestic game and yet live a life significantly removed. The line between County Club journeyman and cricketing millionaire is a fine one indeed, but one that reveals much about the commercial viability of the game at its various levels. Succeed on the televised stage and many doors open to the player, or so it seems. Nonetheless, what impresses me this morning about Bres is what has always impressed me: his ability to detach his cricketing existence from his celebrity life, or at least the distractions of his rise to the Test match stage from that day at Ampleforth College.

Whilst Bres was constructing his flat-packed furniture, the Vikings scrapped to their first 40-over victory of the summer, thanks in the main to a middle-order performance full of the intent and confidence shown in the game's longer form. Set in the public park at Chesterfield, the outfield was boggy and the pitch the slow, deteriorating turner we all expected at Derbyshire's outground. But Derbyshire were not our opponents; rather the Unicorns, County cricket's cocktail of first-class hopefuls and more senior players extending their List A careers. This was a day for substance over style, a 40-over tussle for points on an inconsistent surface suiting the

The stuff of dreams: Joe Root celebrates his maiden Test century.

home side's medium-paced attack. "One of the trickiest one-day pitches I've played on" was Lythy's summary after his match-winning half-century to guide us to our target of 190 with seven balls to spare. A case of a job done, imperfectly but nonetheless with the desired effect.

The stuff dreams are made of

After the three-day victory at Edgbaston, a week free from Championship cricket provided a timely reprieve from the steadily quickening treadmill of the summer. But whilst the players planned a week of recuperation and training, the County Club looked forward to arguably its most important week of the year: Test Match week.

Three days before the Headingley faithful arrived to witness England's second Test against the Kiwis, the County ground on St. Michael's Lane quickly became the domain of the travelling circus of marquee-builders, fast-food sellers and lanyard-wearing officials. Even we Yorkshire players would be unable to breach the airport-style security checks and besides, our presence on or off the field would disrupt the last minute preparations for Headingley's showcase week.

Our home for two days of training would be the Leeds University cricket ground, a developing back-up facility for the Club several miles north from Headingley and away from the distractions of the pre-Test countdown. With June just a week away, hail storms and showers turned batsmen, bowlers and coaches into groundsmen on frequent occasions, pushing the covers on and off the increasingly spongy practice pitches. This was by no means ideal practice conditions, but a useful means of "ticking over" in a week without competition.

For me, a fixture-less week provided a natural break in match-playing routine to reflect on my season so far. My recent return to the first team had given me an insatiable thirst for success with the bat, both in the

Championship and the shorter forms. And I was confident that success would come, assuming I continued to trust the principles that had brought about consistency at the crease in the early weeks of the summer.

"I genuinely believe you are on your way to a big hundred in the coming weeks" said Farby after watching one of my midweek net sessions. "Just keep focussing on what you're doing well and trusting your way". Two innings in as many first-team games had proven the step up in quality needed to be consistent in the first-class game, but had given me confidence that I was heading in the right direction towards fulfilling a valuable role at the top of the order.

Technically speaking, the first two months of the season had furthered the progress I had made through the winter and in Barbados. Essentially, my ultimate aim was to "get into the ball", transferring my weight down the pitch towards the bowler, and each minor tweak and refinement was intended for this most basic non-negotiable. My pre-delivery "trigger" movement – back and across to the off-side with my left foot – was key to setting up a still and balanced position from which to transfer my weight, and two days in the nets proved useful in grooving this technique. With Farby's help, I had learnt that triggering onto the inside half of my left foot was key to enabling me to tip my top half into the ball, helping me to remain tall, "above the bounce of the ball" and with my head above my hands on impact. Trigger back on to the outside of the foot and it would be hard work swaying back into the delivery on its way from the bowler's hand. This back-then-forward sway was something Trescothick seemed to do so effectively at Headingley in our Championship game. Numerous pennies dropped in my mind when working out this subtlety with Farby, for I had occasionally felt myself over-striding into the ball and battling to transfer my weight, even when playing generally well and scoring runs consistently. Consciously repeating this improvement in the week's practice environment would help me bring it subconsciously into matchplay at my next opportunity.

After three days of preparation, the opening day of the Test was a thoroughly anti-climatic washout. But the weather was not the only disappointment. By the morning of the second day, it had emerged that only 10,000 tickets out of a possible 16,000 had been sold for the first day's play, understandably a far from pleasing statistic for our newly appointed Chief Executive, Mark Arthur. In his interview with the Press, Arthur cited the growing difficulty experienced by the soon-to-be eleven international grounds to succeed in the bidding process for international fixtures and the considerable divide in spending capacity between venues in the south east and elsewhere in the country. Recent years passed have produced many special memories of England victories and edge-of-the-seat Test match cricket, so it seems suitable in Yorkshire's anniversary year to highlight the importance of international cricket remaining at St. Michael's Lane well into the Club's next 150 years.

Despite the fact that he stood on a pitch only just uncovered after a full day's rain, Alastair Cook would have had little hesitation in choosing to bat when the coin fell in his favour before play on the second of five allotted days. Summer had seemingly begun at last. The sun was shining, the sky was blue, and Headingley was the picture for which everyone had hoped.

"Bowlin', Donald!" wicketkeeper Alan Mynett bellowed as another ball seamed past the outside edge on a wet pitch at Hoylandswaine.

"No need t'change. We don't like change! Coronay-tion Streeeet, Eastenders, bed. That's a good life. No need for change!" Another ball passes the edge.

"Bay-sics Donald! That's what we're after. Keep it up – there's some cordial on its way." A cheer comes from the pavilion bar. From my fielding position at short midwicket, I know what that means. Rooty's done it!

Six years ago, I remember a 16-year-old boy, very small in stature, with the looks of a choirboy, joining me at the crease in a Roses second team fixture at Headingley. I was on my way to a second hundred in the match, the new arrival in only his second game after his debut at Abbeydale Park the week before. Physical power was lacking but his technique was notably sound, enabling him to accumulate mainly behind square of the wicket, primarily off the back foot, using whatever pace the bowlers offered. Onlookers would have been forgiven for paying little attention to these early days from beyond the boundary rope, but from within 22 yards I had a different view. This young man's demeanour and his contributions to mid-pitch conversation exuded an obvious appetite for a scrap and a cricketing intelligence beyond his experience.

This afternoon I watched a much taller and physically able 22-year-old busily manipulating an international attack on his way to a maiden Test century. This was the stuff of childhood dreams, on a blue-skied summer's day, in front of a capacity Headingley crowd, in partnership with a Yorkshire team mate at the other end. Those 16-year-old habits had become Test match trademarks in this innings of the highest quality.

Former Yorkshire player and Club batting coach Kevin Sharp told me many years ago that "…two Joes will one day open the batting for Yorkshire". This prediction came from his hours spent answering the requests of a small, cheeky, Sheffield-born lad to throw a new ball faster and from a closer distance, preferably at his head. This resolute youngster had something different, apparently, an unflickering desire to step beyond the zone of comfortable practice, extend his limits, and relish the journey with a smile.

This maiden Test century appeared to have so much that is definitive about Joe Root. A love of a challenge, coming to the crease as he did with England tottering at 67-3; a greed for runs when a lapse in concentration in this most purple of patches would have been excusable; a cheekiness, shown in his reverse sweeping of Kane Williamson with a slip in place after tea; and a genuine enjoyment of the game, when the perfection of the occasion threatened to

The first of many: Joe soaks up the Headingley applause.

cause tension at the crease. Tongue in cheek, the man to whom so many have compared Joe Root – Michael Vaughan – made his approval official via the medium of twitter. "Freedom of the city of Sheffield will surely follow…and the Root Stand at Bramall Lane".

Whilst "the other Joe" smiled his way towards a century, his Yorkshire team mate Jonny Bairstow played a similarly important innings at the other end, not only for England's cause, but for his personal hopes of an Ashes inclusion. With talk of Pietersen's imminent return and the shortlist of possible casualties from his recall, this was not an easy setting in which to make a case. And the early stages of Jonny's innings suggested an understandable tension. But with time, and no doubt the help of his cheeky companion at the other end, his partnership with Root began to show glimpses of the 231 scored at a pace for the third wicket against Derbyshire weeks earlier.

Clocking back in

Our nine-day break from competitive cricket came to a close with a Bank Holiday trip to the leafy suburbs of Hertfordshire. Our venue was Radlett Cricket Club, our opposition the curiously named Middlesex Panthers. So whilst the queues for entrance into the third day's play of the Test extended well beyond the end of St. Michael's Lane, we prepared for a 40-over contest in surroundings akin to the set of Midsomer Murders. Inspector Barnaby could have arrived at any stage, or so it seemed, in this manicured oasis of cricketing affluence. The pre-match nets were as well cared for as the corduroys and panamas of the onlooking members. This was archetypal outground County cricket at its most picturesque, modern cricketing razzmatazz with the perfect seasoning of middle-class jazz. Even the fast food caterers exuded their fair share of civility, named as they were as "Elite Barbecue Services".

Predictably, this was a game decided not by whether quick runs would be scored but how many? With the square boundaries relatively short and the outfield trim and smooth, bat ruled over ball in a high scoring contest. This was a frustrating day to be stuck mixing the isotonic drinks, but there is rarely a day when the 12th man's obligation holds appeal. But this was my first first-hand experience of 40-over cricket this summer and a useful glimpse at a game increasingly different from the longest form. The technical basics still hold true, of course, but this was a game now showing more similarities with the 20-over format than the game's red ball version. Bowlers needed variation over pace, batsmen the ability to make risk appear routine, and everyone on the park would be required to contribute competently in two of the three disciplines.

In line with an increasingly frustrating trend, this one-day contest slipped from our grasp well before the final deathblow from the Middlesex middle order. In my early years on the playing staff, a score of 236 from the allotted overs would have been regarded as more than enough to defend with the ball. But on this occasion, everyone knew it was 20 or 30 short of a competitive total. And though the game was balanced with Paul Stirling, Joe Denly and Eoin Morgan all dismissed within the first hour, our brief hopes of a win were quickly quashed by the inventive aggression of Dawid Malan and 'keeper Adam Rossington. With the introduction of the new fielding regulations demanding five fielders within the inner ring, a run rate of six-an-over has quickly become the accepted minimum on surfaces as true as those at Radlett and Headingley. And the home side dealt with this requirement relatively easily, playing positively but with a trust in the technically correct, cruising over the finishing line with over four overs remaining.

Before boarding the bus for an evening trip to Taunton, the dressing room post-mortem was honest and concise. As is often a good sign, a number of the 11 held up their hands and admitted fatal mistakes, accepting that we had fallen short of the day's intention to "nail the basics" with "clarity" of mind. Good teams sometimes lose, and although our one-day cricket was in need of significant improvement before the T20 block, such straight-forwardness in review of performance would surely give us our best chance to correct our shortcomings. Before our week-long southern tour continued along the M4, any remaining post-loss ice was broken with the classic practical joke from Bres. Not that Ballance saw the funny side of the prank – the "body warming sports balm" he mistook for Bresnan's shower gel was still burning his nether regions well beyond Slough.

Back to the drawing board

Pro: "What did you think to yours today, Squiz?"

"Er, well I felt it bounced a bit and left me…I know I didn't push at it…but looking at the footage…I'm wondering whether my bat came down like this [right arm shadows an angled downswing from off to leg]".

Pro: "Right" [extended pause]

"What did you think mate?"

Pro: "Well there's something I've been wanting to mention for a while now but the timing's just not been right…"

Getting out early in the day as an opening batsman really hurts. Not only do you have your unthinkable dismissal to think about, you have the rest of the day to do so. It is not so bad for those in the middle order, for a fair chunk of their day, sometimes the majority, is spent waiting to bat, perhaps a little nervous about their innings-to-come, but far from the potentially depressing inner dialogue of judgmental review. For the uninitiated, that early lapse, mistake or unfortunate uncontrollable can define the day ahead, taking the gloss off events that may otherwise lift the mood.

And today was one of those days. A decent delivery from former team-mate Steve Kirby, my third of the day, which found the outside edge of my bat and settled comfortably in the waiting hands of Marcus Trescothick at second slip. Cue that aforementioned feeling, that struggle to accept the moment just passed and the consequence of that moment for the day ahead. A dismissal comes and goes in a blur, but its consequence draws out infinitely longer, if you allow it.

The early moments of today's play presented the classic mental challenge for an opening batsman. The sun was out, the skies primarily blue, and hopes were high for a win of the toss and the inevitable decision to bat first. We were at Taunton, after all - the County ground causing nervous twitches for many a County bowler to have toiled upon its unforgiving soil. Pitches at Taunton invariably favour bat over ball to an extent far greater than any other ground on the circuit, causing every opposition batsman to mark his fixture card upon the dates when he intends to make hay. All of this hope and expectation draws the mind into the future where preferable outcomes live and away from the present moment, the batsman's most effective space.

Quite honestly, I was happily present for Kirby's second delivery of the day, but that did not ease the painful sense in my gut walking from the field where I was likely to be watching the making of hay rather than doing it myself. On some days we honour this beautiful game, on others we curse it. And 20 minutes into this morning's session, there were curses aplenty.

Pro: "…I reckon your bat face has become slightly open like this [back of the right hand tilted, fingers pointing down]".

"Hmmm…OK."

Contrary to my curious response, alarm bells are poised to be rung – I would rather not be facing technical tweeks mid-game and so soon into my return to the first team.

Pro: "I noticed it in Barbados and I've spoke to the coaches about it…but they advised me to leave it for a while 'cos you were working on other stuff. I didn't want to bombard you with more than one thing to figure out…"

"No, of course, fair enough mate."

Part of me wishes I had received this feedback

earlier, but I can understand why it was withheld. After all, having to address more than one technical improvement at a time may well have delayed my return.

"Well I had been wondering whether my downswing was a bit in-to-out, but my movements and positions feel really good."

Pro: "They are mate – the best they've ever been. I just reckon it's your grip, that's all. Show me your set up".

Between the bags upon the dressing room floor, I take stance against an imaginary bowler. And, after some brief discussion, the grip hypothesis was indeed worthy of investigation.

Pro: "If you can get someone to throw at you, I'll take a look in the nets if you like?"

A back-to-the-drawing-board session of hitting balls and talking batting in the indoor school was the ideal remedy for the morning's self-questioning.

Ninety minutes spent in the nets left me feeling much better about my game and the day, confirming the observations made by Jaquesy and giving me some measurable learning from the most challenging of days. In this modern day of cricket coaching, Pro could feed the bowling machine with his left hand whilst filming my movements with his iPad, held steady in his right. Slow motion replays were accessible immediately, split-screen if required, and a movie of progress emailed to my account within minutes of my hitting the last ball straight down the ground. Priceless.

Whilst I was turning the bat grip in my top hand to find a comfortable fit, opening partner Lyth was cruising his way to his first Championship century of the summer. Budge loves batting at Taunton, and with good reason, but his movements today were as smooth and graceful as they ever have been, enabling him to score quickly on a pitch offering just enough assistance to keep one honest with the bat.

After a first day washout, our first innings batting performance showed much of the discipline and resolve that had been present for the month of May. With a more than solid foundation built, the attacking partnership of Hodd and Rashid was the major factor in our

scoring the fifth and final batting point in the allotted overs, the latter chalking up his third Championship century in as many innings, once again unbeaten. Many an international batsman would be pleased with the batting skill he has shown in recent weeks. "I hope he doesn't get picked for the Lions," Budge said from the dressing room as Adil punched another to the cover fence off the back foot.

As the pitched dried under the southwestern sun, so did any notable sideways movement fade, leaving an under strength Yorkshire attack with quite a task with the ball. But Sidebottom, Patterson, Pyrah and Ashraf stood up well to the challenge, restricting the Somerset line-up to three an over on a ground where four is nothing new.

"What was it like on the replay, Dizz?" Galey asked knowingly as he entered the dressing room at the lunch break. "Missing leg, missing off…and hitting middle about half way up!" came the reply.

A nip-backer from Sidebottom at the Sir Ian Botham End had hit Trescothick half-way up his right shin, just a matter of balls into his innings, and every Tyke to a man had arms aloft in appeal. After Somerset's batting horror show at Horsham, where they collapsed twice in the match last week, everyone in the County ground knew that the wicket of their captain was the game-changer. "It's all on Tres," Galey would shout from mid-off, confirming the home side's reliance on you-know-who.

"Not owwwwwt!" was the answer from umpire Nick Cook. We all believed he was wrong.

Though the Somerset tail scraped past the follow-on target of 301, eight wickets down, maximum bowling points and a lead of 140 were telling consolations for another impressive performance. Trescothick's let-off had proved a pivotal moment in the match. It is easy to say in hindsight, but had that decision gone in our favour the game may well have followed a different course.

So at five o'clock on a sunny Taunton evening, the fourth of the match, captains Trescothick and Gale shook hands in acceptance of a draw, just as they had in the

Green and pleasant land: a view from the players' balcony at Radlett CC.

equivalent fixture at Headingley. Both circumstances and conditions here were quite different, but in both cases we had held the upper hand with bat and ball.

After the tenth and final Somerset wicket, Kirby caught Ballance on the stroke of lunch, 63 remaining overs presented a few in our top six with a valuable opportunity to spend some time at the crease. For me, it was chance to put the technical improvements I had felt in the nets into practice when it counted. But 19 balls into my innings, a delivery from Kirby set up an action replay of my first innings dismissal, ending my role in the match.

My movements were as good as ever, the

openness of my bat face corrected with comfort, and my state of mind relaxed and focussed. Despite my obvious need for a score of note, I was really enjoying my batting. Why was the outcome no better? What had I done wrong? Could I really have done anything different?

There is a fine line between learning and over-analysing and this was no time to be caught up in critique. I was in a good place, my technique improving with time, and I could feel myself heading along the right track towards that significant contribution. But against bowling of first-class quality, that hits the pitch hard with the new ball, playing the ball late was key, and I could certainly improve that area of my game. I had two runs in two innings on the friendliest surface in the country, and a measly total of 27 from my first four innings back in the first team. Not exactly the stats I had in mind on my recall to the side. Though other members of the top six continued their own respective struggles, was my future in the side uncertain? A trip to Scarborough beckoned – a place holding good memories this summer – and I had my fingers crossed for another opportunity.

After a tough day at the cricketing office, a five-hour coach journey was low on my list of preferences. Propping up a bar with a frustration-numbing beer would have been much more appealing. But after a week away from home, and the prospect of cricket in the league tomorrow, my usual seat on the coach awaited. Besides, the modern-day cricketer travels in a style not experienced by those retired not so long ago.

The Yorkshire team travel the motorways of England in a coach comparable to the first-class floor of a passenger aircraft. Leather seats surround communal tables with cup holders for the mid-journey cappuccino. Multiple television screens show sky television en route or double as computer screens for the games consoles on board. Fridges hold the victory beers and the milk for one's morning coffee, made in the fully equipped kitchen at the rear. Quite a change from my early day's as a player, spent hastily flicking through the ring-bound pages of a map in my capacity as navigator and travelling partner to Anthony McGrath.

Nowadays, gone is the navigator's apprehension; hours go by without us knowing our whereabouts on the M1. Players become absorbed in an iPad game of Tiger Woods Golf or their iPhone playlist, or sleep off the effects of a long day in the field. Wicketkeeper Hodd flies the flag for the traditionalists with a liking for an occasional crossword, whilst others lose themselves in a world of technological entertainment. Others still open their laptops to write the day's entry in their dressing room diary. "How many words to go, Squiz?" someone shouts from the back of the bus, catching sight of me staring into another potential chapter.

CHAPTER FIVE

June

That sinking feeling

Dizzy approaches me in the dressing room at an unfortunate moment – I am wearing nothing but a towel around my waist.

"Can I have a minute, Squiz?" he asks with a quick return to the coaches' dressing room. Players never enter the coaches' dressing room without worthy purpose. On this occasion, though that purpose is not mine, I know what it is. With Martyn and Dizz present as I enter, I take a seat in awkward silence, as if in a confessional box. I was right. The purpose was as I expected.

Getting dropped from a side really hurts. And in this case, not yet a month since my recall to the first team and just four - admittedly unsuccessful – innings, it hurt that little bit more. When you know what is coming - those inevitable words - the stomach turns, the adrenaline pumps preparation for an irrational outburst, and the ego lies bruised. Bruised by the emptiness of being unwanted, judged and criticised and by the knowing that it is too late to make amends. There was nothing I could have said, or should have said, that I would not have regretted saying at a later time.

My ego was a raging someone inside of me begging to express his anger and rage. But he would not be allowed to do so on this occasion. The reasoning was clear, but I did not agree with it for a moment. Visualisations of a comeback century at North Marine Road could stop. I would not be there. Instead, there were second team nets to report to, bags to pack for a week in Leicestershire and - just what I needed at this time of emotional knock-back - emergency childcare to arrange to cover my unexpected absence.

Reflections upon another one-day loss for the Vikings were far from mind on the drive home to Harrogate. On paper at least, the visiting Gloucestershire side should have been no match, but this was another example of our 40-over cricket lacking the clarity of a pre-match plan, at least with the bat. One-day cricket is a difficult and unpredictable game to master without such structure and, as has been the case this summer, performances with bat and ball appear reactive, lagging behind those of the opposition in a game when timing is all-important.

The day's silver lining came in the form of a List 'A' debut for young Ben Coad, an increasingly impressive and reliable bowler of medium pace from Ripon. His complement of overs produced a debut wicket and a consistency of length and line for which "Coady" has become renowned in the Academy and second team. Being "the pick of the bowlers" on debut is something about which few Yorkshiremen can boast.

Though our one-day performances had proved consistently below par, it was fair to say that the rotation-policy of senior bowlers in the 40-over format had left us with an under strength attack on numerous occasions. Resting a player who is fit and able to play, though a bold selection decision, is something becoming increasingly common in the modern world of professional team sport, the classic case being the top flight football Club resting its key men for a Cup match carrying far less meaning than the upcoming league fixture in the race for silverware.

Similarly, in a cricket season demanding much from a limited battery of quick bowlers, the debate lives on over whether a side can realistically challenge for all three trophies in a domestic summer. As has been the case for us this season, a successful run in the Championship can quickly lead the four-day game to the top of a Club's list of priorities, leaving at least one of the shorter formats as an opportunity to blood upcoming talent.

One may argue, perhaps, that well-paid sporting professionals should be required to compete at every opportunity, entertaining the paying spectators and serving their employers. On the other hand, coaches and players alike may curse a fast-bowler's misfortune of sustaining a season-ending injury in a limited-overs dead rubber when September promises a sniff at the Championship race.

It has to be said, the current structure of the 40-over format does little to encourage full-blooded participation. Several losses early in the group stage leaves a Club with negligible chance of a Lord's final and little to gain from the continued involvement of their four-day match-winners.

Nonetheless, winning is a habit in any form of the game, and our motivation remained to win at every opportunity in the 40-over competition. If we were to do this, however, we would need a clarity of respective roles and a proactive approach.

"C'mon the cow-tipper!" comes the shout from mid-off. It is a sunny day at Grace Road, Leicester, and Matthew Hoggard is the reference, running in to bowl to me with a pink one-day ball in his hand.

'Hoggy' is in typically eccentric mood.

"Captain…", he begins at the end of his follow-through, "…it is against my religion to take wickets against Yorkshire! You should know that by now."

Hoggy is turning out for Leicestershire two's in a 40-over fixture preceding its three-day equivalent. With no first team game, the Foxes boast a full complement of first-class seamers – Hoggard, Nathan Buck, Anthony Ireland and Alex Wyatt. But the "cow-tipper" is not in the best of form, coughing and spluttering between deliveries.

"I caaaan't breeeeeeathe!" he shouts in a way only Hoggard can.

The process of getting left out of a side extends beyond the initial bombshell. As the reality of life beyond selection sinks in, the ego takes a series of smaller jabs to the body after the shock of the opening right hook to the chin. In my case, the first of a series of jabs came as I arrived for second eleven nets, the day after the evening before. It was real – for the foreseeable future, I would be part of a 'dinkies' side of teenagers and junior professionals. There was not a capped player in sight, just a team of enthusiastic youngsters making their way. The second jab came shortly after, as I boarded the Club minibus for our evening excursion to the Midlands. For two and a half hours, talk was of school exams, twitter and the unmentionables of teenage conversation. "I should not be here" insisted my egotistical inner voice.

Having slept on my withheld feelings of anger and frustration, a phone call to Dizzy was right and proper in my efforts to move on from the disappointing news. Such follow-up phone calls are bitter pills to swallow, but essential in maintaining clear lines of communication with the coach. In this case, my conversation with Dizz was clear and constructive, both parties explaining their positions and concluding by agreeing to disagree. We could now move on. Besides, allowing bravado to cause a breakdown in communication at this stage can be damaging for both player and Club, tempting though it is to avoid the awkwardness of honest disagreement.

That sunny day at Grace Road could not have gone better, for the teenaged team or myself. My innings of 91 from 86 balls, ended only by a call of "Yes…No…Sorry!" from my anonymous batting partner with eight overs to go, was the ideal response to my being left out. On a slow but true pitch, I made a concerted effort to hit the ball late and with intent, and subsequently scored all around the ground at will. The bat face was full throughout and my movements as precise and relaxed as they felt in that second innings at Taunton. Walking from the field, I could have asked for no greater compliment than that provided by an onlooking Jack Birkenshaw, of Yorkshire, Leicestershire and England. "That's the best I've ever seen you play, Joe," he said.

A challenging month in the first team had brought little reward for my hard work. My game was improving, or so I felt, but the statistics did not lie. Few runs scored and a considerable time spent making them. Without overplaying the discomfort of my situation, I stood at a crossroads in my season. My choice was clear: continue along the path of turgid progress and absorption of pressure; or take forward the lessons from Grace Road, enjoying the freedom of playful commitment to strike the ball with intent, as I knew I could, thus transferring pressure on to the bowler. One path seemed far more fulfilling than the other. Perhaps it was the time to commit to a fresh and liberating approach? One that made me harder to bowl at, more versatile in all forms of the game and potentially a more fulfilled cricketer. Besides, I had little to lose and much to gain.

A near-century no doubt helped, but a day shepherding the 'dinks' was extremely enjoyable. This was not a group of naïve schoolboys; rather, an exciting unit of hopeful professionals-to-be, playful in their ways and keen as mustard to learn. A credit to Academy Directors Ian Dews and Richard Damms and a spine tingling view into the future of the Club.

No performance was more exciting at Leicestershire's County Ground than that of the 15-year-old Matthew Fisher. His figures of 7-1-25-6 were the second best in the Club's history of second XI one-day cricket, and included three of his six dismissals in an over of perfectly-pitched yorkers. His approach was naturally aggressive, his action gracefully textbook, and his physical attributes ideal for a career with the new ball in hand. "Where should I pitch it to a left-hander, Squiz?" was his innocent question after his opening dismissal. "Just hit the top of off stump, mate," my simple reply.

Coming on first-change up the slope, his seven overs showed pace and an ability to swing the ball, all with a smile on the face. Though I am reluctant to attract attention to Matthew's obvious talent at such a young age, there is no avoiding the fact that this is nothing but an exciting prospect for cricketing years to come. His opening spell reminded me of another teenaged Tyke, Tim Bresnan, bowling up the slope at Grace Road during my first-class debut almost a decade ago.

Reflecting upon a resounding win for this near-Academy side over a strong Leicestershire Seconds was a welcome antidote to the difficulty of my own personal situation. Sunday's news was difficult to take and impossible to agree with, but I had come a long way in a short time on the Dinkies' minibus, metaphorically at least. This carefree group of hopefuls had reminded me of the importance of play, in its truest and most enjoyable sense, and of the selfless innocence of a team enjoying each other's success.

True, it was easier for this bunch of schoolboys to approach a day's cricket in this way – they had few other responsibilities upon which to focus – but that liberating message remained in my mind. The closer a player gets to the advent of his professional career, the more important it is to return to that playfulness of youth, that exciting rollercoaster of learning enjoyed when the game was our hobby, not yet our profession.

Though first-world issues cloud this clarity as cricket becomes more of a financial means to an end, this instinctive, unpredictable game-playing is why we cricketers feel those butterflies when Spring comes around each year. Out of an emotionally challenging week, this would be the learning that would take me forward.

In reply to Nottinghamshire's first innings total of 443 at Scarborough, compiled in an uncharacteristically turgid manner, Yorkshire are 27-3 inside the 11th over on the second evening of the game. Nightwatchman Patterson has just nicked a ball from Luke Fletcher into the waiting hands of 'keeper Chris Read, exposing the middle order with the ball still new. In a state of urgency in the dressing room, Captain Gale has hastily padded up, grabbing the pads beside his kit bag in his usual spot. Unbeknown to him, they are the right-handed pads of Azeem Rafiq, present at the ground for a week of training and rehab. Gale makes it through to the close unscathed, yet to get off the mark.

Within a few balls of the restart the next morning, the Nottinghamshire fielders are asking the skipper about his unusual superstition. He is wearing the same pads he wore the night before, after all. Surprised and confused by their query, only then does Yorkshire's number four realise his mistake. With his pads, left-handed of course, remaining on the dressing room shelf above his hook, he continues his innings with a smile and a shrug of the shoulders.

A minute short of nine hours cricket later, "Galey" walked off the field to a standing ovation from the North Marine Road crowd, with 272 runs to his name. His score was the 13th highest in Yorkshire's history, the third highest since the war and the best tally since Lehmann made 339 against Durham in 2006. The wrong pads had been ever present in the highest score by a Yorkshire batsman at Scarborough. But more pertinently for our captain, his double century brought to an end arguably the most challenging period of his career with the bat and his first score of three figures since June, 2011. His hunger to make amends for his recent struggles was clear throughout this vigil full of discipline and drive.

Though the Nottinghamshire bowlers may have smelt Yorkshire blood on that unsettling second evening, that passage of play was the only one to suggest a positive result out of this four-day fixture. A solid Yorkshire bowling performance had curtailed the attacking instincts of the visiting top six, but failed to dismiss the line-up after inserting them at the toss. Led by Gale and the increasingly consistent Ballance, a centurion for the second time this season in partnership with his captain, the first innings batting display prevented any prospect of loss but took the game to an inevitable draw, petering out after tea on the final day. Nonetheless, the stalemate was by no means damaging for our top-of-the-table prospects, with eight points keeping us in touch with leaders Sussex approaching the Championship's half way point.

Glimpses of a promising future

Sunday at North Marine Road was a day of Yorkshire Cricket in its truest sense. Lines of expectant members, queuing on to the road from the turnstiles with Yorkshire Post in hand, greeted my arrival at the ground, over two hours before the scheduled start.

Between innings in this 40-over encounter with Leicestershire, the signature panama of Geoffrey Boycott stood out above the crowd of surrounding spectators hustling for the President's autograph.

The sun was shining and Galey had made the most of the blue skies and true pitch, choosing to bat first at the toss. Dickie watched from the balcony. Recently appointed Chief Executive Mark Arthur was in attendance to get a taste of County cricket by the seaside. Chants of "Yourrrrrkshire, Yourrrrrkshire, Yourrrrrkshire" rang out amongst the slightly inebriated in early afternoon. But most of all, this day's cricket was a view into the not-too-distant future of the Club, and the emerging talent that would define its path. The thousands in the terraces were there to witness the potentially memorable early days of some fledgling professional careers.

In response to a first team injury list teetering upon definition as a crisis, Dizzy selected four Academy bowlers to be led by Liam Plunkett on his welcome return to first team action. Two of the four teenagers, Ryan Gibson and Matthew Fisher, made their Yorkshire debuts in the match after impressing at Grace Road earlier in the week, whilst Will "Wilfred" Rhodes and young Ben Coad continued their List 'A' careers with promise.

At 15 years and 212 days, young Fisher attracted most of the inordinate media attention. Six days earlier, "Pup" was revising his GCSE French whilst the Seconds built their score at Grace Road. Today, as long-distance lenses snapped every movement of his pre-match warm-up, Sky television cameras filmed the staged stroll of his mother and two brothers along the boundary rope in front of the pavilion.

"I wish I could play in front of this crowd every week," he would later say to me as we crossed paths in the field. There were no signs of the headlights startling this supposed rabbit; this was the youngest post-war player to appear in a County competition celebrating every moment of his surprise inclusion.

Though not as surprising as that of my younger teammates, my inclusion was by no means a prediction of mine after losing my place in the Championship side a week before. But it was my first opportunity wearing blue pads this summer and my first batting at four in as long as I can remember.

Galey's week long runfest has come to an end with a thin edge to 'keeper Niall O'Brien and I am in. With Adam Lyth my partner and 17 overs bowled, my role is to maintain momentum in this innings towards a minimum target of a six-an-over tally of 240. I'm in a no-nonsense mood, keen to get to the crease and start as I wish to go on. I begin my innings well, striking the ball decisively to the boundary sweepers and running hard between the wickets. Nathan Buck goes past my edge twice in succession and the Leicestershire fielders sense a release of building pressure.

"It's ok, stay relaxed, line him up straight and keep playing it late". Moments later, a length-ball from Buck splits the gap between extra cover and mid off perfectly. The Scarborough amphitheatre confirms its approval. That feels good.

After a breakthrough innings in the Twos on Tuesday, my 58 from 63 balls was a timely confirmation of my commitment to a positive-minded approach and a key part of our tally of a slightly below par 258. These were early days in this new, liberating approach to my batting, but I now had the confidence that I could adopt this more attacking style with consistency. I had been harder to bowl at this week, asserting pressure on bowlers who were mindful of my ability to cut and score from width, in particular. And most of all, batting was fun. I looked forward to getting into the nets each morning and into the middle, to hitting the ball and letting my instinct guide me forward. I was playing with a smile on my face.

On his day, 'Pudsey' Plunkett is the cricketer we would all love to be, whacking sixes into the stands and bowling bouncers at near 90mph. And today was no different. His 53 from 23 balls gave us vital momentum in the game and our battery of teenagers a target to defend. And the 3,400 spectators were fully behind their team, amongst them the Fisher family and supportive friends from Sheriff Hutton Bridge CC.

At 56-2, the 15-year-old debutant was thrown the ball.

"What pace does he bowl?" asked Galey, recognising that I was one of very few to have seen the young "Fish" bowl.

In truth, neither captain nor coach had seen either debutante with the ball in hand, either in the nets at Headingley or in live matchplay. Their inclusion and respective performances were therefore testament to the wisdom of Farby's recommendations and to the apparent trust amongst the structure of coaching staff.

Within moments, the home crowd were behind the day's headline maker with vocal support, fully justified by an opening spell of well-paced deliveries right on the money.

"Not bad for a 15-year-old," Galey later remarked. "I bet he pins plenty of under 15s on the 'ead at that pace."

After the Lord Mayor's show, so to speak, Ryan Gibson came into the attack with the visitors 185-5 after 30 overs, building momentum in their chase. His performance was no less impressive than that of his younger team mate, particularly when he had Michael Thornely caught behind the wicket for his maiden first eleven wicket.

Not to be outdone, 'Fish' then returned for his second spell and dismissed the new batsman, Shiv Thakor, without scoring. Mother and brothers were on their feet; the crowd cheering with a volume resonated by the North Marine Road amphitheatre. There were fewer watching here than at Leeds a week before, but the noise would have suggested quite the opposite.

As he had at Grace Road days earlier, 'Fish' looked to the sky in his follow through, in honour of his late father, at this memorable moment.

"You nearly had me welling up again, mate," I would later joke. In truth, such cricketing moments present a sobering bittersweet perspective tinged with both joy and sadness.

The two debutants had swung the game in our favour with eight overs still remaining. But the Leicestershire lower order bounced back, aided both by a well-timed batting powerplay and the inaccuracy of our youngsters' death bowling under the pressure of a run chase. Sadly for the hopeful crowd, an unbroken stand of 71 led the visitors to victory with five balls to spare, ruining the fairytale beginning for our fresh-faced few.

"Keep looking after him," said Matthew's brother Adam as I left the changing room after the game, laden with bags. He made a good point, for his younger brother would need all the support and encouragement the Club could provide in his fast-tracked rise through the professional game. Though I was reluctant to join the media circus that accompanied this teenager's success, I could not help but acknowledge the memories it had given me of a similarly young Tim Bresnan making the first of many steps forward in his career. Despite the disappointment of another one-day loss, this was a day to remember for the County's most recent debutants and those looking forward into the future of the Club.

From One Home of Cricket to Another

We were into the belly of the season, that so-called conveyor belt of fixtures that prevent any sense of knowing what day it really is. Neither Monday morning blues nor that Friday feeling exist at this stage of the year; the day is either a match day, a training day, a travelling day, or a rest day, and we all become absorbed within our cricketing bubble, relatively unaware of what is happening on the outside.

And so, after a late night arrival home from Scarborough, the bags were packed for another week away, and an early morning departure on our team bus cum first-class lounge. But this would be no ordinary week away from home. The formal invitations placed upon our seats confirmed as such.

"Nigel Adams MP, Secretary of the All Party Parliamentary Cricket Group and Lords and Commons C.C. requests the pleasure of the company of Joe Sayers at a lunchtime reception on the Commons Terrace to mark the 150th Anniversary of The Yorkshire County Cricket Club".

It was 1998 when Yorkshire last played Championship cricket at Lord's, where we would take on a Middlesex side tied with us on points in second place in the table. And so, over a beer with Our Geoffrey, the MP for Selby and Ainsty had decided to mark the occasion with a sesquicentennial celebration in his place of work, the House of Commons. For many of us players, this was a once-in-a-lifetime privilege, and a memorable way to start the week of our eighth Championship match of the summer.

"Do yu' know who that is, Budge?" someone shouts from the back of the bus, gesturing to a 15-foot statue in the gardens across the road from Big Ben. "Errrrrr...." comes the hesitant reply. "I'll give you a clue," shouts the playful questioner. "He sells car insurance on the telly..." Still no light bulb moment as we step off the bus, suited in unison. "Ooooo, yes!" another voice shouts in impersonation of the aforementioned insurance 'salesman'. Still no answer. Winston Churchill deserved better.

The inconceivable sense of history consuming a visitor to the capital is no more apparent than in the Houses of Parliament.

"That tree's probably older than my country," said the antipodean Jaques as we approached the security-checked entrance across the surrounding lawns.

As a visitor, one cannot help but consider the lawmakers, law-breakers and the royalty to have walked the carpeted corridors of both Houses and the weight of their conversations.

Our conversations were to take place upon the Commons Terrace, the south-facing

Debutant Matthew Fisher cannot hide his excitement before his record-breaking appearance in the YB40 match against Leicestershire at Scarborough.

Fisher celebrates his first professional wicket with two teammates slightly longer in the tooth.

Matthew Fisher back at Easingwold School after historic debut at Scarborough for Yorkshire County Cricket Club.

outdoor balcony running the length of the Houses along the river Thames. Compere Harry Gration and a merry collection of politicians and Yorkshire members warmly greeted our televised arrival. Sponsors stood beside sesquicentennial vinyls and plasma screens showing the now familiar highlights reel of our 150 years.

Closey was there, Goughie took time out of his TalkSport radio schedule to be there and even Ed Miliband made a brief and smiley appearance. After the welcoming from our host, Geoffrey took to the microphone without delay. "A warm welcome to all you Yorkshiremen…and to the rest of you who wish you were from Yorkshire".

Ice broken, our President proceeded to confirm the special nature of this occasion and of his passion for the history of "the greatest cricket Club in the world". He spoke of the importance of young Yorkshire players becoming familiar with the feats of Yorkshire finest; of Verity's 10-10 ("…they were lucky to score ten") and of Rhodes' dominance with bat and ball. "Not only did Wilfred take over four thousand wickeets…FOUR THOUSAND… he nearly scored as many runs as meeeee!"

After the canapes and cricketing conversation, our tour of the Houses took us on to the viewing gallery in the Commons where, as if organised by our host, another Yorkshireman of profile, Foreign Secretary William Hague, was addressing his listeners. The details of his statement about GCHQ were over our heads, but that did not matter.

This was a memorable way to mark the start of a potentially memorable week, and a refreshing change from the repetitive nature of pre-matchday practice. It was also an event confirming the extent of the Club's remote following from those based in the southern counties. Later that week, Middlesex captain Chris Rogers would admit his surprise over a pint in the Lord's Tavern that Yorkshire "had brought more supporters than us" to the Home of Cricket.

Hoddy summed up the day's unofficial headline perfectly as he walked onto the hallowed turf.

"From one Home of Cricket to another", he said, referencing the seaside outground of his adopted County. It was the first day of our Championship match at Lord's and the weather was not befitting the venue. Sporadic spells of drizzle and gloom made this day's cricket feel like the first or last of a summer, not the first in a four day fixture bringing us to the Championship's halfway point.

Hoddy's remark, of course, had its fair share of irony and Yorkshire bias. And though North Marine Road possesses an intangible cricketing romance, Lord's is truly the Home of the game we love. The Grace Gates, though somewhat narrow for the easy passage of our first-class lounge on wheels, leave us under no illusion as to the refinement of the grounds within. Beyond the engraved pillars, the oversized parasols of the seafood and Champagne bar border the way towards the pavilion entrance, manned by gentlemen attired in ivory blazers with a trim of MCC egg and bacon. Without fail, they greet us with a "Good morning" on our arrival and an unconditional "well played" on our leaving each day, regardless of the numbers beside our name on the scorecard. Within moments, one feels uplifted by one's surroundings but surprisingly at home.

Up the flight of stairs in front of me, the library is to my left, the bar to my right, both pristine in their decoration. Up another flight, and through the door curiously marked "Dressing Room No. 5 and Secretariat", and I am met by a smartly suited man at the door of the visitors' dressing room. It is Pete, the formal and yet friendly dressing room attendant making us feel that little bit more at home.

Nine years ago, in a rain-break partway through my innings in a Varsity one-day game run chase, Pete brought me a china bowl of the highest quality jelly beans to give me the sugar rush I needed. "There you go, my boy," he must have said in his notable Welsh accent. I remind him of that day as I enter and he smiles. "If that'll help, Sayers, I'm sure I could get you some more".

The dressing room benches are padded and deep, above them the honours boards charting the Test hundreds and five wicket hauls of England's visitors over the years. In the centre of the room, upon a large wooden table cum chest of drawers and cupboards, is a large bowl of fruit, boxes of cereal bars and a stack of fresh white towels. There is Molton Brown hand soap beside the sink, a fridge full of isotonic drinks beneath it and silver spoons – from Sheffield I might add – with which to stir your morning coffee.

In contrast to other visitors' dressing rooms on the circuit, deliberately undersized and without the conveniences enjoyed by the home side in question, this could simply not be any better. To my left, and beyond the painted double doors, is the dressing room balcony, small but perfectly formed, overlooking the ground beneath us. There is a smell of tobacco, rising up from the pipe of an M.C.C. member sat outside the pavilion below, reading his pink pages before play. And the view upon the balcony is world famous – the Mound Stand to our left, the Media Stand "gherkin" ahead, and the sloping outfield as lush and green as ever, overlooked by Old Father Time.

"Look up, not down," is the piece of advice given to an undecided captain before the toss at Lord's. For there is invariably a decent and uniform covering of grass upon the Lord's square and pitch, and the overhead conditions play a significant role in how that grass behaves. If the skies are overcast and the air dense with moisture, the grass and softened pitch surface is likely to offer seam movement for the bowlers, particularly with the new ball. Conversely, if the skies are blue and the sun shines, all that grass will generally do is create a little more pace and carry in the pitch. So with the sun just beginning to break through at half past ten on the first morning, Captain Gale decided to bat first. Not that his decision was an easy one, for half an hour earlier, the sun was nowhere to be seen. But as one of the many general rules of captaincy suggests, if in any doubt, bat.

Within an hour of the opening overs, the players were off the field, much to the frustration of the travelling Yorkshire members, but understandably for a combination of bad light and intermittent drizzle. That in fact was the pattern of the first day, short spells of cricket curtailed by unseasonal gloom and drizzle.

Each such rain break gave question-master Lyth the chance to test out his teammates with a series of football-based trivia questions churned out by an online trivia machine much to his liking.

"'Ere we go lads", he would say. "'av got a good one 'ere". Everyone poised for the next question, some more eager to answer than others.

"Which football league Club…'as a name… that starts…with five…five…continents?" Silence.

"Don't you mean con-so-nants Budge?" Patterson asks, poised to ridicule his question-master. Needless to say, by the stroke of tea, brought forward due to another spell of gloom, the contestants had lost their will to answer Budge's teasers.

The first day at Lord's belonged to one man. With just a handful of deliveries remaining in the day, Alex Lees faced the off spin of Oli Rayner, unbeaten with 96 runs to his name. A day of rain breaks and restarts had been a test of his concentration; a pitch offering movement up and down the Lord's slope a test of his skill. Rayner brought his leg side sweeper up to present a risky opportunity for a boundary. And Leesy took it, at the second attempt, slog sweeping the off-spinner over the leg side field to bring up his maiden Championship century for Yorkshire.

Just three days earlier, a Yorkshire debutant had saluted his late father on taking his maiden first team wicket at Scarborough and here at Lord's, of all places, Leesy did the same, looking skyward with tears in his eyes upon reaching this special landmark. A moment he would never forget, and one of which his late father would have been extremely proud. Gorging upon his own return to form with an unbeaten 59, his captain was there to congratulate him and shepherd him to the close.

"Not a bad 'owse is it lads?" said a tweed-jacketed Michael Vaughan as he entered our dressing room shortly before play on the second day. Vaughany was in London in his capacity as a television

*On the team coach to London,
Alex Lees spends some time
reading some of the many column
inches written about team mate,
Joe Root*

Geoffrey Boycott reflects upon his playing days with members of the squad in the Members' Bar.

From left to right: Liam Plunkett, Ryan Sidebottom and Richard Pyrah posing for photographs at The House of Parliament

commentator for the ongoing Champions Trophy, but could not miss the opportunity to watch his beloved Yorkshire at Lord's.

"I see they've still not put my hat trick on these boards. Three for six I took on Sat'dee from the Nursery End". In jest, the former England skipper picks up a pen and writes the aforementioned figures in large capitals upon the white board beside the door.

"HAT TRICKS AT LORD'S" his title, beneath which he continued "8TH JUNE 2013, M.P.VAUGHAN, 3-6".

With the second day's play almost underway, no one felt sufficiently curious to delve into details. It later emerged, however, that the unfortunate three Vaughan victims were J.P. Morgan employees paying an incomprehensible amount of money for their chance to hit MPV's offies into the Mound Stand.

After overcoming the emotion of the evening before, Leesy edged his first ball of the morning, a back-of-a-length delivery leaving him down the slope, to 'keeper John Simpson, and I was in. I had watched almost every ball of the Lees-Gale partnership in the detached state of focus most common with all next-men-in, and now it was my turn.

Leaving my seat on the players' balcony, I collected gloves, helmet and bat from my place in the dressing room and headed for the door. At Lord's, one's route to the middle is by no means ordinary. Down one flight of stairs, and then another, right at the bottom and through the double doors. Waiting beyond those doors is one of the most special sights in world cricket, The Long Room, full with egg-and-bacon-wearing members, some sat in their seats, others lining your route to the field, and all offering encouraging applause. Bradman, Jardine and C.B. Fry look down upon your purposeful walk from within the frames of their portraits. The hairs of the back of the neck stand in respectful awe and excitement and the adrenaline pumps.

With just two overs until the second new ball, and important batting points to achieve within the allotted 110 overs, this was a key time in the match. Several hours of positive footwork at the crease would get us right to where we wanted to be by the evening session of this, the second day.

Unfortunately for me, however, Mother Cricket had other ideas. The seventh ball of my innings was my last; nipping back down the slope and trapping me leg before. Umpire Trevor Jesty confirmed my fear with a raise of his outstretched finger; out for a single run for the fourth time in five innings.

The disappointment hit me harder than ever. I wanted nothing but the most cliched of sporting responses; to dig a hole in the sloping turf and jump in, never to emerge. Once again, my innings was over within minutes of its start, ended by a delivery too good for my defence. I had so looked forward to incorporating the attacking intent of last week's one-day cricket into a Championship match when the team needed it most, and making a claim for future inclusion in the side. But it was not to be. The weight of disappointment was once again interrupted only by the familiar series of inward-looking questions. I felt in decent shape, calm at the crease and focussed upon the ball. My practice and preparation was good and I felt confident that the numbers next to my name would reflect this hard off-the-field work.

Good players make significant scores on one out of five occasions, so the cricketing theory goes, better players twice as often. And though I had made two key contributions within the past week's white ball cricket, my last five Championship innings had passed me by without a notable score, and it was becoming harder to remain positive.

Asking WG for advice

Experienced players know when that mysterious concept of "form" is eluding them, when the technique, the mindset or the attitude, or any combination of the three, falls short of the mark. And the same players also know when those three important elements are in good working order but are failing to produce the numbers. I was not going to kid myself at this challenging time – my technique had been in need of refinement a fortnight ago, and was most likely the reason for at least three of those five disappointing outcomes. But my game was now in much better order, my bat face full, my pre-delivery movements sufficiently early and consistent to give me time to respond. My quick-scoring success against a white ball was sufficient proof of this fact. But again the outcome was far, far from satisfactory, and on this sole occasion a poor reflection of the place I was in.

The extent of my frustration led me out of the dressing room within moments of unstrapping my pads. I needed an escape, a place where I could reflect, turn emotion into rationale and begin to accept my predicament. I found that place on a park bench within the gardens of Lord's, with a bronze statue of WG for company. Perhaps he would have answers to my questions?

Within earshot of an occasional ripple of members' applause and the sound of the capital's traffic, I sat upon one of the many park benches, searching for a light at the end of my batting tunnel. I was working so hard, preparing so well and giving all I possibly could to my cause, but without reward. Reasonable form had been exposed as simply not enough, and I had to improve to ascend the slippery slope of a damaged confidence.

With time, the bruises to my ego began to fade, and I could begin to resolve the chaos of my emotional reaction. Despite a series of scores verging on the embarrassing, my technique had improved and the past seven days had proved a positive commitment to a new-found way, full of an intent to score at every opportunity. True, my future in the four-day side was by no means assured, but that selection was beyond my control and should not create distraction from my continuing journey as a player. With the assurance of technical refinement, of paramount importance was the continued cultivation of a positive attitude on and off the field, and a full-blooded belief that I would come through this challenging time. I knew I could do it and,

after a 40-minute silent conversation with WG, I returned to the dressing room a calmer and more positive man.

In the middle, Adil had been manipulating the Middlesex field, as would a skilful schoolboy in the playground. His wristy flicks to the midwicket boundary accompanied playful dabs past the outstretched hands of the slips, taking us up to and beyond a competitive total. At the other end, Galey progressed inevitably to a second Championship century in as many innings, reaching the milestone with a characteristically flat-batted drive to the cover boundary. Though lower order wickets fell far more frequently than we would have liked, our positive intent took us to a first innings total of 390, short of an ideal 450, but nonetheless a sizeable score on a pitch still offering assistance for the seamers. With just over two days remaining in the game, forcing the follow-on would be key to our prospects of a win.

As we were hoping in taking to the field, the pitch continued to offer seam movement up and down the slope, making our first innings total appear more than competitive. After the dismissal of opener Robson shortly before the close on the second evening, the remaining nine Middlesex wickets fell in relatively quick succession, leaving the decision to impose the follow-on a no-brainer for skipper Gale. The loss of Rogers in the first over of the home side's second innings – his second within the day – exposed the middle order, not only to the impressive comeback of Plunkett, but to Rashid, who spun the ball increasingly from the Nursery End. Winning four-day matches as the summer progresses requires a spinner capable of rising to the challenge in the second innings, and Adil did this in style, completing his first five-wicket haul of the season with two wickets on the final day. Openers Lyth and Lees promptly reached a target of five runs within minutes of our second innings and a comprehensive victory was complete on the stroke of lunch on the final day. It was Yorkshire's first Championship victory at Lord's since '87 and a win sending us to the top of the table.

Captain Gale soaks up the surroundings upon the players' balcony at Lord's on the morning of day one.

Yours truly making weather predictions during the one of many breaks in play at Lord's.

In 2004, I had the pleasure of leaving the field an unbeaten centurion after winning the Varsity match at Lord's with a six over the square leg boundary. The applause from a near capacity Long Room is a cricketing memory that will forever stay with me. And today, the members were again on their feet, applauding a Yorkshire side that had outplayed a home side tied in second place in the Championship a week earlier. This was reward for yet another four-day performance full of discipline and trust in the key basics of the game, particularly from the bowlers. Their aches and pains were eased and quickly forgotten shortly after victory, not by physio or travelling masseuse, but by a pleasure every visiting player looks forward to when playing at HQ: the Lord's lunch. Traditional cricket spread this is not; there are no triangular sandwiches or sausage rolls in sight. Rather, after taking your seat in the top floor dining room of the pavilion, you are treated to a three-course meal, if you wish, of a quality befitting a fine dining restaurant. A china bowl of sweet potato soup preceded a main of lamb cutlets, both served by the attending waitresses, before a tiramisu dessert falling short of the dietician's approval. The team was high on the enjoyment of good food, great company and the fulfilment of a four-day win. There could not possibly be a more stylish way in which to celebrate.

On a rare summer's afternoon free from cricket, and with the joy of our ten-wicket victory fresh in our minds, bus driver "Rafa" – so called for his likeness to former Chelsea boss Benitez – was under strict instructions to take us to Covent Garden. The motivation: continued celebration, with cold beer in hand, upon a sun-drenched balcony, toasting our efforts as a team. There are few opportunities in a cricket season to rest briefly on one's laurels and enjoy a challenge overcome, such is the "professionalism" of the modern game, but this certainly was one of them, and we would enjoy it. Only a scheduled bus trip to Bristol could curtail the celebrations, but this was a memorable day, one we would talk about in years to come.

All eyes on KP

Form is an intangible and mysterious thing. Something every sportsman or woman strives for on a daily basis, a state of well-grooved and effortless effectiveness bringing about the best possible outcomes. Generally speaking, to those looking in from a position outside the world of professional sport looking in, a sportsman is either in or out of form. The media may take a similarly bipolar view. But to those within the game, though the most consistent of players enjoy the rewards of the most preferable state – good "nick" – the majority exist in a state of flux somewhere upon a spectrum between the two extremes.

Unfortunately, I had reached a point of uncomfortable acceptance that I was battling for good form. What that meant, exactly, was open to debate. For my performances in one-day cricket and with the second XI had suggested quite the opposite. But in the Championship, a series of low scores and a developing pattern of dismissals told a different story. At the crease, considering my predicament, I could honestly confirm a healthy state of calm concentration and focus upon the ball. After all, a run of so-called poor form can so often be caused by the most obvious of failings – a distraction from watching the ball from the bowler's hand. But Jaquesy's observation about my unnecessarily open grip at Taunton and the nature of my dismissals – too often beaten in defence by stock deliveries from the seamers – provided evidence of some necessary technical improvements. If it were not for the absence of Jaques and Ballance, for reasons of injury and illness respectively, there was no ignoring the fact that I would not have been in the chosen XI for an important fortnight's four-day cricket. I was fortunate to be in the side, and there was no better time to break the tiring pattern of unsatisfactory outcomes.

One man who had done so in style was our captain. After a comparatively lean period at the crease extending back beyond this time last year, and an early season period scrapping to find technical consistency, Galey had made

Surrey's Keven Pietersen making his much-publicised return to action in the Championship match at Headingley.

amends with a spell of critical and consistent run-making. In hindsight, his half-century in the first innings at Taunton proved a pivotal knock, giving him the confidence to go one step further, and beyond, as he did in his record-breaking vigil at Scarborough.

And in this week's Championship fixture, at Headingley against the brown-hatted Surrey, Galey continued where he left off at Lord's. He had lost an important toss on a gloomy and humid morning, and seen his side inserted on a green and lively surface. Such misfortunes create vital periods in a Championship season, spells of four-day cricket when a side must stay in the game when conditions weigh heavily in the opposition's favour. And in such circumstances, Galey counters with adrenalin-fuelled bullishness with the bat. As at Scarborough a fortnight earlier, another Gale-Ballance partnership rescued back the initiative lost against the new ball and quickly placed us in another first innings position to drive a Championship game. A third century in as many attempts for captain Gale was absolute confirmation of a man riding a wave of good form after a period with which I could empathise.

Our captain's batting partner for much of that first afternoon was another man enjoying the peaceful playfulness of good form. Not that many can ever remember Gary Ballance being in anything but good health with the bat. Falling ten runs short of a deserved century was of obvious disappointment to Gary on his return to the side from a week-long illness, but his innings was the comparatively quiet compliment to his partner's and equally vital in the circumstances.

Furthermore, it was a timely lift for the most recent Yorkshire batsman to be recognised for his consistency by the national selectors. Gary would leave us at the close of the play on the second evening, with his bags packed for a journey to The Oval where England's T20 squad were making preparations for their series against the Kiwis, squeezed into the international schedule before the imminent pre-Ashes build up. Such circumstances for a County cricketer – leaving a domestic fixture for international duties before its conclusion – have become increasingly common in the modern game. Though no sweeping generalisations could be made about the trend, in this particular case, Gary's absence would be significantly felt by a County side already straining to manage the graduations of Root, Bresnan and Bairstow.

The domestic game exists as a nursery for the national side and a County Club of Yorkshire's size aspires to produce successful international cricketers. But in challenging economic times, the depth of squad required to cover for a number of possible international call-ups is no help for the balance sheet read out by the Financial Director at the pre-season AGM. Nonetheless, as one door closes, another opens and, in this case, that opening door presented emerging batsman Jack Leaning with a Championship debut, even if only for the second innings.

The build up to this particular Championship fixture had attracted an inordinate amount of press and media attention, and we all knew why. Yes, the newly promoted home side were top of the league at the halfway point of the four-day season, and there was talk of a charge for silverware in the anniversary year. Furthermore, the away side's Director of Cricket and first team coach, Chris Adams, had been shown the door just days before the match, having failed to achieve a Championship victory. Acting caretaker manager Alec Stewart was present to lead his side. But they were not the most prominent reasons for the attendance of a travelling circus of lanyard-wearing journalists and television production vans.

This four-day match would have significant bearing on the international summer and, more specifically, the upcoming Ashes, for it marked the comeback of England's greatest hope, the irrepressible Kevin Pietersen, 100 days since his last competitive innings. And, by the way, a determined Pietersen was not the only concern for the Yorkshire attack; teammate and recently signed overseas player Ricky Ponting promised to bring a few more spectators through the turnstiles. Messrs

Pietersen and Ponting were the obvious target of the cameras and autograph hunters, the latter appearing to enjoy playing second fiddle, the former in his element in the spotlight.

I am in the middle at half past ten on the morning of the first day, doing as I always do before the start of a four day fixture, becoming familiar with the pitch, the background viewing behind the bowler's arm and the surroundings in general. A melee of players, scorers, cameramen and television presenters crowd the playing area beside the nets. The Surrey scorer approaches coach Stewart for any last minute confirmations of team news. "Ponting out" mouths Stewart. "Hand injury". Moments later, before the toss of the coin, the absence of Australia's former captain is confirmed. News travels fast back to our dressing room. In post-toss television interview, Galey insists upon his slight disappointment in not playing against a player and leader of Ponting's obvious class, but we all know his overriding emotion is a relief to have avoided the need for a plan to break the Ponting-Pietersen partnership.

Our first innings total of 433-9 declared was considerably above par on a pitch continuing to offer carry and seam movement, and another example of a Yorkshire side driving four-day fixtures with sizeable first innings totals. Though significant periods of play had been lost to the weather, yet again there was a sniff of enforcing a follow-on and pushing for a positive result. And 17 minutes into the third day, with the visitors 62-3, that improbable surge for victory seemed all the more possible.

Mr. Pietersen had other ideas. By all accounts, this was a man in the search for some pre-Ashes form, that confidence-building feeling of smooth footwork and sound timing ahead of his imminent international duties. But ignoring an early "play-and-miss" at a Sidebottom delivery we were sure had found his outside edge, his innings offered no suggestion of the suck-it-and-see exercise it had been built up to be.

The first thing you notice about Pietersen as he arrives at the crease is his size. This is a man with the height and physical presence to match his desire to impose and dominate with the bat. Only his unnecessarily long-sleeved Surrey jumper and strong, exuding smell of deep heat hinted at a body recovering from recent weakness. Quickly thereafter, you notice his power, used to dismiss any delivery slightly off line or length. The ball may be airborne on occasion, but it would take some catching.

His first 50 came relatively quietly from 71 balls, a strike rate that would not necessarily displease a top order player in 40 over cricket. His second came from a mere 35 balls and was anything but quiet. "KP's going through the gears lads, and he'll give us a chance," was Galey's rallying call upon the dismissal of one of his partners. And go through the gears he did, starting positively but with low risk from ball one, and engaging the clutch at will to raise the run rate and rapidly reduce the first innings deficit.

Therein lay an admirable part of this game-changing innings. For sure, his unbeaten 177 from 188 balls was a display of individual batting "genius", to quote Surrey acting assistant coach, showcasing a wide array of shots and field-manipulations. But its real value, as far as his adopted County was concerned, was the fact that it was performed in such circumstances in the match. Only Pietersen himself could confirm the extent to which he was motivated by his team's predicament, but few batsmen would, or indeed could, display such a positive intent to impose scoreboard pressure on a bowling attack in search of enforcing the follow-on. With three first innings wickets down and 221 still required to avoid the follow on, the majority of middle order batsmen would go about building a slow and steadying partnership to appease the dressing room.

To call his style rambunctious is to do Pietersen a disservice, for his single-minded attack on the bowler is far more calculated than this suggests. His physical height is used to full advantage, standing tall above the top of the bounce to seize upon any opportunity to drive, thereby pressurising the bowler to pull back his length. Short of a length deliveries that would usually threaten the outside edge or cannon into the splice are forced through straight midwicket, thereby pressurising the bowler to offer width. And when he does, Pietersen invariably scores through the off side, off front or back foot, and with utter commitment to the stroke. Under such pressure, bowling one's best delivery is a difficult test of mental strength.

K.P.'s innings was without doubt a game-changer, as the Americans would say, and gave Surrey's mere mortals at the other end an unofficial licence to play with attacking freedom. Only shortly after taking our second new ball, and much to our surprise, Pietersen and partner declared the innings, well beyond the follow-on target, and 80 runs shy of our first innings total. And a brave and admirable move it was on the part of captain Vikram Solanki, for there remained 27 overs to achieve a further batting bonus point. But to Surrey's credit, and to that of a Championship points structure encouraging cricket that risks loss in search of victory, their decision moved the game forwards and create the possibility of a positive result for both sides.

The technical penny drops

It is 7.10pm on the third evening of the game and from my seat in the players' viewing gallery, there is not a single person to be seen. Wearing just my playing shirt and a towel around my waist, I am sat reflecting upon my day with attention divided between two screens. The first, that of our analyst's laptop, shows replays of each delivery of my short but unbeaten stay at the crease before the close. The second, a small wall-mounted television screen, is showing England's 20 over run chase towards victory in the Champions Trophy final at Edgbaston. I am more interested in replays of my innings, for I am keen to measure progress in my technique before restarting my innings on the fourth and final morning. The game is interestingly poised, as a lead of 132 with nine wickets remaining is insufficient for us to approach the final day with an air of having nothing to lose.

The latest, and hopefully final, chapter in my technical conundrum is giving me hope of a return to consistent form. And the replays of matches this season back up my hypothesis. Simply speaking, cricket is a side-on game of straight lines, whether it is ball or bat in hand. And to achieve these straight lines, a cricketer needs good alignment to his target. That is to say, in my case at least, if I were to draw a line from toe to toe in my stance and continue that line down the pitch, it should gladly arrive at the bowler's hand, the source of my target – the ball. In my short innings before the close this evening, this was clearly the case, and that was good. But a similar line from back to front shoulder told a different story. Over time, and probably due to a lot of time spent improving my hitting through the off side, my shoulders had become aligned not to the bowler, but more closely to the stumps, or the umpire, thus giving me a somewhat "mixed" batting action, if you will. Cutting a long technical indulgence short, this meant it was bloody difficult to achieve the most basic of batting aims – a straight bat in downswing. Balls angling across me exposed a downswing coming across the line of the ball from off to leg, and quite often found the outside edge of my bat. The Taunton saga about my open-grip had been a further complication, exaggerating the "in-to-out" shape of the swing of the willow. All such technical complications seemed to fade when I went about striking the ball with intent, but the need for improvement remained.

So action replays of my facing Jonathan Lewis' last-ditch efforts to claim Surrey's second wicket before the close were showing a small improvement to my shoulder alignment but not enough to eliminate the aforementioned problem. There was work to be done and I was not only relieved to have found the missing piece of the jigsaw, or at least be somewhat closer to it, but excited about the progress I could make. "I could sit here for hours," I thought, in the peace and clarity of a problem being solved.

Meanwhile, Rooty and his teammates were edging encouragingly closer to a seemingly below par target set by tournament favourites India in the Champions Trophy. Surprisingly, a rain-soaked Edgbaston had produced pitch conditions more akin to the subcontinent than the drizzly Midlands. Just as it had during our Championship match, the grassless and tacky Edgbaston surface offered considerable turn for the battery of Indian spinners, who were feeling increasingly at home with every over bowled.

After two sizeable first innings totals, the third innings of any Championship match can be a potential banana skin for the batting side and, on the fourth morning of this four day fixture, everyone involved was fully aware of the potential for an upset. In our favour, we had nine second innings wickets in hand and a lead of 132, but all was not as it seemed. Gary was on T20 international duty, Patterson had limped into the dressing room with an X-ray showing a broken toe, thanks to a Chris Tremlett yorker, and Siddy was out of action with stiffness in his lower back. Added to which, the visitors' declaration had made clear their intentions to chase down a victory target of any sorts in the final session, particularly with you-know-who in the ranks. So there was work to do, and we knew it.

"In years gone by, lads, we'd 'av lost today," came the summary from Galey after a five o'clock handshake between the two skippers, accepting the stalemate of a draw. We had come through the day unscathed, surviving the best of the Surrey efforts to force their first win of the four-day season. And our captain was right. During less successful seasons of Championship cricket, the tricky third innings may well have been our undoing, leaving the door open for a Surrey chase in the final hours of the game. But we could feel encouraged by being difficult to beat, even if this Championship draw felt underwhelming when compared to our recent victories.

The 3-word game plan

We had come to a natural break in the season, a pause in the repetition of Championship and 40-over cricket, and a time when cricketers, coaches and travelling members take stock of the summer's journey so far. Nine out of 16 Championship games had come and gone, and the Division One table could not have read better. Newly promoted Yorkshire firmly at the top of the division, with four wins and a lead of eight points from second place Sussex. The opening round of the four-day competition, in hindsight, had delivered a sobering punch that eliminated any romantic complacency remaining from pre-season. And the subsequent single-minded discipline with bat and ball had brought consistent results rewarding our trust in the basics. As a friend quite rightly noted in a text message this week, "…you can't win any silverware by June, but you can near enough lose it". Talk of Championship silverware was inevitable and admittedly justified – we must not underestimate our chances – but the summer had not yet reached its halfway point, in days at least.

Such speculations of silverware could wait, for what stood immediately before us was a new chapter in this cricketing year. A period that led to international recognition for the Club and its players last summer, boosting our push for Championship promotion. For the next few weeks, or at least until our next Championship match at Chesterfield, the purists of the County game could retreat into hiding, to be replaced by those more attracted to the advances of the modern game, and those who enjoy the spectacle of a sell-out as much as any cricketing nuance.

It was time for Twenty20 cricket, the shortest form of the game, arranged in a block of fixtures intended to most likely coincide with the sunniest of English summer's evenings. And in this much discussed economic landscape, the forthcoming weeks of well-marketed razzmatazz would present each County Club with a money-making opportunity too good to miss. Gate receipts would increase, as would the bar takings and merchandise sales, all in response to a form of the game far more commercially viable than its longer and more esoteric equivalents.

For us players, changes would be similarly marked. The slow and steady treadmill of Championship cricket would be replaced by a weekly schedule more akin to that of a footballer preparing for twice-weekly matches. Training would be short but sharp, the maintenance of fitness and energy levels key, and longer periods of downtime would provide welcome relief from the niggles of sustained Championship matchplay.

Adjoining Championship and 40-over matches require a significant switching between skill-based modes for a player, but the shortest form of the game demands a further step away from one's day-to-day techniques and some time revisiting the necessary specifics. Batsmen would be charged in working out their respective methods to consistently score eight runs or more from an over, embracing higher levels of risk and a fair dose of invention. Bowlers would be required to adjust the length of their stock ball, execute yorkers at will, and introduce unpredictable variations to their repertoire.

In the not-too-distant past, T20 was invariably played with a certain abandon revealing its popular reputation as nothing more than one of the game's temporary experiments. But now, it is arguably the most fiercely fought domestic competition, offering both the minnows and the bigger fish the prospect of silverware and considerable prize money. It has also become a game highly respected by its players, a game demanding high levels of – admittedly unconventional – skill.

In cricketing terms, the days before our first T20 fixture would be vital in making the transition from one format to another. On unfortunate occasions in the past, the summer's schedule has offered no opportunity to file away the practices of four-day cricket and, unsurprisingly, our T20 cricket has suffered. But on this occasion, a day of rest and two subsequent days of T20 practice would give us some valuable, but not ideal, time in front of the T20 drawing board.

And whilst television highlights of the world's T20 tournaments would throw spotlight on the eye-catching and unconventional brilliance of a few, our game plan would look to achieve three key aims, as it had throughout the highly successful 2012 campaign. Simplicity, Clarity and Enjoyment. Easy words to say, more difficult to achieve, and ruthlessly effective when employed.

Snatching defeat from the jaws of victory

Though a full week of preparation for the summer's T20 tournament would have been useful, the two days of match practice possible went encouragingly according to plan. There is no better way to practice the shortest, most instinctive and unique form of the game than to get stuck into competition, and in two 20-over fixtures played between opposing halves of the squad, the majority put to good use some reminders of the T20 basics.

I had little to lose over the two days. For though my one-day performances had been encouraging, my selection for the opening match of the T20 competition was unlikely, and this carefree approach did me no harm. "That's the way you should play in all forms, Squiz!" was the matter-of-fact message of approval from Galey after consecutive days of eyebrow-raising striking in the nets and the middle. I could not help but feel that the T20 block had arrived at the perfect time.

Key to a successful bid for Championship silverware is a strong start in the early stages of the season (even if the opening week does not go to plan). Similarly, progress through the competitive group stages of the T20 competition relies very much on a winning start. But in the shortest form of the game, there is far less time to right the wrongs of the early fixtures and halt the momentum of a losing habit. So our opening fixture, a home tie against struggling Derbyshire, was a good opportunity to put theory into practice and get the summer's T20 ball rolling.

To our frustration, however, we left Headingley after that opening match with spirits dampened, not only by the pre-match drizzle and evening gloom, but by losing a game we should have won. At least we should have won when the visitors' equation for victory read 28 required from the final three overs. Earlier in the evening, a Vikings total of 119- 8 from our allotted overs was way below par, despite a surface softened by rain and offering seam movement rarely seen in this form of the game. But four wickets in nine balls led Derbyshire to 70-7 in reply, thanks to an aggressive display from Jack Brooks. Or should I say "The Headband Warrior"? For that was his nickname heralded by the marketeers at Headingley, and those selling replica headbands in the Club shop. Purists may cringe at this cricket-cum-capitalism, but in many ways this is the unapologetic fun-loving we have come to know.

A worrying trend

What better way to dispel the disappointment of an opening loss than with a weekend trip to sunny Scarborough? For that was the venue of our second match, against north east neighbours Durham, at North Marine Road. And just in case a sunny day, capacity crowd and a straw-coloured pitch were not enough to build expectations for Whitby-born Budge, the public address went just one step further.

"…and opening the batting with the Vikings' captain is your local hero, from just down the road in Whitbeeeee… Adam Lyyyyyyyth!"

"No pressure then, Budge!" Galey remarked with obvious irony as he took guard before the first ball.

The celebratory atmosphere did all it could to push a clambering Yorkshire performance over the line, but an obvious common thread of shortcomings between this game and the first led us to the same result in a similar fashion. A total of 146 was insufficient batting first, curtailed inexplicably by the part-time spin of the visitors. And in the defence of that total, our seamers failed to execute the plan that had worked so well en route to the T20 final last year – the stubborn and unfaltering bowling of yorkers in the last four overs. Durham got over the line in the final over and, though the sun-drenched crowd left having enjoyed another edge-of-the-seat thriller, us players would spend the long drive home from the east coast considering a plan to stop a worrying trend.

T20 fixtures come thick and fast once the tournament is underway and for a winning team, this frequency provides the perfect opportunity for a successful streak. Similarly, though a losing trend is just as likely for a team falling short, another match soon after a loss is a useful remedy for disappointment and a chance to "get back on the horse". But in our case, the next T20 encounter was no easy horse to mount.

CHAPTER SIX

July

Footballers for the day

In a world where footballing demigods exist under the scrutiny of a celebrity-loving microscope, County cricketers travel from game to game in a state of relative obscurity. True enough, there are daily autographs to sign, perhaps a television interview to give after a match-winning performance, and the acceptance that one's daily statistics are accessible to anyone who takes an interest. But the extent to which one's day-to-day existence as a working cricketer is invaded by the public glare is far smaller than for those much better known – and better-off – sporting counterparts.

But for at least one day of the cricketing summer, County cricketers from either side of the Pennines have a much more different sporting experience. One in which one's every move on, and in some cases off, the field is made within the judgmental view of a raucous crowd and television commentators. A day when the adrenalin pumps faster and harder than on a midweek morning of Championship cricket, not only during the hours of play, but long after the lubricated crowds have left the ground for the nearby bars. Frankly, a day upon which the journeymen of County cricket get a subtle taste of what it must be like to be a footballer.

Of course, the day in question hosts what many see as the flagship fixture of Yorkshire's cricketing summer, at least from a commercial point of view. The Roses T20 match; a two-and-a-half-hour "bish bash bosh" of the most competitive T20 cricket, with northern bragging rights at stake. The opening match of the competition attracted 3,700 through the turnstiles on St. Michael's Lane, a healthy turn-out; 12,000 tickets had been pre-sold for

the Roses encounter, the remaining 4,000 taken well before the toss. This is a fixture much the same as the tournament's others in so many ways, but wrapped in the most possible hype, expectation and T20 razzmatazz one could expect. "Any chance of a complimentary ticket mate?" comes one of many pre-match texts from a long-lost friend. It is the perfect advertisement for the game's shortest form, the ultimate justification for the T20 revolution, and so much more than a game of cricket. The 16,000 present are not just there for the cricket, nor the Roses rivalry, but the spectacle itself. Andy Murray's bid for a place in the Wimbledon final would not keep away those who sensed a game worth watching.

Much to the relief of the Club's Financial Director, the skies are blue and there is no chance of anti-climactic rain. "Bumble" is on the outfield, microphone in hand, emphasising how the atmosphere in the ground is that more often found at a one-day international than a domestic match. "Huuuuuge pressure for theeeese lads," he confirms to anchor Charles Colville. There are just over two hours to the start of play and from my seat in the players' dining room, I can see a melee of people unfamiliar to Yorkshire match regulars. Cameramen, technicians pulling cables out of holes in the outfield I did not know existed, petite production assistants with head-mounted microphones and customary clipboards. Oh, and the Lancashire lads, preparing with a pre-match net practice upon the square.

On the television in front of me, highlights of the 2005 Ashes build upon the escalating expectations of the first Test now just days away. Beside me, tucking into a chicken salad, is the man stood at mid-off in that replayed match, Michael Vaughan. "What you up to, V?" someone asks from the other end of the table. "Just come for a watch,

Gary Ballance hits out in the Twenty20 match against Derbyshire at Headingley. There are few better strikers of the white ball than this man in County cricket.

lads", Vaughany replies between mouthfuls of coleslaw. The televised Vaughan over his shoulder appears quite different from the one in front of me. The modern-day Vaughan has made the transition quite naturally from player to media man, with picture-perfect appearance and well-rehearsed turn of phrase. "Do you miss it, V?" I ask as his attention is drawn to the screen. "Batting?" he replies, "No. I'd much rather watch someone have a net than strap on the pads myself these days".

In the adrenaline-fuelled opening spell of the 2005 Lord's Test, Hoggy has swung one through the imposing drive of Matthew Hayden and Steve Harmison has drawn blood from Rickie Ponting's cheek. At the other end, Justin Langer appears well-set, cutting anything slightly short and wide of off stump and working anything straight off his hip to fine leg. His positive movements and obvious intent to score hint at the game I would like to develop in myself.

The return of Phil Jaques to fitness meant disappointment for Budge – the man to be left out – but the reassurance of batting experience when it was needed most. His unbeaten 66 from 57 balls was the anchor for our total of 152, showing the value in batting around a top order player, but for the third time in succession, we were short of a par score on a unfaultable surface. As Galey confirmed in his post-match interview, our position at the halfway point matched that of our first two games. We had nothing to lose.

With three overs of the Lancashire reply remaining, Director Moxon remarks from the back of the pitch-side dug-out.

"Here we go again lads. Third time lucky".

His reference was to three T20 matches following a very similar pattern, leaving our opposition requiring near ten runs per over from their final three.

"I'd rather be out there than sat 'ere" he continues. "At least I could do somethin' about it!"

Ten needed off the final over, Siddy's last one, and we all know what he is going to bowl. Six yorkers, aimed directly at the painted line between the feet of the batsmen Steven Croft and Kabir Ali. With Lancashire needing nine from five, Croft swings and edges a perfectly pitched yorker past the diving hand of 'keeper Hodd to the third man boundary. Siddy looks to the sky in frustration, knowing he's done all he could, then turns to return to his mark. On his way, he looks up unintentionally to the Carnegie Pavilion, packed with corporate guests and officials. And amongst the thousands of faces, he sees only one, that of his wife, Kate, head in hands, unable to watch. He didn't know where she was sat, or if indeed she was watching.

Five needed from four. It will take some defending from here. Single. Single. Two world-class yorkers from Sid. Three needed off the last ball. The noise is deafening. Is this what a one-day international is really like? Another yorker right on the money, squeezed out to the cover boundary by Croft, for a brace. Siddy thinks we've won – he celebrating, arms aloft. Hoddy too. Have we? Some of the crowd think we have. No! A tie! We've tied. What now?

The script writers could not have written it better. The crowd could not have been entertained by a tighter or more unpredictable contest. The television producers could not have seen a more television-worthy display of domestic cricket. But in another game we should not have won, and then perhaps should have won, we had tied. So how should we feel? Whilst some of the players bowed heads with the thought of what might have been, others smiled in relief of a defeat avoided and the sharing of spoils. Generally, everyone involved would to and fro between contrasting states of review, but our overriding emotion would be of disappointment that in a game requiring proactive clarity and intent, we had produced another performance more hesitant and reactive. We were getting there, but slowly.

In the aftermath of the Roses match, Galey was complaining of a pain in his left hand. A firmly hit Croft off-drive had caused him considerable pain in the palm stopping the ball at extra cover, and that was nothing new. Of more concern was the swelling on the back of his hand, suggesting something more serious than a so-called "fielder's hot spot" of bruising.

Stepping into the skipper's shoes

"You got a minute, Squiz?" said Dizzy as I walked through the dressing room door before our fourth T20 match of the group stages. Dizzy's usual ice-breaker had mainly been a pre-cursor to bad news.

"You're opening today mate. Go and enjoy yourself. We're really pleased with the way you're striking 'em."

True to predictions, Galey had suffered a break in his hand and I was his like-for-like replacement. The media circus was back in the Headingley car park and our opponents were Leicestershire, a side I had seen my fair share of in the summer so far.

Budge was bound to be disappointed to be overlooked for a return to the side, but this was a great opportunity for me, and I deserved it. I had fully committed to the process of redefining myself as a more positive, instinctive player and exposure to the shortest form provided a timely stage for my showcasing this liberating approach.

In Galey's absence, the captain's armband went to Azeem Rafiq, Yorkshire's youngest ever captain after his successful time in the role last summer, and a cricketer experienced beyond his years with a white ball in hand. "Rafa" is the epitome of the "no backward step" philosophy of T20 cricket, embracing a challenge head-on with an instinctively attacking approach and a quiet enjoyment of a gamble. Off-spinners are often made of more conservative stuff, perfectly happy to build pressure under the radar with accurate consistency, but this Yorkshire spinner is an "offie" with a leg-spinner's mindset, backing himself all the way in the confrontations he seeks.

In my first T20 match for some time, fielding first gave a welcome introduction to the characteristic intensity and speed of the 20-over game. In this form, Championship cricket's session-long spells of pressure-driven momentum are condensed into minutes, even overs, which come and go in a flash. So were the Leicestershire batsmen on this occasion, as the Club shop's favourite bowler ripped through the top order in a spell of 5-21 from his four consecutive overs. The second of Jack's five victims was thanks in the main to a "wonder catch" from Gary Ballance, running towards the boundary from his position at mid-off to complete a diving effort with his left hand just inside the rope. Within minutes, the replays were spreading virally through the social networks of the internet, for this was a clear indication of how performances in the field can alter the course of a 20-over contest. Naturally, when asked to comment upon the catch after the match, Gary gave a characteristically modest and simple summary. "I just put my left hand out and it stuck!"

As he so often has in all forms this summer, Jack had beaten the opposition batsmen for both pace and length, hurrying onto them much quicker than expected. And a Leicestershire total of 113 for 9 left us in a situation similar to that presented to our opposition in each fixture so far in the competition.

"Get me off my seat in the dug out," was Farby's instruction as I strapped on the pads at the halfway point.

"Go and strike the ball."

He was right – a positive start and the game would be ours.

Within moments of our winning runs being scored, I am sat beside skipper Rafiq in the dug out, as television presenter Matt Floyd walks past to prepare for his after-match summary. "Where did you get those shots from?" he asks in surprise. "Been working on 'em, Floydy," I reply. Matt was more accustomed to the Sayers of old as Oxford University's workmanlike number four.

We had our first win, achieved comfortably with more than three overs to spare, and it felt good. My innings of 28 from 23 balls was a key part of the effort, and the statement I so wanted to make had been made in front of the 4,100 spectators and the television cameras. Though scores in the twenties are rarely something to write home about, this was my most meaningful display of the commitment I had made to a more attacking way with the

Fire in the belly: stand-in captain Azeem Rafiq showing his competitive edge in Twenty20 action.

bat, a way firmly encouraged by Dizz, and I could take the confidence from this cameo forward. "Great intent up top, Squiz," were the exact words I wanted to hear in the post-match analysis from Dizz, underlining the step forward I had made.

As an emerging junior professional at Yorkshire, I played within a side of well-known ex-internationals in the advent of their careers and would often take note when they could enjoy a few moments with their sons and daughters on the outfield at the close of play. So it felt at once uplifting and surreal to see my son, Sebastian, racing around the Headingley outfield after the winning runs had been scored, chased by his wearying father. Seeing the joy on his face and that of Lisa, my wife, looking on from behind the boundary boards, finished off a memorable afternoon in the sun.

A Friday night to forget

The country is basking in the summer's heatwave, with daily temperatures consistently flirting with 30 degrees centigrade, and I am en route to Chester-le-Street, Durham, for another Friday night T20 furore. The poetic tones of TMS can only just be heard over the hard-working air conditioning. At Trent Bridge, it is the first Test of the much-awaited Ashes series that England are supposed to win with ease, but newly appointed coach Darren Lehmann seems to have brought together an Australian team with different ideas. Just past Scotch Corner on the A1, and Jonny has just fallen to the left arm spin of debutant Ashton Agar who, after a game-changing 98 in his first Test innings – at number 11 no less – is grabbing all the headlines. In his usual matter-of-fact style, Geoffrey summarises his godson's dismissal with obvious disappointment. England are in trouble. "Well I reckon England are going to neeeed 200, at leeeeeast," he says, referencing the home side's faltering second innings in recovery from a first innings deficit. "Two-fifty, and I fancy 'em, Jonathan". The Trent Bridge surface is turning more than expected, and getting lower for the quicks. There's nothing like the Ashes to stir up some cricketing drama.

A Friday night's T20 cricket at Chester-le-Street had little to no drama about it. From the opening overs to Durham's inevitable deathblow, we were thoroughly outplayed, and we knew it. "Colonel" Mustard took advantage of our wayward start with the ball on his way to a highly impressive 91 from 52 balls, setting the tone for his team to continue the onslaught, tallying 215-6 from their allotted overs. That proved too much work for us with the bat, and a losing margin of 76 runs confirmed how far short of the mark we really were.

Thankfully, days at the cricketing office as bad as this happen rarely, but coach Gillespie was right to ask some searching questions in the after-match post-mortem. On occasions such as this, it is easy to make excuses, avoid responsibility, and let the disappointment linger way beyond the drive home with woolly and non-committal words after the match. But as we all know, Dizzy is from a different school, a cricketing culture of winning and winning often, as part of one of the best Test teams of all time. And so his post-match words had one purpose: to ascertain why we had lost so badly and draw a line under the display, leaving disappointment in the dressing room. Essentially, we had been inexcusably lethargic and timid in the field and for some reason, had lost trust in our simple and proven plans with the ball. The first half lost us the game and there were no excuses. "This is NOT how Yorkshire plays T20 cricket boys," said Dizz, and he was right. This was how we used to play the shortest form, lacking clarity of mind and simplicity in planning, and making the game a lottery not worth buying a ticket for. The result was disappointing, not least for the man sitting next to me in the dressing room, "Pudsey" Plunkett, who had sights set on a victory against his former side. But days like this happen in professional sport, and it is often in response to such shortcomings that cricketing team cultures define their way. The southbound A1 would see none of our lingering disappointment.

Gamesmanship at its best

The group text came through as I drove home from Hoylandswaine on Saturday evening, and the news was deeply shocking. Dizzy's Dad, just a few days after flying across the world to visit his son, had passed away and, naturally, Dizzy would not be with the side until further notice. An immediate sense of perspective hit every recipient of the message.

"Let's win this game for Dizz, lads," came the rallying words from the deputising Moxon before the toss at Chesterfield the following day.

The marquees were erect, the sun shining, and the crowds squeezed into their boundary-side seats for this T20 match against Derbyshire, marking the start of a week's County cricket at Queen's Park. This was a quick opportunity for us to dispose of the baggage from Chester-le-Street and keep our slim hopes of T20 qualification just about alive.

Queen's Park is a curious venue for County cricket in its most modern form, situated as it is within a public park, as its name suggests. The crooked spire peers above the surrounding trees upon a County outground typically small in size and endearingly fraying at its edges. Inside the brick built pavilion, pictures of Saturday's league cricket heroes adorn the walls. The tea ladies have done it all before, serving boiled potatoes and cold meats with a smile. Above all, the place gives you a sense of those gone before and the tales of Derbyshire cricket before pyjamas and white balls. But today, the crowd anticipated something slightly different.

Pre-match preparation went as well as ever for me, but not so for a young autograph hunter stood just beyond the boundary rope an hour or so before the start. According to plan in pre-match nets, I managed to strike a ball from Iain Wardlaw over an imaginary long-off's head for six. The kind of sweetly timed shot that gives a batsman the relaxed confidence for which he searches in the build-up to a game. Unfortunately, the cries of "HEADSSSSS!" from anyone tracking the ball from my bat failed to alert the imperfectly

placed young lad, and the ball struck him square in the face. Luckily on this occasion, a few stitches in the bottom lip would repair the damage, but the incident illustrated two related issues in the shortest format of the game.

Firstly, the obvious and growing danger to spectators from balls being hit into the stands, not only during the game, but particularly before the start, when sixes or high catches struck from the middle often land within the nearest bank of seats beyond the rope. However good your eyesight as an onlooker, there will be occasion when you are unaware of a ball descending upon an unfortunate path, and all players fear the potential tragedy when the unlucky victim requires far more than a few stitches. Secondly, and in relation to the aforementioned danger, we must also acknowledge the dangers of playing T20 cricket at venues such as Chesterfield. Of course, the intimacy of such an outground makes for an atmosphere suggesting an attendance far greater than is reality, but as bats get bigger and batsmen more adept at striking the ball hard into the crowd, it should not just be the fielders on their guard for a hard, white ball coming their way. Pedantic concerns, perhaps, but it is hard to believe that there are not more injuries to enthusiastic spectators as the T20 revolution continues.

"C'mon lads, no backward steps 'ere. Keep tekkin' wickets!" comes the shout from stand-in captain Rafiq. The left-handed Dan Redfern had just driven a flighted off-spinner from Rafiq into the hands of a diving Pyrah at extra-cover, and the hosts were beginning to wobble at 64- 3. Albie Morkel is walking to the crease. In earshot of Derbyshire's potential match-winner, Rafiq continues his rally.

"ere we go lads! Let's see if he'll drive his first ball down long-on's throat again! C'mon! Loadsa' pressure on this one! Overseas player lads! It's all on him!"

Half an hour earlier, Azeem had given the team talk we all needed. The Chesterfield pitch had curtailed our total to 142-9, seemingly another below-par score with the bat roughly 15 short of a competitive target. "We've nothin' to lose

Captain Andrew Gale in action in the Roses Twenty20 match at Headingley.

'ere lads. Let's give us all in the field. No backward steps!"

Azeem's face-to-face showdown with the home side's most dangerous player typified the approach he was looking for from his team. The ball was turning, spin was the key, and both men knew it.

"You and me then, c'mon!" came the matter-of-fact reply from Morkel, accepting the mid-innings duel.

The ego-driven scrap was exactly what our Barnsley-reared off-spinner wanted; that self-imposed pressure to come out on top against his prey of choice. "The harder he comes at me, the better", so Azeem believed.

As it happened, Morkel survived unbeaten in an unsuccessful chase, scoring 26 off Plunkett's last over to flirt with an improbable victory, but Azeem finished with 3-22 from his four overs, drying up the early innings momentum with fellow spinner Rashid. Morkel capped off an outstanding all-round display with 51 from 31 balls and was magnanimous in defeat. "I loved your aggression, mate," were his words to captain Rafiq upon his after-match handshake. When carried out with maturity, this sort of professional gamesmanship adds to the intensity of the domestic game, better preparing young players for the pressures of the highest level. So-called "sledging" it is not; simply the conscious staging of competitive cricket strictly within the spirit of the game. This Yorkshire spinner would leave Chesterfield full of the confidence that he had taken on one of the best T20 hitters in the world and produced a match-winning performance under pressure. Morkel would have thrived upon an intensity of competition with which he would have become familiar in the IPL. And whether they were aware of the head-to-head contests in motion in the middle, spectators would head for home having enjoyed a English County match with a ruthless edge that makes for dramatic sport.

Geoffrey's prediction comes true

Since the introduction of the game's shortest, most specialised format, it has often been asked to what extent T20 cricket affects one's approach to the four-day Championship form of the game. How hard is it to adjust from one form to another? Should players be required to flip between playing modes in a matter of days, or even overnight? Can T20 cricket have a positive effect on four and five-day matches? And in the future, can we reasonably expect players to be consistent across all forms? They are all valid questions that many a County and International cricketer would have answered in his time. Generally speaking, those players keen to move with the times and extend their playing days would downplay the limitations of a growing number of fixtures and wider variety of formats, but what really is the truth about the T20 effect and its future for us players?

One glimpse at the scorecard for our Championship game at Chesterfield, inappropriately squeezed between T20 fixtures, would suggest a significant effect made upon the purist's game by the shortest form. The ground was relatively small, granted, and the pitch good, but Yorkshire's first innings total of 617 for the loss of only five wickets came comfortably at more than four runs per over, including just over 60 overs of seam bowling going for well over five runs per over. The home side lost 20 wickets quickly to lose inside three days, but their 504 runs still came at a rate comparable with that of their opponents. Derbyshire's bowlers mustered only 20 maidens out of over 152 overs bowled.

Some say "the stats don't lie", others believe you can make numbers say what you want, but it appeared beyond coincidence that the scorecard would suggest such attacking intent from batsmen fresh from striking a white ball over the ropes.

In truth, it would come as no surprise that the daily practice of T20 batting has the expected effect upon one's Championship game. The ball may be red, the game slow and steady in its rhythm, but the batting instinct remains programmed to score whenever possible with power and intent. Wickets may fall to shots more often seen in the powerplay overs, or brought about by a batsman's second-guessing of an attacking instinct. Fewer balls will be left, for sure, and greater pressure placed upon the bowlers.

To which end, the adjustment from pyjama to purist form can often be more difficult for the bowlers than the batsmen. Our Championship success had been so much about the discipline of our quick bowlers bowling a fuller length intended to hit the batsmen's knee-roll of his pads, or the top of off stump but in T20 cricket, a delivery of such length invariably gets dispatched into the stands. For the quicks, the shortest form is about starving the batsman for room to swing the willow, hitting the pitch hard on a length appropriate to hit him in the nether regions, or on the toes towards the end of the innings. Slower balls are a key variation and swing away from the bat is often frowned upon, only creating width for a batsman keen to free his arms.

So our bowling performance at Chesterfield would rank amongst the most impressive of the season, not only for its stubborn consistency and discipline, but for the effectiveness of the adjustments made from white ball cricket. The T20-induced instincts of the Derbyshire batsmen were strangled by the persistence of the familiar four: Sidebottom, Brooks, Patterson and Plunkett, and victory was sealed before the close on the third day.

In any sport, and as Premiership managers will no doubt say, challenging for silverware is so often about taking the spoils from your "must-win" games, and this was certainly one of those. Our fellow promotees from Division Two were floundering in the top flight of the Championship, and anyone seeing them on their fixture card would seek vital points to climb the table. There were still six Championship games remaining, and a lot of cricket to be played, but news of Sussex's defeat at the hands of Middlesex compounded our quiet excitement of another step taken in the

right direction. A step towards being in contention when the Championship run-in approaches.

The week's bowling performance was a relentless team effort to win the game; the batting was simply about one partnership, and one half of it in particular. After the early dismissal of Budge on the first morning, Leesy and Pro compiled the highest ever second wicket partnership for Yorkshire against Derbyshire, driving us into a position from which the fresh-legged bowlers could set about winning the game. Though vital, Phil's contribution of 139 to the 311 partnership runs proved secondary to the exploits of his younger partner, who made a record-breaking and chanceless 275 not out from 436 balls. After his maiden Championship hundred at Lord's, Leesy became Yorkshire's youngest to make a double century, and with a raise of the bat in acknowledgement, surpassed the personal best of Director Moxon by a single run before the declaration. In his own words, he was going through a "really rewarding and extra special" period with the bat, graduating to first class level with statements full of his characteristic determination and self-assurance. Impressive steps for any 20-year-old making his way, quite something more for this lad from Halifax unfortunate to have been dealt the hardest of hands in his recent family life. Though his successes made my inclusion at the top of the order all the less likely, I could not help but be pleased for an honest, home-grown batsmen reaping the rewards he so deserved. Apparently Geoffrey had forecasted the rise of the latest Yorkshire opener many months ago on that January evening at The Crucible Theatre. No surprise there.

Strangled by spin

"Rooty's bossing Test cricket now!" exclaimed The Headband Warrior as he ran past me towards his fielding position at short fine leg. Midway through Nottinghamshire's innings in this T20 match at Headingley, the public address has just confirmed the Test score from Lord's, where Australia face a mammoth fourth innings chase towards a near-impossible victory. "He's writing his own script!" said another as we convened in the huddle at the fall of another Outlaws wicket. After his second innings 180, English cricket's "golden boy" had just taken two Australian wickets on the turning Lord's surface on his way to the Man of the Match award and a Test victory inside four days. The 7,100 at Headingley cheer in approval.

Nottinghamshire have a very strong T20 side, at least on paper. Their strength, particularly in their batting, was clear from the moment I walked into the players' dining room before our pre-match warm-up. Alex Hales, Michael Lumb, Samit Patel, James Taylor and David Hussey could take on a strong international attack and succeed, and there they were, eating pre-match meatballs in preparation for swinging the willow.

Contrary to their billing, the aforementioned top five failed to do as they wished, scraping to a very gettable 155 from their 20 overs, thanks to some clinical hitting from captain Hussey in the late overs of the innings. And with ten overs remaining in our chase, the game was ours to win. I had raced to my highest score of the tournament so far, taking on my former teammate Ajmal Shazhad in the process, and we were well set to achieve the challenging but reasonable run rate required.

Cue the most obvious and frustrating trends of our T20 batting campaign: the slow and subtle strangling of our early innings momentum by bowlers of the slower variety. From a position ahead of the game at the halfway point of our chase, the far-from-threatening whiles of Patel, Graeme White, Steve Mullaney and Hussey dried up our scoring, leaving us unable to find the all-important boundaries and an emphatic 26 runs short of our target. A run chase of two halves had left us short by an embarassingly considerable margin and we all knew it.

"We are simply not good enough against spin!" came the declaration from stand-in skipper Rafiq. "We have to practice better and play better when pace comes off the ball!" He was right. Martyn put our challenge into context. "We're not out of this competition. The equation's simple. We win our last three and we're through. But it'll spin at Old Trafford on Wednesday, and we've got to be better against spin."

It fell to me to provide the diplomatic and philosophical version of that stark reality to the Press after the game. We were all in agreement of our shortcomings and keen to make progress in preparation for our next T20 match, the return fixture of the Roses rivalry. What better place to put it right?

Personally, despite my disappointment of our floundering in the final stages, I felt nothing but uplifted by my progress with the bat and my opportunity to say so into the microphones. I was taking significant steps along the path of redefining my batting ways, as Dizzy had so encouraged, and there was talk amongst the interviewers of "shaking off a label". There was some truth in that, for sure. I was beginning to show the instinctive flexibility of my talent, raising eyebrows in the process, leading a few onlookers to question my categorisation in the early days of my Championship career. The shortest form of the game leaves a player with nowhere to hide, exposing any lack of confidence or hint of hesitancy. In equal measure, the game rewards the sort of fearless optimism I was feeling, and I could not wait to get back to the crease.

Textbook in reverse: Phil Jaques displays the perfect reverse sweep against Lancashire at Headingley.

A game of inches: an outstretched Rich Pyrah just misses out on a diving catch in the Roses Twenty20 match at Headingley.

Not for the want of trying

I have many fond, and some not so fond, memories of Old Trafford, the home of our neighbouring rivals over the Pennine hills. The red-bricked pavilion offering a square-of-the-wicket view from its sun-drenched balcony; Dominic Cork, Glen Chapple and Sajid Mahmood kissing a shiny new ball off a barren slab of a wicket; Darren Lehmann toasting the Lancashire crowd in a way only he could after a game-changing catch; that ill-fated first morning of the Championship match in 2009 when I knew I had something more than a cold.

It is unsettling, therefore, to arrive at the same ground and to lose one's bearings. To see references to the cricket ground in your mind's eye but feel that you are somewhere else.

But this was somewhere far more impressive. A newly renovated – no, transformed – Old Trafford, with wickets rotated 90 degrees, old pavilion respectfully modernised and surrounding stands coloured in "Lancastrian rose".

"Where should I go?" were my first words to the security guard on parking my car on the "wrong" side of the ground. Past The Point, the ground's most eye-catching feature, was the answer, and on past the bars, highlights-showing television screens and colossal temporary stand to the reception of the new pavilion. The view from the dressing room balcony was so much better than it used to be. Elevated and behind the bowler's arm, it did as a dressing room balcony should. And from there, I could see where a sunburnt David Byas used to sit, square onto the wicket, from his usual seat outside the old away dressing room.

"Lads…as a Yorkshire player…there is simply NO better place to win than Old Trafford." They were Martyn's words before the start of round two of the Roses tussle. A pre-match power-cut had done nothing to dampen the atmosphere and the capacity crowd was as partisan as its equivalent at Headingley. The Sky cameras were predictably present too, eager to see another hard fought Roses clash in the group stages.

Unfortunately, however, our batting display offered far less than the game's billing deserved. Slow to adapt to a typically bare but tacky surface, we were timid with the willow yet again, strangled by the medium paced cutters and variations of the home attack. The dugout was a quiet place to be for those 20 overs, and the mood was no better in the dressing room. Understandably, but inexcusably, the newly painted walls of the Lancashire dressing room took a hammering from my anonymous neighbour after his dismissal, unable so he was to contain his frustration. Packing my kit an hour later, I would find pieces of plaster in my bag.

"Are you loose, Pete? You're on next over that end!" I joked to umpire Hartley well before the halfway point of the Lancashire chase. Turning to the former Yorkshire swing bowler's skills would not have done any harm if it had have been possible, as the game was racing to a premature end. Openers Stephen Moore and Tom Smith had thrown caution to the wind as you can more easily do in chasing a low total, safe in the knowledge that a positive start will extinguish any remaining hope in the fielding side. For what seemed like far longer than half an hour, boundaries came with embarrassing frequency, each celebrated with verses of "Lanky, Lanky, Lanky, Lanky Lan-ker-shire!" of increasing volume.

From bad to worse

With the game almost gone, and with the Red Rose faithful in well-lubricated voice, Moore swept a delivery from Rashid towards the square leg boundary, and I set off from my position at deep backward square leg to prevent the boundary. The outfield was quick, but I was on track to make the kind of diving stop that has become common in the modern game, arm outstretched and wrist firm to knock back the ball in a superman-like pose on the turf. But just as I started my descent into the dive, I saw in my peripheral vision a long-strided run that could belong to only one man in our side, Wardlaw. Within moments, his long strides became a sliding effort at a stop for the same ball, leading not with outstretched arm but feet and spiked bowling boot. The rest was predictably painful. It was too late to pull out of my full length dive, and too late to prevent Wardy's boot and then knee careering into my left thigh.

We both stayed down, genuinely shaken by the impact, and somewhat embarrassed to see the white ball trickle over the rope between us. Standing to my feet, more in competitive response to the home crowd's jeers than a reduction in pain, I went about "running off" the impact as would a Sunday league footballer. But my efforts we futile, and my left leg well and truly "dead", leaving me with no option but to hobble from the field and up the endless stairs of the new pavilion.

No more than 20 minutes later, I am lying on the physio bed in the dressing room staring at the ceiling spotlights, with a bag of ice strapped to my thigh. "Plenty of ice, Squiz," instructed Physio McAllister, adding "it'll be stiff for a least a couple of days. Friday could be problem", referring to our next and penultimate T20 game at Trent Bridge.

A short while later, I hear the sound of spiked boots on metal stairs. The game had obviously finished, and with it our hopes of progressing in the competition. There would be no need for a post-mortem this evening. Words could not describe the manner of our loss nor our disappointment shortly after.

Impressive though Old Trafford's pavilion is, its size and distance from the players' car park is little help for a hobbling, kitbag-laden cricketer with one functioning leg. The drive home was a low point of my summer, as with every push of the clutch pedal, my swelling leg cried in painful protest. An evening to forget.

What a difference a year makes...

Moving into the T20 phase of the season, riding high from our resurgence in the Championship, the dressing room mood was one of optimism and eagerness to get going. Video clips had been played in team meetings of a 2012 campaign that brought the Club recognition on an international stage. Sixes from David Miller and Ballance, ramp shots from Rafiq, that catch-cum-offload from Root, and yorker after yorker from Ashraf. Every player in that meeting room wanted a piece of the sequel, taking the team onto Finals Day for a crack at the second most sought-after trophy in English domestic cricket.

But with two group games to go, we were out of the competition. On no occasion had we found the carefree confidence or fearless approach that had served us so well 12 months earlier. And the disappointment within the squad was almost tangible. Though our Championship season was progressing beyond the expectations of most, this young, fit and athletic group of cricketers fancied throwing themselves into the fastest and most powerful form of the game and coming out on top. But we had produced performances well below our expectations, strangled by some average batting and inaccurate with the ball.

The remaining two fixtures gave us nothing to write home about. In fact, they were more extreme examples of the worrying trends that had killed of our chances of group stage progression. Part-time opposition spinners emerged with flattering figures, our middle order succumbed to self-imposed pressure, and the opposition's top order got away to match-winning flyers in the opening powerplays. Our T20 cricket had gone from bad to worse, leaving us with the North Division's wooden spoon one year after falling just short in the competition's finale.

Our performances in the shortest form were, in many ways, a microcosm of our failings in 40 over cricket and, though our four-day cricket had been a rewarding highlight of the season, our white ball cricket had been equally disappointing. The T20 curtain could not come down soon enough.

CHAPTER SEVEN

August

Watching from the physio's room

Injury is an occupational hazard for a sportsman, a dealt hand that is as inevitable as it is difficult to accept. On occasion, the hindsight of poor preparation or training may suggest it was preventable. But invariably, it is an uncontrollable fate, the outcome of being in the wrong place at the wrong time, perhaps a little too often.

If this summer concludes as we so wish, we will look back upon an unprecedented number of unfortunate injuries, each of them caused by impact of some sort. Brooksy's thumb broken in his follow through against Somerset; Patto's toe broken by that Tremlett yorker at Headingley; Galey's hand broken diving at extra cover; my thigh the victim of that Cantona-esque kick; Rafiq's wrist in need of x-ray thanks to a Boyd Rankin bouncer. It is a credit to the depth of our squad that our success, admittedly in just the four-day game, has been maintained in spite of such setbacks.

An injury of any kind leaves a player in a lonely place. A place full of frustration at being unable to do more, in which you curse the run of events leading to your demise, and become tired by the aches and pains of the unavoidable rehab process. You become a note on the physio's whiteboard, a work-in-progress wrapped in strapping and bags of ice, and a player hoping to be conspicuous by absence. Invariably, however, it is easy to feel overseen, even forgotten, as the game and the team you left behind shift focus to the next fixture, the next challenge and the next team selection. Even those players accustomed to changing games in their favour may be temporarily filed away in the minds of those watching the successes of a new-look team. Professional sport waits for no one, even the most loyal and consistent servant of yesteryear. And whilst the able-bodied go about their athletic rituals, the injured are left with the mind-numbing repetition of gentle hops, skips and side steps on the progressive route to recovery.

At least I would have company with whom I could share my misfortune – "Pro" was one place above me on the physio room whiteboard with a "Grade II" tear to a muscle he never knew he had, somewhere between his ribs. Apparently, it is a muscle of key importance in the completion of any cross-batted stroke, whether it be a sweep, cut or pull, as any such efforts greeted him with searing pain.

It is the first morning of our return to Championship cricket, marked by our hosting last year's four-day Champions, Warwickshire, at Headingley. It appears summer is on its way out, for this morning the Headingley turf is covered in a thin film of late-summer dew. It is too early for the arrival of the most punctual members for the day's Championship cricket, but my day is underway, circling the boundary rope with half an hour's running to strengthen my injured left leg. "Pro" has taken the outside lane to my right, and we level-peg until it becomes clear that his intercostal is in far better nick than my left thigh, enabling him to open up a lead.

In the middle, Warwickshire's Director of Cricket, Dougie Brown, stares pensively at the surface beneath his feet, offering a comment or two to stand-in captain Varun Chopra. Pressing his outstretched palms into the pitch, he appears undecided about how it might behave when play gets underway. Patto's arrival at the wicket is greeted by a knowing grin and a nod from Dougie. "Plenty of grass, Patto" he confirms, perhaps fishing for a nugget of insight from Yorkshire's new ball bowler.

Shortly after, my middle-distance ordeal is complete, and "Pro" and I walk to the middle to form our own opinions about the pitch. "Looks like the Sussex pitch," says Pro, referencing the thick and tufty carpet of grass covering a relatively firm surface underneath.

An hour later, Pro and I are partway through the second half of our morning's training, a series of relatively gentle weight-based exercises in the East Stand gym, when the voice of announcer Tony Loffill comes through the sound system speakers. "...Warwickshire has won the toss... and...invited Yorkshire...to bat". Jaquesy's reaction was instant. "Oooooo, they've f****d it up Squirrel! They've seen the grass and f****d it up!"

Throughout my career at Headingley, and that of those gone long before, the decision at the toss has never been an easy one. Years ago, visiting captains would have arrived at St. Michael's Lane very much aware of the characteristic seam movement with the new ball, a tendency for variable bounce on days three and four, and the somewhat mysterious effect of overhead conditions on the behaviour of the pitch. More recently, even Yorkshire's captains have been misguided in their expectations of a bowler-friendly surface, and the ground's reputation has shifted to one facilitating a more balanced contest between bat and ball.

This season, however, has seen a further shift in pitch preparation for Championship matches. On the request of Director and First XI coach, first day surfaces have been hidden beneath a much thicker and lively covering of grass, with a view to producing more pace and more carry for the quicks to the waiting 'keeper and cordon. The theory, at least, is that pace in a pitch favours the most skilful cricketers with bat and ball, producing attractive performances and, more importantly, positive results when there is negligible reward for a four-day draw. And aside from the featherbed produced for the home fixture against Derbyshire – which, incidentally, lacked sufficient grass cover – the pitches have behaved as intended, offering just enough assistance for the bowlers but just reward for those batsmen adept in countering the pace and bounce.

So on that first morning at Headingley,

Warwickshire's decision to insert Yorkshire was understandable, but perhaps not the most positive. For unless the pitch is damp, it is quite often a statement of positive intent and confidence to bat first and drive the game forward with a score in excess of 320 at the first attempt. To do so, however, requires due caution against the new ball and disciplined patience for three sessions of batting, at least. The decision to bat first can often backfire in such conditions, but a batting performance that is respectful but not fearful of the surface can place a side in a position to drive towards victory.

A Club within a Club

It is Yorkshire Day and, in recognition, our very own Tim Bresnan has declared upon the world's social networks how he intends to celebrate. "Might take the whippit for a walk in my flat cap [and] stop on [the] way back for a pint of real ale". It is the day before the game, and all players are called into the dressing room for a meeting before practice. Captain Gale stands to his feet. "As we all know, lads, very few people in the history of this Club have been good enough, and fortunate enough, to wear the Yorkshire cap". Those more experienced in the room know what is coming. "But there are two lads in this room who, having joined the Club only this year, have put in consistent performances deserving of such reward". From the bench behind him, he picks up two caps, both pristine, both Oxford Blue, and both stitched with Lord Hawke's Yorkshire rose in full bloom. "So, Brooksy and Puds...I would like to present you with your...well-deserved... Yorkshire caps". From their seats beside each other in the dressing room, Jack and Liam stand and acknowledge the applause of their team-mates, before accepting the most official symbol of acceptance by their adopting club.

Somewhat tongue-in-cheek, but with an underlying gesture towards the preservation of tradition, physio Scot McAllister addresses the group with an historical note for the most recent additions to the exclusive Club of capped

Yorkshire players. He talks of the origin of the Yorkshire emblem, the visiting Vikings and the Ridings they named. Some smirk in harmless ridicule whilst others look on with curiosity, but everyone in the room joins in the recognition of common ground, common cause and shared identity.

Never one to miss an opportunity to uphold tradition, Patto raises his hand to attract attention. "So lads", he says with eyes upon Brooks and Plunkett, "…as is customary on such an occasion, and so we can all celebrate your success… you'll both be expected to buy 12 bottles of the Champers to toast your good news". The proposal is greeted with an inevitable cheer. There's no such thing as a free lunch, after all.

Dizzy remains in Australia with his family, Martyn still deputising until his return. Before practice gets underway, talk from captain and stand-in coach looks ahead to the "business end" of the Championship campaign. In the Press, there has been talk of "six cup finals" for the White Rose County. Keen to extinguish the fires of expectation, the words of Gale and Moxon are anything but headline-making. Galey talks of "enjoying the challenge ahead of us" and how we would only be under pressure if we were scrapping for our Division One survival. Martyn stresses the importance of a commitment to processes, to addressing fully what lies in front of us, this game, this hour, this ball, and allowing the events of the season to fall into place. Everyone is fully aware of our opportunity. For a number of us, it is the first time in our careers that we approach the final straight of the Championship season with our noses in front. Expectations of those looking on will rise with every point won, and we will be forgiven for buying into the hype on occasion. But the game is always right, and Mother Cricket will reward the most deserving. Besides, the defending Champions are on their way.

The first hour of the Warwickshire match revealed a pitch very much in line with Pro's expectations. The tufty carpet of grass had produced the bounce and carry witnessed to a similar extent in the opening game against Sussex, and Warwickshire's fielders had the air

of a side happy to have inserted the opposition. They would have been particularly encouraged after the early loss of Lythy, caught at slip having pushed at a full pitched away swinger from Chris Woakes. The dismissal was a classic example of the difficulty of driving on the front foot against the new ball at Headingley. Budge did little wrong and the ball was only fractionally short of a half volley, but such length can be the most productive for a bowler at the ground.

Predictably, after the full-pitched swing of Woakes and Keith Barker came the aggressive pitch-hitting of Rankin and Rikki Clarke, the former's stock delivery rarely bringing the batsman forward. Though the ball invariably flew through to 'keeper Tim Ambrose above head height, it infrequently threatened the pads or stumps and offered our top order welcome reprieve. Not that we were racing towards a three-figure total, for this would be attritional cricket, a battle for the batsmen to ride an early morning wave of hostility and invest in some time at the crease.

It is 11.04am on the second day and in the players' viewing gallery there is standing room only. Typically, such interest from beyond the rope indicates a top order player approaching his century, but there is no such occasion to applaud today. The score is 299 for 9 and after five runs came from the second day's opening over, we need just a single more to bring up our third batting point of the match. Such milestones are invariably glossed over in a Championship match, seen as just another step towards the magic first innings total of 400, but not today. Everyone recognises that, with just five Championship games remaining after this one, every point counts. Chris Woakes stands at the top of his mark. "C'mon Woakesy", someone shouts from the back of the gallery. "Give Brooksy a clip of his legs". Moments later, and against his wishes, Woakes does just so. Brooksy clips a full-pitched delivery down to fine leg and the 300 is up on the scoreboard. Lesser cheers have been heard in the viewing gallery after a one-day win. This was a point of great significance, at least through our eyes.

The fact that Jack was out shortly after was of little matter. Though 320 would have been a realistic first innings target, the visiting batsmen would have to work hard to surpass the 302 on the board.

In my capacity as 12th man, mixing the drinks for the day, I acknowledge a signal from "Pudsey" Plunkett from his fielding position at fine leg. He is flapping his arms like an albatross coming in to land and it can only mean one thing. "Red Bull for Puds, Squiz," comes the call from Martyn, confirming his request. Our tall fast bowler is partway through a long spell from the Kirkstall Lane End, and needs every bit of the caffeine hit to maintain his pace and aggression. Though those of lesser pace find a fuller length and movement in the air most effective, Puds looks at his best when he hits the pitch hard, using his height and athleticism to extract steep bounce from short-of-a-length. Shortly after, he takes his fourth wicket of the innings - Javid caught behind the wicket – leaving the visitors eight wickets down with a deficit of more than 100.

As I drop the drinks bottles within the huddle of players beside the pitch, Galey notes the arrival of new batsman Barker at the crease. "Surely Barker's due a failure against us now?" he murmurs honestly with a wry smile. The lower order left-hander had scored some vital runs against us in recent seasons. "C'mon lads! Give 'em nothin'!"

A first innings lead in excess of 50 would have been significant on a pitch continuing to offer assistance for the bowlers. But as though he knew that, Barker frustrated us for over two hours with the bat, not only edging his team to a respectable position but, in partnership with his partner Jeetan Patel, beyond our first innings score, giving his team a lead of seven and the psychological edge. Cue the classic banana skin of four-day Championship cricket: the tricky third innings with the bat.

The windscreen wipers are working at full pace on my route to Bromsgrove for my return to competitive action – a second XI three day game. "Surely there'll be no play tomorrow?" I cannot help but think. The rain is showing no sign of relenting and the fixture card suggests nothing more than a village cricket club for tomorrow's venue. It all adds up to a probable day off, or at least watching the mopping-up process from the pavilion.

As the rain persists, the radio tells an interesting story from the County circuit. There is good and not-so-good news from reporter Kevin Howells. Our nearest competitors in the Championship – Sussex – have lost at the hands of the favourites for the wooden spoon, and Durham have failed to make the most of their game in hand, losing to Middlesex at Lord's. The not-so-good news is the summary of our position on the third evening of the Warwickshire match at Leeds. Despite the occasionally volatile nature of the pitch, a lead of 141 with three second innings wickets remaining is simply not enough. Perhaps rain tomorrow would not be such a bad thing, after all?

Behind the bike sheds

England had retained the Ashes, not in the nail-biting fashion the neutrals and journalists so wished, but with the assistance of the most Lancastrian of weather patterns. Whilst one adopted Yorkshireman, Darren Lehmann, or "Boof" to his cricketing friends, reflected on what might have been had the rain stayed away, three young members of the current Yorkshire squad performed a rather soggy "victory" parade beside the boundary rope at Old Trafford. Most of the rain-soaked spectators had gone, but the most hardy remained to obtain the autographs of Root, Bresnan and Bairstow, not ignoring their England team-mates.

The Australian performance had been one to make Boof proud and would most likely have led to an outright win before the close on the fifth day, barring interruptions for rain. England had seemingly drawn upon its trump card – the weather – when it was most needed, and everyone knew it. This was not the way we would have preferred to retain the famous urn.

Liam Plunkett (left) and Jack Brooks (right) receive their first XI caps from Andrew Gale (centre), becoming the latest members in an exclusive Club of capped Yorkshire players.

In fact, it was somewhat of an anti-climax. Nonetheless, the night was England's to celebrate not just an escape from probable defeat, but the exploits that brought about successive victories in the first two Tests.

Predictably, the wicket at Barnt Green CC was no match for the elements, but nothing more than a postponed start was likely on the second day. The delay gave the members of the "Dinkies" dressing room the chance to peruse the latest catch of the Ashes-following paparazzi, a photograph of Yorkies Root and Bresnan puffing on a celebratory cigarette outside a Manchester bar. The ensuing debate was just what we needed to pass the time.

In line with other mainstream professional sports, cricket in its most modern form has quite clearly followed a scientific path in recent years. Performances are filmed and replayed, objectified by salaried analysts using a growing variety of metrics, and ultimately classified. Meanwhile, a player's preparations for a summer begins before Bonfire Night with a weekly programme of hard to cover and weights to lift. Fitness testing, at one time an annual event, has become a run-of-the-mill procedure, and minimum accepted levels of fitness are non-negotiable for anyone intent on picking up a bat or ball in March. In some cases, diets are monitored and managed whilst daily urine samples provide a measure of fluid – and alcohol – intake from the night before. The game may never quite employ the formulaic approach of the Oakland Athletics in baseball's "Moneyball" story, but all the talk continues to be about the cliched "one-percenters", those apparently minuscule improvements that make all the difference to the Championship table.

To this end, the sight of Rooty and Bres

Adopted Yorkshiremen Plunkett and Brooks with their newly-awarded first XI caps.

with fag in hand after sunset may irk those of this scientific and objective mind. Some may argue that Yorkshire and England's men of the moment should be the clearest of signs of a progression from the "beer and fag" brigade of the previous generation. Others may even be disappointed that the clean-faced role models of the Ashes campaign have been caught publicly flirting with a lifestyle not associated with professional sport at the highest level. Besides, in this time of cricketers as athletes, would you see Mo Farah or Jessica Ennis letting their hair down in this way after a high-pressured event?

Without question, Yorkshire's finest are role-models for the younger generation, the face of cricketing brands, in truth. An international cricketer's public image is arguably of more commercial value than ever before, endorsing anything from trainers to tea bags, and must, therefore, be cultivated with care. The photos of the cricket-following paparazzi can often, therefore, be damaging, not only for this personal brand, but also for that of the team. Furthermore, and particularly partway through an Ashes series, such images can be an unwelcome distraction from what really matters on the field of play.

But let's not get carried away here. These were not images of inebriated cricketers falling into taxis with multiple female friends. These were snapshots of a quiet moment of relaxation between team-mates, perhaps reflecting on a special day in their respective careers, or looking forward to their intentions for further success. Despite a challenging week scrapping for position with Australia, their performances had been outstanding, and largely consistent. They had been making Country and County proud on a weekly basis, playing significant roles in the successes of both. Did they not deserve a moment of harmless indulgence, when the objective metrics of their daily lives could be filed away, at least until tomorrow? And after all, at a time when marketeers create polished and impenetrable facades of our sporting stars, surely these images portray a side more endearing, even refreshingly human? Either way, this insight into the after-hours

lives of our international stars is less a measure of their adherence to the strict criteria of modern-day sport and more an indication of how far the game and its public image has come. The days when public celebrations with pint and cigar were accepted without question are long gone. These are the days when a private moment of reflection between players provides headline news on the celebrity pages.

The soppers and sawdust have done their job at Barnt Green CC, and the sun is out. Better put the spikes on…

Welcome but far from convincing

A cricketer's life takes you to some curious pockets of the cricket-playing world. The thundery rain in Bromsgrove has turned the wicket ends to mud and put pay to any chances of play at Barnt Green Cricket Club, the venue of this week's second XI game. So here I find myself, a short walk beyond the high street Poundland and Phones4u, in the nearest reputable coffee shop I can find. I could be in one of so many places on the County circuit, one of so many cloned retail centres around the Country, decorated with the vinyls of the commercial names we know so well. A day in the life of a professional cricketer is often priveleged, sometimes even glamorous, but today is not one of those days. Outside the coffee shop window, Bromsgrove's shoppers are getting wetter by the minute.

At Old Trafford, the inevitable last day rain has not yet materialised, and England find themselves in a little bother, 37-3 at the lunch break. The now infamous Decision Review System has just taken its latest victim, Pietersen caught Haddin bowled Siddle, much to the public disapproval of the England balcony and the Manchester faithful. Australia's new ball attack have just produced over an hour's Test match bowling of the highest quality, making Yorkshire's Root work for every one of his seven runs, and yet all the talk in the Sky Sports studio is about the shortcomings of the technological aids supposed to eliminate all doubt.

Herein lies the greatest shame of this ongoing debate about technology-led umpiring in Test cricket's highest profile series. The fast-footed brilliance of centurion Clarke, the characteristic counter-punch from Pietersen, and the entertaining ebb and flow of this Ashes Test had come secondary to the controversy of the DRS. The regulator's latest introduction had detracted from four days of fascinating cricket, with England on the ropes but scrapping to retain the Ashes with anything but a loss.

Aside from that, and addressing the technology itself, the disappointment of all cricketers and cricket followers lay in one simple truth; that a measure introduced to eliminate human error at the highest level had in fact only changed the nature of such uncertainty. A scientific model failing to produce the absolute truth had simply supplemented the naturally flawed performances of an imperfect umpire. As retweeted by Ed Smith recently, sport review technology had "replaced one form of grey area with an increasingly precisely calibrated grey area".

From my view as a physicist, or a retired one at least, cricket has met with the limitations of science. From the early days of my career, scientists of a sporty variety have made the purist's game increasingly objective and measurable, compartmentalising a Gower-esque cover drive to the essential elements from which it was made. Increasingly so, graphs have been drawn, performances measured and the intangible made formulaic, all in search of those "one-percenters" casual psychologists value so much.

And this has led to a misfit of a marriage, this meeting between the intrinsic uncertainty of sport and our will to make it measurable. Whether KP did nick that full-length ball from Siddle only God knows, if you believe in that kind of thing. Pietersen will have a good idea whether he did, "Hot Spot" suggested "No", "Snicko" affirmed "Yes", and we were left uncertain.

The chaotic nature of sport is so often the reason for us being drawn in and seduced by its uncertainty, so why must we reduce the performance errors that make this drama possible? Even before Newton felt the impact of that apple, science has been constructing models to approximate natural chaos, and this tussle between cricket and the DRS is no different. The familiar process has repeated throughout history: scientific models are made, successfully applied, and then refined or disposed of when their limitations are exposed. In years to come, therefore, must we look forward to a truly objective and measurable form of Test cricket, when every human error is quantified and labelled by a machine of Absolute Truth? Cricketing fantasy, perhaps, but I know what I would prefer - that flawed, error-ridden and unpredictable game we have all come to love and debate.

The rain outside the coffee shop window is getting heavier, Bromsgrove high street is looking a sorrier version of its earlier self, and breaking news is coming from the County grounds on either side of the Pennines. To quote the unavoidable twitter, "Yorkshire have retained their lead at the top of the County Championship and England have retained the Ashes. Neither convincing; both very welcome." The rain has curtailed the efforts of Australia and Warwickshire to force a final day victory in their respective matches. With the loss of three England wickets before lunch, the former looked possible. And having dismissed Yorkshire for 180 in their second innings, Warwickshire's victory appeared even probable, at least out of view of the clouds. Had the rain come to Yorkshire's rescue or prevented a low-scoring victory? The relief of coming through unscathed would surely outweigh Galey's disappointment of victory chances washed away by the elements.

Business on and off the field

In front of a full house at Chester-le-Street, Rooty is off the mark with a back foot punch for two off Jackson Bird, making his Ashes debut. It seems like yesterday that Joe and I were 22 yards apart in Yorkshire shirts. These days, my former opening partner looks as comfortable as the man at the other end, England's captain Alastair Cook.

This morning, I am in corporate company at the fourth Ashes Test, high above the play in the hospitality boxes, talking cricket and business.

With customary bacon sandwich in hand, I chew the cud with James Whitaker, formerly captain of Leicestershire, and now acting in his capacity as England selector.

"What do you make of Ballance, Joe?" he asks as the players take their "Buxton Drinks Break" at the morning session's midway point. "And Plunkett's been doing well, I see?" My responses provide James with nothing new in the way of insider information, simply an endorsement of his approving views of Yorkshire's frontrunners.

Conversation moves on to James' roots in North Yorkshire, or Skipton to be precise. We talk of his playing days at Grace Road, of Leicestershire's dominance in the Championship before promotion and relegation, and his plans for a winter overseas. "What's the official line on DRS (Decision Review System) then, James?" one inquisitive businessman asks from within earshot of our conversation. The cost of lunch for this England selector is a willingness to entertain the paying guests with snippets of the modern game's most controversial news.

The cricket in the middle is attritional, a battle against bat and ball on a seamer-friendly surface. It seems the Aussies are bowling to a specific plan to Rooty, bringing him forward in defence, against his wishes to "hang back" on his back foot against the new ball. Captain Cook will be happy to walk in at lunch unbeaten, regardless of the score.

Breaking news at the hospital

News from down the road at Headingley is of "one of the most complete innings" from Gary Ballance in our dead-rubber of a 40-over game against the travelling Unicorns. The game is of little consequence, but one cannot pick and choose the timing of good form, and the innings will do Gary no harm as we approach the Championship run-in.

I had twitter to thank for my update, for I was sat impatiently in the reception of Chapel Allerton hospital, awaiting my call for an ultrasound scan on my Achilles tendons. As so often happens, one injury had exacerbated another – the bruising to my left thigh causing increased soreness in areas already stiff from the summer's workload. And time would tell whether I would remain on the injury list on the physio's whiteboard as we entered the final month of the season. I had my fingers crossed.

Fortunately, the scans revealed tendons free from debilitating tears, so the race was on for a speedy return to competitive action.

Another hiatus in the Championship fixture list allowed the one-day season to take two steps closer to its anti-climatic end. Our form in 40-over and 20-over cricket had been the antithesis of that in the longer form of the game, so the week's fixtures against the Unicorns and Somerset offered little more than an opportunity to restore respectability to our limited overs season. Though some of the first XI's regulars used the games to find or continue good form, experience was given to young players emerging in the squad, such as Lees, Gibson and Coad. At this time of year, worthwhile plans extend beyond the end of the season to next summer's competitions, when experience gained by the aforementioned may prove valuable. I made my first XI debut in a dead-rubber of a one-day game at the end of the 2003 season, a few months before making my Championship debut the following summer, and Rooty did the same. Steps forward in these games may seem small or insignificant at this stage of the summer, but in later hindsight they prove so much more than that.

The morning after a resounding win over the Unicorns, news was officially broken of the most recent addition to the Yorkshire playing staff. With Ballance selected for the Lions and unavailable for the first of five remaining Championship matches, Dizzy confirmed in the Press that the Club had "moved swiftly to strengthen the side…[bringing in] a proven international batsman…with a proven first-class record". The man about whom Dizzy spoke was Kane Williamson, the 23-year-old New Zealand top-order batsman, and he would remain part of the squad until the end of the season.

Settling in nicely: new signing Kane Williamson on his first day in a Yorkshire shirt.

The news came as no surprise and it was certainly true that a player of Kane's ability was likely to give us our best possible chance of performing well at the "business end" of the season. The signing of an overseas batsman was not good news for me or my plans for a first XI return, admittedly, but for the Club, confirmation of the signing was exciting indeed.

I first met Kane last season in the dark and dingy dressing rooms of the Bristol County ground, where he and I sat waiting for an urge to provide a post-match urine sample to the visiting drug-testers. So we were brought together by circumstance, and conversation was predictably concise. "Any luck yet mate?" he would ask, enquiring as to whether the two litres of isotonic drink had done as intended.

"Not yet mate. We could be here for a while…"

A day earlier, Kane had impressed me with the bat. Coming to the crease early in Gloucestershire's innings, having been inserted on a wet pitch, he played the seaming ball skilfully late, apparently at peace with the patient wait for offerings short of a good length from Sidebottom, Patterson and Bresnan. His century was the key part of the home side's total, preventing us from driving the game forward as we so wished, and obviously catching the approving eye of Yorkshire coach and captain. If he plays like he did that day for the next five weeks, we will certainly not be short of Championship runs.

Siddy eyes the 700-mark

The first day in the Yorkshire career of our newest recruit did not go to plan. Having not batted in a first class match since the second Test against England in May, Williamson steered his first ball in a Yorkshire shirt to third slip and fell for a debut duck, leaving his adopted side 137-4. It was the opening day of a four-day contest against Nottinghamshire, the return fixture of the hard-fought stalemate at Scarborough, and we had been asked to bat first on a particularly green Trent Bridge surface.

Typically in such situations, there would be cause for concern. The top order had almost come and gone, the promising overseas batsman had been dismissed for a duck and two potential match-winners with the bat – Ballance and Bairstow – were absent from the ground. The former had been selected for the England Lions and would not figure in the Championship match. The latter, however, would shortly arrive, having been left out of the Test side to take on Australia at The Oval and set about a journey north on the M1. His imminent arrival was the reason for a little less concern than the scoreboard encouraged. The Yorkshire dressing room simply hoped he would arrived in time to take to the crease.

The unfortunate man to step aside for Bairstow's arrival was, naturally, wicketkeeper Andrew Hodd. Earlier in the season, Rich Pyrah had been relieved of his duties in the Championship match at Edgbaston, when Tim Bresnan turned up from England duties in a similar scenario. Substitutions of this type are unavoidably frustrating for the man missing out, but a clear bonus for the side benefiting from the boost in resources.

Fortunately, Bairstow arrived in time to strap on his pads. Soon after he did so, his duties were called upon, walking to the crease at No. 8 in the order. And if managers could make substitutions in cricket, they would do well to beat the effectiveness of this one. For the presence of Bairstow had two important effects. One, the dampening of the home side's hopes of wrapping up the Yorkshire tail

without further damage; and two, a timely boost for our overnight ambitions. Finishing unbeaten on 24 at the close on day one, he gave his less able partner the hopes of a useful partnership and his side the belief in the possibility of an imposing first innings score.

Regardless, a score of 327-8 represented a good day's work for Yorkshire, particularly having been inserted on a seamer-friendly pitch.

Ask any County cricketer which ground he most loves, and invariably you will receive a predictable and perfectly justifiable reference to the Home of Cricket, Lord's. But shortly after, and perhaps in the same sentence, you will hear mention of Trent Bridge. For it is one of the most aesthetically pleasing cricket grounds on the Test and County circuit, a harmonious marriage of the traditional and the new, a reflection of a modern game ever-evolving with a respectful eye on the past. Members can view proceedings from the seats fit for a television commentator, high upon the upper terrace at the Radcliffe Road End, or intimately close to the passing players outside the pavilion steps. The ground has the scale to host the highest-profile of international games, and yet keep the all-important air of a club cricket ground. And, as most fast bowlers will admit when nudged for an explanation, the food and the showers are as good as you will get.

Despite these attractive qualities, it can often be a difficult place for a visiting team to force a victory in under four days. The away-team's top order invariably has its work cut out by a new ball swinging significantly (some believe in the role played by the surrounding stands making this so), whilst visiting bowlers must dismiss the Nottinghamshire batsmen early to avoid falling victim to their attacking instincts with the willow. And though a points system encouraging positive results has led to Trent Bridge surfaces favouring the bowlers on days one and two, a particularly effective drainage system has left pitches once green lacking the life to move the game forward as they dry.

The Yorkshire player to know such subtleties

best is undoubtedly Ryan Sidebottom. Having been central to the success of the dominant Nottinghamshire side of the recent past, he showed every bit of said experience with the new ball in his hand. Just as he did on in Barbados five months earlier, and at Headingley in the T20, he hit the Nottinghamshire top order hard, on this occasion dismissing both Alex Hales and Michael Lumb without scoring, and Samit Patel shortly after. With his next wicket, that of Riki Wessels, he went to within one wicket of the career first-class aggregate of his father, Arnie, who took 596.

Sidebottom's four were bettered only by the five of Steve Patterson, who took his career best figures of 5-43. Befitting his label as "Yorkshire's unsung workhorse", 'Patto' goes about his business quietly, finding his successful niche as the man renowned for steady and reliable consistency. And such reliability was proving a key part of the team's success, for at this point in the season he was our leading wicket-taker in the Championship, with 38 at an average of 21.50.

Earlier in the day, he had played a priceless role with the bat, supporting his partner Bairstow in a partnership of 91 that realised our overnight hopes of a score in excess of 400. Jonny's 62 from 70 balls was a typically rambunctious reminder of what England were missing at The Oval.

The exploits of Patterson and Sidebottom with the ball left the home side in fatal trouble, and only a rear-guard action from Ajmal Shahzad and Andre Adams could delay the inevitable follow-on, after their dismissal for a total of 150, 257 runs adrift of our first innings score.

But Sidebottom was not finished in his pursuit of wickets against his former side, dismissing Steve Mullaney before the close and helping us reach what would surely be an insurmountable position, barring interruptions for rain. And then on day three, Ryan took his tally to three in the innings and seven in the match, going one wicket past his father's total first class tally of 596 wickets in 43 fewer matches.

Reflecting upon his achievement, he said "...it's an honour and a privilege to go past Dad. He had a fantastic career himself and I've always wanted to follow in his footsteps."

Wary of the temptation of onlookers to associate his achievement with the twilight of his career, he was quick to dismiss his status as the veteran of the side.

"...I've still got a few years left in me yet and I'd like to go way past [Dad] if I can. I think 700 [wickets] would be nice..."

And it would be a brave man to bet against this long-serving Yorkshireman. For 'Siddy' has evolved with the fast-changing game throughout his career, not only developing the specific skills for success in the shorter forms of the game, but maintaining high levels of fitness when many of his fast-bowling competitors have given in to the aches and niggles of a career with the ball. And like the Super League stars he follows intently on a Friday evening, he is hardened by the day-to-day workload of a professional sport, and loves nothing more than a head-to-head scrap for an inch over the gain line. This product of the Yorkshire school of fast bowling may not have the pace of his fresh-legged days, but he has lost none of that red-haired fire; that childlike passion for playing the game he loves; or the priceless ability to swing the red ball back into the pads of a right-handed top order batsman. And for those reasons, amongst many others, the 700-mark might not be such an unrealistic dream...

Predictably, and to our relief, the Nottinghamshire middle order could do little to stem our progress towards inevitable victory on the third day. The six remaining wickets were shared amongst the attack, but Rashid's figures of 8.3-1-22-3 hammered the all-important final nails into the Nottinghamshire coffin. Mushtaq Ahmed played a vital role for Sussex in their Championship winning years, mopping up the tail with his natural variation from the wrist and smartly placed "in-out" fields. And in a similar way, and as he had in the second innings at Lord's months earlier, Adil proves too skilful a bowler for opposition batsmen unsure about whether to attack or

Not done yet: Ryan Sidebottom delivers the perfect inswinger on his way to surpassing his father's record.

Jonny Bairstow, Adam Lyth and Ryan Sidebottom lead the Yorkshire team out in the Championship match against Durham at North Marine Road.

defend. His third, and our final wicket, Harry Gurney caught Jaques for nought, came too late for victory by an innings, but that was of little inconvenience for openers Lyth and Lees, the former scoring three boundaries from five deliveries to take us over the line.

Victory was ours, well within three days, at a venue renowned for its difficulty for visiting sides, against a full-strength Nottinghamshire top order, at a stage in the season when it mattered most. A 33-point lead underlined the message this victory sent to our nearest rivals for Championship silverware, and gave us valuable breathing room at the top of the Division, at least until Durham caught up their game-in-hand. The stage was set for a top of the table clash between north-eastern neighbours at Scarborough – the script could not have been written any better.

For the time being, however, coach Gillespie had other ideas, namely the celebration of a resounding Championship win, in true antipodean style. The "cold treats" mentioned in his twitter feed would taste so much better upon reflection of a game that had gone almost perfectly to plan.

The curtain comes down

The final 40-over match of the summer, a home fixture against Glamorgan, told the telling tale of our one-day campaign and, in stark contrast, that of our opposition too. Almost four months earlier, the first of two contests against our Welsh counterparts – a soggy encounter at Colwyn Bay – had ended in disappointing defeat, leaving us with some clear lessons to learn if we were to open our account in the one-day competition. But as we all now know, those key lessons were not learnt, or at least employed, in subsequent matches, and our limited overs cricket continued as it began, in underwhelming style.

Early losses in the group stages of the competition made our qualification for the knock-out stages all the more improbable, leading the coaching staff to preserve our full-strength line-up for the Championship challenge, but that did not detract from the Group C table making disappointing reading. Nine losses from 12 left us one place above the Unicorns conglomerate, embarrassingly far from a challenge for qualification, let alone silverware. And after the well-documented successes in the Twenty20 competition in 2012, our white-ball cricket in 2013 had fallen well below expectations.

It was not all doom and gloom, however, because the one-day season had given valuable experience to potential first XI regulars of the future. Promising displays have come from Academy players Will Rhodes, Ben Coad and Ryan Gibson, each making their Yorkshire debuts in the competition, not forgetting headline-maker Matthew Fisher, who became the country's youngest post-war cricketer.

The YB40 competition had been central to the season of another emerging player, Dan Hodgson, whose career best 90 in the final fixture of the summer underlined the eye-catching progress he had made in both the 40-over and 20-over competitions. 'Hodgy' started the season in a somewhat precarious position, as the third in line of three Yorkshire wicketkeepers, but success with the bat - in his characteristically wristy style – came in the second XI and coincided with Bairstow's departure to the Ashes, bringing about an opportunity at No. 3 in the 40-over line-up. If a disappointing one-day season for the Club had a silver lining, the consistent progress of this quiet achiever would be it.

Hodgy's 90 from 98 balls was central to Yorkshire's total of 215-5 from the allotted overs, with encouraging contributions coming also from new boy Williamson and the in-

form Lyth. But Glamorgan edged over the line with seven balls to spare, thanks in part to a typically bullish 31 off 17 balls from Graham Wagg, thereby securing their progress to the last four of the competition and going on to become losing finalists to Nottinghamshire at Lord's.

Our 40-over campaign had finished how it had started, with some nearly-cricket leaving us frustratingly short of the victory line. That had been the trend from a frustrating season of one-day cricket, at times promising much and building pressure against the opposition, only to suffer from a subsequent release at a key stage of the game. A year earlier, if our skills with bat or ball had left us short of the mark, our fielding had papered over the cracks, quite often turning a game on its head with an effective combination of aggression and on-field energy. But for a frustrating variety of reasons, this enthusiasm in the field – a trademark of coach Gillespie's one-day cricket blueprint – had been conspicuous by its absence, exposing the slightest of errors from the bowlers. Throughout the two domestic white ball competitions, we had failed to achieve two key elements of the previous year's success: a carefree abandon with the bat, so often taking us to competitive totals in 2012; and the unwavering nailing of yorkers in the final throes of our fielding innings, strangling the opposition with predictable effectiveness. There were no excuses to be made, but so much of our limited overs anti-climax could be explained by the absence of these parts of the puzzle.

Ignoring the obvious distraction of an imminent title challenge in the Championship, attention would now turn to plans for a new-look one-day competition in 2014, a 50-over contest mirroring the international game, played in a block of fixtures mid-way through the summer. Regardless of our finishing position in the four-day competition, motivation would certainly be high to right the wrongs of our white-ball campaign. But for the time being, the coming down of the limited overs curtain would be met with certain relief.

The tables turned

It is the day before the mass exodus to the Scarborough Festival and I am looking for mail in the players' pigeon hole of the Carnegie Stand offices. The room is near empty, as it happens, but for a familiar voice employing its usual turn of phrase in a quiet corner to my left. The voice is Galey's, answering the interview questions of Head of Marketing and Communications, Danny Reuben, in preview of tomorrow's much-hyped contest against Durham at North Marine Road.

As he often does, our captain plays a diplomatic straight bat to the series of gently leading questions, playing down the top-of-the-table clash as "just another game" giving his team the opportunity to "do the basics well", as they had for the previous 11 Championship fixtures. As he rightly said, though the Division One title would be decided within four weeks, "there's still a quarter of the season to go [and] a lot of cricket to play". A lead of 25.5 points from second-placed Durham was significant by anyone's standards, but Paul Collingwood's men knew as well as anybody that victory over Yorkshire at Scarborough would place the Championship run-in in a much different light.

Between his dead-batted responses, Galey could not ignore an unavoidable issue for him and his management team before the toss a day later – the embarrassment of riches in the batting department, and therefore the question of which unfortunate batsman would miss out upon selection. Jaques was back from injury, Ballance returning from Lions duty and Bairstow once again available. Williamson had to play, having only just been drawn in, but Lyth and Lees could both argue strong cases for inclusion, the latter with a near triple century and a century to his name in a matter of games.

"So who will be the unlucky man to miss out?" came the question from behind the microphone. Rather smartly, Galey sidestepped the question with the aplomb of a well-trained politician.

If I had been fit, I may well have been involved in this interesting debate. The fact that I was not made it no less fascinating. For this selection headache shone the spotlight upon a County coach's predicament that is becoming increasingly common.

The story began weeks earlier, when the respective successes of Bairstow and Ballance in England shirts (the latter for the Lions) brought about the suggestion that both may be selected for the upcoming ODI series against Australia. That suggestion was highly believable, for Jonny had shown good form under pressure in the Ashes, whilst Gary's match-winning consistency was becoming all the more expected.

Understandably, news of the possible withdrawal of two key members of the Championship top six set the alarm bells ringing. Jaques and I were still unfit for selection, despite marginal progress in our rehab programmes, and the alternatives for selection from the second XI, despite their promise, were admittedly a little green for graduation.

And so it was perfectly understandable and of no surprise to hear of the selection of Kane Williamson as an overseas batsman. His presence, when combined with the return of myself or Jaques, would fill the boots of the absent two, and the jigsaw would be complete.

As hindsight now shows, the true run of events was not quite as smooth. Despite their form and success, Bairstow and Ballance both avoided selection for England's 50-over side and remained automatic selections for the Yorkshire XI. Then Jaques completed his rehab, declaring himself fit for selection and ever-eager to figure in the four-day side.

Herein lies the increasingly common problem faced by a County coach – the impossibility of predicting one's resources in light of international call-ups at any one time. One could argue it is an enviable problem to have, for any side would love such selection dilemmas on a regular basis. But at a time when commercial profits are hard to achieve in domestic cricket, signing an overseas player as

*Cometh the hour:
Phil Jaques on his
way to a second
innings century
against Durham.*

cover for a possible loss is an untimely expense and somewhat of a gamble that prize monies won – as a result of the signing or otherwise – will outweigh the costs of the adding to the wage bill.

The rumours as to which unfortunate batsman would be mixing the drinks simply added to the pre-match hype of this pivotal fixture in the Championship season. There was talk of record crowds on their way, hopeful of the Yorkshire lead at the top of the table being extended to title-winning proportions. Twitter was frequented by Yorkshire fans on their way to "Scarbados", such was the forecast, befitting of a perfectly-scripted context for the fixture.

Victory against Durham would have the Championship all but sealed, in the eyes of many, at least. But a high-scoring draw would mark a productive week of cricket also, preventing Durham from closing the gap as the season's end drew closer.

And the pitch at North Marine Road reflected this scenario, for it was not the typical Scarborough surface promising an even contest between bat and ball and the likelihood of a natural result. Rather, it offered less assistance for the seamers than one might expect, being slower than usual in pace and advantageously placid for those batsmen at the crease once the new ball softened. It was a pitch designed to make an away victory difficult, barring a home performance against the form book. The toss, therefore, would provide an important opportunity to drive the game with a sizeable first innings total.

It is the week following the Scarborough four-dayer and I am sat in the changing rooms at the Academy training ground, in Weetwood. Down the road, our usual home has been overtaken by Rooty and his team-mates, busy preparing for the imminent one-day international. Thanks in the main to my injury-forced isolation from first XI affairs, it is some time since I have spent time with the usual company.

Before we set about our routine warm-up, conversation turns to the previous week's cricket at North Marine Road. 'Budgie' Lyth offers his analysis in somewhat of a nutshell.

Dizzy fronts up to the Press after our table-turning loss against Durham.

*"We bowled s**t, we batted s**t. That was it."*
New boy Williamson contributes with a smile as we take to the field. "Good summary, Budge! You are not far off there".

The match against Durham had not gone to the romantic script pieced together in preview. In fact, it had ended in a loss very damaging to our progression toward Championship silverware. It was only our second defeat in 31 matches, but it had come at the most untimely of points in the season, and left our opponents with the upper hand entering the final four weeks.

The toss was indeed important, and was won by the visiting captain, Paul Collingwood, who chose to take first use of a favourable batting pitch. And though 'Siddy' continued where he had left off at Trent Bridge, trapping both Keaton Jennings and Scott Borthwick leg before inside his second over of the day, the subsequent scorecard told of 138 overs dominated by a fast-scoring line-up of Durham batsmen. Mark Stoneman, Ben Stokes and Michael Richardson each got their names on the honours boards of the away changing room with respective centuries, and other key contributions brought about an imposing first innings total of 573, scored at more than four runs per over.

In a break in the morning's training at Weetwood, Jaquesy explains the shortcomings of our bowling performance.

"Siddy bowled well, but other than that we generally bowled too short". Bowling too short at Scarborough was a common mistake made by those unfamiliar with its marked bounce and carry to the 'keeper – the sight of such carry behind the wicket tempting many an attack into over-indulgence in bouncers.

Jaquesy continued. "[Durham] just scored too quickly for us to build the pressure we have been building. Apart from the Sussex game, that's just not happened this year".

The magnitude of the visitors' total and the speed at which their runs were scored left us with a clear and simple task: to bat well for the lion's share of two days to prevent our Championship rivals from converting their position of strength into victory.

At the close on the second day, a Yorkshire score of 182-3 represented a promising platform upon which to build. The highlight of said foundation was the form of recent acquisition Williamson, who walked from the field unbeaten with 76 runs to his name. Members departing North Marine Road for their nearby B&Bs would be hopeful of him going on to a match-saving score.

The third day started with increasing promise that the members' prayers would be answered, Kane and Bairstow edging us to a position of tangible comfort, at 211-3. But, as one might expect from a top of the table clash between two competitive sides, progress

towards the follow-on target did not continue as planned. In a quick change of the game's momentum, seven wickets fell for just 63 runs, Kane departing for 84, leaving us dismissed for a precarious 274. Onlookers unaware of Durham's selection news would have been forgiven for assuming a five-wicket haul from the usual spearhead of the visitors' attack, Graham Onions. He was on the sidelines, however, nursing a hand injury that kept him out of consideration; the wickets had been shared between an under strength and relatively inexperienced attack. Quite suddenly, we were in clear danger of a four-day defeat, and there was work to do, following-on in our second innings.

In interview at the close on day three, Jaques could be very happy with his day's work. When the team is in trouble, it needs its most adept and experienced players to remove it from danger, and "Pro" had gone some way to doing that, unbeaten as he was on 151. A Yorkshire score of 276-1 was two in excess of the team's first innings score and left us just 23 runs short of Durham's sizeable total. We could not have asked for a better response to our first innings collapse and much of the morning's worry had dissipated. With one day to go, every Yorkshire run would count double in effect, building our lead in the game whilst taking up valuable time for the visitors to carry out an improbable chase.

Of course, though Jaquesy's century was central to our riposte, he needed the assistance of a partner to build the partnership of 257 inside 60 overs. And after falling 16 runs short of a first innings century, Kane went a few steps further, finishing the day with thoughts of the ten runs he still needed to take him to three figures on day four. In fact, the Kiwi had achieved a rare feat on the third day, contributing to both a century partnership in the first innings and a double century stand in the second, all within the day's allotted overs.

"He just looked very assured," said Brooks, reflecting upon Williamson's performance days later at training.

"The new ball seamed, as it does at

Scarborough, but he played it very well, and just looked intent on batting all day. Nothing seemed to faze him either. I reckon he's a tough cookie".

Brooky's observations were very much in line with memories of Kane's century for his Gloucestershire side last year, in trying conditions. It was no surprise that, despite the anti-climax of his first ball dismissal at Trent Bridge, the late-season signing was beginning to produce exactly what the coaching staff were hoping.

And though the home win we were hoping for looked improbable at the third day close, this pivotal game in the Championship season was still wide open with a day to spare. There was work to do, but the forecast was good and there were sufficient batting resources sat waiting to secure a hard-earned result on the final day.

Amidst the unpredictable scrap for momentum in this game, it was a damaging trend that brought about our downfall. At the close of day two, our first innings battle had built a position of promise, only to see it lost before lunch the following day. And with similar effect, hard yards with the bat had built another stable base by the close on day three, with Jaques and Williamson hungry for a triple century partnership.

But again, the overnight break preceded a turn of the tables, with 'Pro' adding just a single to his overnight score and Kane just seven more, falling within a boundary of his first century for the White Rose.

The beauty – and cruelty – of four-innings cricket is that it takes persistent and consistent dominance to win a game, and just a matter of overs to effectively lose one. And in line with this adage, a second batting collapse in as many innings proved fatal for our hopes of coming away unscathed.

Three important wickets fell before lunch, and Scott Borthwick took as many after the break to wrap up the lower order, leaving his side just 121 runs to score within 37 overs after tea to hammer home the win. In the words of centurion Jaques, we had "batted without discipline, losing wickets at key times, having worked hard to build partnerships". Cricket of this frustratingly insufficient quality is sapping for a side, taking all possible effort to repeatedly recover from self-imposed strife.

Calls of "You never know, lads!" would not have been far from the mouth of captain Gale when he took his side to the field for the final session of this four-day scrap. And 'Siddy' offered an early taste of the improbable, dismissing Stoneman first ball and raising a number of appeals for leg before.

But the man who wrapped up our tail, Borthwick, then wrapped up the match for his team with a counter-attacking 65 from 85 balls, making the most of our last throw of the dice for quick Durham wickets.

After all the build-up, the promise and the talk of a victory at Scarborough that would near-enough seal the sesquicentennial silverware, our Championship hopes had suffered a blow of equal and opposite effect. We were now just a handful of points ahead with three games to play, and our north-eastern neighbours had a game in hand. A third title in six seasons for our opponents now appeared possible, a similar fate for us less likely than it had seemed just four days ago.

CHAPTER EIGHT

September

Out of our hands

"Oh s**t, 'av you seen the score, Squiz?" said Brooksy, staring into his smartphone. "Sussex are 81-6!"

The game to which Brooksy referred was the all-important game-in-hand of our closest title contenders. At home on the predictably spicy Riverside pitch, Durham were taking on our next Championship opponents, Sussex, and were going too well for our comfort.

By all accounts, a home team first-innings total of 245 was more than competitive. And when former Tyke Mitch Claydon had night-watchman Jimmy Anyon caught and bowled for 19, a first innings deficit for Sussex looked inevitable.

We are at Weetwood, filling our fixture-free schedule with fitness training and net practice whilst the England boys make preparations for the ODI. A few of us make the most of a break in the net practice rota, taking a seat outside the pavilion.

"Who's in next?" someone asks, forming predictions of Durham's advance. "Brown, I think," comes the reply.

We never thought we would say it, but we need Sussex to recover well. After coming out on the wrong side of the cricketing equivalent of a "six-pointer" at Scarborough against Durham, a title that was once in our hands is now our nearest rivals to lose. If the unthinkable – yet predictable – happens, and Durham beat Sussex this week, the Division One lead will be taken from our grasp with time running out.

For the moment, at least, we have become helpless watchers of our online scorecards, refreshing their content with obsessive regularity. There is nothing we can do.

The game moves on

Thanks to the persistence of my Achilles tendonitis, the summer's schedule is now far from busy and I am forced into an unavoidable break from competition. To ease my frustrations, I take the train to London to meet up with all those friends from whom I am ex-communicated in the summer months.

It is a rainy Friday evening and I am aboard the seven o'clock train from King's Cross to Leeds. Predictably, it is uncomfortably packed with people looking to escape the rat race for the weekend. As the train approaches its terminal at Leeds, I see a familiar face reaching for his overhead luggage at the opposite end of our coach.

"I thought it was you, Ed," I confirm, as he turns beside the train's automatic door. It is Ed Smith, former Kent, Middlesex and England batsman, now an author and journalist of growing reputation.

He looks different from the Ed I remember, inevitably older and slightly greyer around the temples, but clearly in good health and form. Without hesitation, he puts forward an explanation for his chosen attire.

"I've been swimming in London – that's why I'm wearing these shorts!" Long to the knee and checked in blue and red, these could not be described as an orthodox choice for a casual swimmer. Furthermore, it seems we are both in agreement that they are not the ideal complement to Ed's pale pink shirt and navy blue blazer.

"I'm going to get some right stick off the boys when I arrive at the hotel! Might just have to sneak in through reception without notice".

The 'boys' to whom he refers are the Test Match Special (TMS) commentators, staying the night at a luxurious hotel in one of the more trendy parts of Leeds.

Ed is due to join the TMS team for tomorrow's one-day international between England and Australia at Headingley. After hosting the Kiwis for an early-summer Test, the Club are looking forward to a profitable day of international cricket, but the forecast is not good.

"I expect I'll be on the early train home tomorrow", Ed says in reference to the imminent rain.

Before we go our separate ways, I take the opportunity to ask Ed about his life as a journalist and commentator, born out of his success as a dressing-room diarist. His response is genuine, believable and full of positive remarks in description of his developing career.

"One thing you realise though, Joe," he says, pulling our conversation to a natural conclusion, "is that, after a while, no one really remembers your career once you've done".

A disheartening line with which to bid our farewells, but a telling one nonetheless. Sport waits for no one. The game must go on.

A Headingley hat-trick

To no-one's surprise, Ed and the weather forecasters were not wrong. Persistent rain from the early hours led to an inevitable washout of the one-day international at Headingley by lunchtime, leaving the Club frustrated by the unfortunate hand dealt to them by the elements.

It was nothing new for the administrators at Headingley, however. It was the third washout of a one-day international for the Club in five years, after similarly disappointing events in 2009 and 2012.

The much-discussed balance sheet would not suffer unduly, thanks to the usual insurance covering against such losses of revenue, but the same could not be said of the impression of those ticket-holders walking away disappointed. After a glorious summer of consistent sunshine, this was a bitter pill to take for everyone involved.

Dizzy sets about his now-trademark regime, pacing around the outfield boundary barefoot.

Our lead lost

We all thought Sussex would put up more of a fight at The Riverside. Batting totals of 112 and 116 led the away side to a margin of defeat larger than Durham's highest total in the match, and would have suggested a contest played between sides at opposing ends of the table. But Durham's surge to a second consecutive victory against their nearest rivals was as impressive as the Sussex demise was disappointing.

Durham's resounding win in this, their game-in-hand, gave them a lead of 14.5 points with just three games to go. Where had our substantial lead gone? The title looked so much closer to our grasp only a fortnight ago.

The only consolation was the fragility of Sussex's confidence, for they would be our next opponents. If our attack could penetrate their top six as the Durham bowlers had, that badly-needed win may be within reach.

Meanwhile, Durham would travel to Derby, the home of a Derbyshire side equally in need of a victory, in their case to stave off relegation back to the second Division.

Dizzy laps it up

It is the third day at Hove, and for the second time in as many weeks, Yorkshire folk are being frustrated by the September rain. Play has been delayed until 2.10pm, leaving just 42 overs remaining in a day that is pivotal to our chances of success this week.

Making the most of the opportunity presented by the delay, Dizzy sets about his now-trademark regime, pacing around the outfield boundary barefoot. Onlookers viewing Dizzy's "hard yards" as a protest against the decision to postpone play in such light and sporadic drizzle could not be further from the truth. Of course, coach Gillespie would welcome the decision for play to start in spite of the conditions, for his batsman are less than 50 runs from the home side's first innings total with six wickets in hand. But his continuous

bare-footed laps of the boundary, or "earth walk" as he calls it, is nothing more than an effort to keep off the pounds.

After Durham's table-changing win over Sussex last week, this four-day contest against the same opposition was vital to our chances of regaining a lead at the top of Division One. And it promised the prospects we were hoping for on day one, when the hosts' fragile batting line-up fell to 137-6, having been inserted by captain Gale. England wicketkeeper Matt Prior had been bowled by Patterson for 23, leaving only Ben Brown as the last recognised batsman of notable ability. A profitable hour with the ball and the first step towards vital victory would be complete.

Brown had other ideas, guiding his tail towards a first innings total of 292, himself finishing unbeaten on 84. In doing so, he had tempered our momentum in this game, shepherded his side to a competitive total, and delayed our efforts to impose a first innings lead.

As Dizzy felt the earth beneath his cold feet, our position in the game was, yet again, a promising one. At the close on the previous evening, and thanks in the main to 93 from Lythy and yet another half-century from Williamson, we were very well placed to surge ahead to a first innings lead and place that Sussex top six under significant pressure. A score of 246-4 left us just 46 runs behind the home side's total, with Ballance and Rashid still awaiting their chance with the bat.

When Lythy makes a significant score, he often does so in the most effortless and stylish of ways, timing the ball through the off-side as though refining his technique in the indoor school. But his first innings effort was forced to be more watchful in style, such was the accuracy and stubborn consistency of the attack.

As he has done of so many occasions this summer, Sussex's overseas signing Steve Magoffin gave the toughest of examinations to the defensive techniques of our top order, on his way to 25 overs at a cost of just 29 runs. Line and length is Magoffin's game, but his performance was simply more than a show of accuracy, and made Lythy's progress all the more difficult and our position at the close one to be proud of.

When play finally got underway on the third day, our second position of notable strength in the game was lost all too quickly. Williamson departed without adding to his overnight 80, and our efforts to adhere to Galey's encouragement and "play positively" towards a desirable first innings lead led to our losing six first innings wickets for 76 runs in just 24 overs. Slow left-armer Ashar Zaidi, effectively on trial for the home side after his successes in the Lancashire league, finished with 4-57.

Our collapse with the bat was as much down to our own ill-discipline as the whiles of Zaidi, but a lead of 34 highlighted a missed opportunity to achieve a potentially match-winning lead in excess of 100. Victories in four-day cricket require a concerted and consistent performance throughout the match, and on this occasion, it seemed the position we had worked so hard to gain had been somewhat squandered within just over an hour's cricket.

The silver lining of the dark cloud that was the afternoon session was the passing in first class matches of the 1,000 run mark for the season by Gary Ballance. His subsequent dismissal would have been disappointing, but the achievement of the much-adorned milestone is something to be celebrated. As arbitrary as it sounds, the season tally of well over 1,000 runs tells a story of consistent professionalism and persistence. It is indicative of a batsman who has scored important centuries at key points in the summer, survived the inevitable lean patches that come through misfortune or human error, and made quietly significant contributions on the days in between. It is difficult to achieve the 1,000 run milestone without being a key part of a team's success, and Gary has certainly been that during the past six months.

Before the minimal deficit was wiped out by the Sussex batsmen in their second innings, Siddy and 'Pudsey' Plunkett dismissed Wells

and Yardy respectively, giving us just a hint of what-might-be after the home side's second innings collapse the week before. But much to the frustration of skipper Gale, bad light made even the spin of Williamson and Rashid an unfair challenge in the eyes of the umpires, and the day was cut short.

No doubt frustrated by the untimely disruptions by the elements, Galey posed an interesting question to the game's authorities in his after-match interview on day three. In response to the news that Durham had brought forward the start time of their next game, against Nottinghamshire in a few days time, to 10.15am, Galey was quite clear in his view.

"Maybe that'll be an advantage to them," he said, citing the decreased likelihood of a day cut short by bad light in the evening.

Contriving a contest

Durham captain Paul Collingwood would not have been surprised by the bowling figures from Hove on the fourth morning. The pitch was good, and barring another collapse, the dismissal of eight Sussex batsmen in sufficient time to chase down a gettable target was a tough ask for the Yorkshire attack. The spells of Magoffin had proved it difficult to score against consistent bowling on this pitch, but less of a challenge to merely survive.

And so, seeing a creative opportunity, Galey agreed with his counterpart, Ed Joyce, that Yorkshire would chase 300 for victory in this match from 60 overs. An intriguing competition in anyone's book, but there remained the small matter of how the current match situation could be fast-forwarded to the agreeable deal.

The cricket that followed the captain's negotiations was not for those singing the praises of a high-quality and ultra competitive English domestic competition. In the morning session, 32.5 overs of highly questionable bowling were delivered to the Sussex batsmen, from which 285 runs were scored with enviable ease. Chris Nash raced to an unbeaten 167 from 137 balls, Rory Hamilton-Brown to 126 from 83 balls, and the distasteful deed was done. The cricket that followed promised to be of a different type altogether.

In the not-too-distant past, negotiations such as those to have taken place between captains Gale and Joyce were commonplace, as a means of ushering a three-day match towards a positive result. In the modern day, such contriving of a result attracts considerable criticism from a division of the on looking spectators, understandably keen to watch competitive cricket between two sides thinking of nothing less than defeating their opposition.

But as stakes have risen and Championship "dead-rubbers" have become all the more a rarity, the points taken by a captain for a drawn game are of little value in his side's bid for silverware or survival. Though the cricket required to set up a final day chase is that more often seen upon a school playground, the resulting contest should be worth the wait.

Besides, it is arguable that captain Collingwood may have done just the same if his side were in a similar position.

So the stage was set, a target of 300 required from two sessions to achieve the vital victory that would place our rivals Durham under sufficient pressure going into their contest with Nottinghamshire next week. Liam Plunkett, naturally aggressive with the bat, was sent is a makeshift opener. The game yet again was full of promise.

A double disappointment

Much to both sides' frustration, the afternoon session was blighted by spells of rain and bad light. Though Lythy continued his form from the first innings, moving encouragingly to an unbeaten 40, there was nothing he could do about the increasingly heavy showers that led the game to an inevitable stalemate. As painful as the morning's cricket was for some to watch, the acceptance of a rain-affected draw after such efforts to force a result would be far more difficult to take. Confidence was high that the victory target would be achieved, but there was nothing more uncontrollable than the weather.

But as the rain got heavier at Hove, there was news to come from Derby that would be far more damaging to our title hopes. Derbyshire wickets had been falling fast.

At the start of the third day, visitors Durham had begun 41 runs adrift of their hosts' first innings total, and nothing other than a draw could be envisaged. Both sides had found it difficult to score on a pitch lacking in pace, after all.

A Durham lead of 27 gained a useful third batting point but, with time ticking away in the game, bonus points promised to be the extent of their spoils.

But almost as if it were meant to be, after a slow but steady start by the Derbyshire top order in their second innings, their next nine wickets fell for just 37 runs in the space of 20 overs. They had capitulated to 63 all out at the hands of Graham Onions, who took 5-23, bringing his wickets tally to the season to 60 from just 10 appearances.

The victory target for the visitors was a cricketing stroll in the park, achieved with relative ease for the loss of a single wicket. Their nine-wicket win had taken them 27.5 points clear at the top of the table and just one more win away from the Championship title.

For all its sins, the online world of twitter provides a straight-to-the-point microcosm of such events from differing views. The tweets of Yorkshire's Gale and Durham's Mark Stoneman could not have summarised the contrasting situations better. "Disappointing day," wrote the Yorkshire skipper. "Couldn't have done any more. Bloody weather!" His rivals' opening batsman saw events differently. "The lads keep finding a way! #winning". Stoneman was right, after all – his side had produced match-winning cricket when it most mattered, and were justified in their position at the top of the table with just two matches remaining.

A man in form: Gary Ballance cuts the ball to the boundary in the Championship match against Middlesex at Headingley.

Autumn arrives

The view from the players' dining room in the Carnegie Pavilion is a sorry one. Watched by a notably small crowd in the Headingley terraces, the Middlesex fielders have taken to the field wearing as many layers of thermals, shirts and jumpers they can get their hands on, each appearing deceivably rotund in the process. Autumn has arrived, or so it seems, with a cold wind, fading light and a blanket of cloud.

After all, it was the St. Leger stakes at Doncaster racecourse last Saturday, and according to my granddad, "upon the tail of the last horse in the Leger comes autumn". Not far off this year, granddad.

Having been inserted by the visiting captain Chris Rogers, our innings has got underway to a concerning start. With half an hour gone, the scoreboard reads 9-2, with Kane Williamson not yet off the mark.

All indications are of the seamer-friendly pitch upon which everyone would have counted. At least, both sides would have been hoping for a surface naturally producing a positive result in this, Yorkshire's penultimate game of the campaign. This would be a day of gritty northern cricket, a day when cricket – and cricketers - of substance would come out on top, in spite of the far-from-glamorous setting.

A short while later, I am in the players' viewing gallery, known affectionately as "the letterbox" by the players (in reference to its dangerously low ceilings and obvious dimensions), watching Williamson and Galey tackle the challenge posed by the conditions under their feet in the middle. Galey, as he always has since our days in the under-12 Yorkshire schoolboys' side, counters the bowlers and conditions with adrenalin-fuelled attack, punchy with his hands and aggressive in his shot selection. Fighting fire with fire has always been his way, and more often than not his strength.

In contrast, Kane manages the conditions in a way quite different from his captain. A good length, seaming delivery from Middlesex new-ball bowler Tim Murtagh, ideally-paced for the conditions, is played not only with due respect by Kane, but with such 'soft' hands and so late that the ball comes to a halt within a bat's length of his feet. Moments later, the same happens. Both deliveries from Murtagh would have dismissed many a quality right-hander on a day such as this, but this 23-year-old Kiwi is more than equal to the task.

"How does he do that?" asks Lythy. "Most of us'd be nicking that!"

"It must be disheartening to see that as a bowler, Dizz?" I ask our coach, prompting a reflection upon his career.

"It certainly is, Squiz. Not quite as disheartening as hitting the middle of Sachin's barn door of a bat on a flat one in Mumbai though." I could not argue with that.

In his next over, Murtagh delivers a ball of slightly shorter length, again seaming away sharply off the grassy surface. Kane's hands remain consciously beneath his eyes, the blade unmoved from the original line, and it deviates safely passed the edge. To the novice onlooker, this play-and-miss would appear to indicate skills lacking in the batsman. But quite the opposite was true, for those able to play the ball as late as Kane survive the seaming ball most frequently.

"He reminds me of Benky," says someone in the letterbox, referring to the style of Dale Benkenstein, the prolific middle order batsman for Durham in recent years. And there is some truth in the comparison. The stature, the arm guard, the preference for back foot strokeplay, the ability to play the ball late – these are all signatures of their respective ways.

Inevitably, the grey blanket of cloud has produced its first offering of rain, and the players have left the field for an early lunch.

"Have you seen the score from The Riverside, Dizz?" asks Brooksy in the dining room. "They're 72-9!"

News of the score is near-fatal for our dwindling Championship hopes. Nottinghamshire had chosen to bat first at the toss, and been subsequently dismissed for 78 runs, 20 minutes short of the lunch break. The title was a step closer for the hosts.

A short while later, and with the play at Headingley stuttering along between the frequent showers, news comes through of a game at Chester-le-Street continuing to move forward at a pace. No fewer than 15 wickets had fallen within the first 48 overs of the day and there was a slim possibility that the visitors would take a first innings lead.

"The pitch inspectors'll be up at The Riverside," came the obvious retort from the huddle of players queuing for a warming lunch at Headingley.

At the close of the first day in Durham, Collingwood had his own batting exploits, as well as the ordinary shot selection of both sides' batsmen, to thank for the quietening of the complaints about the pitch. "Excessive" movement apparently there was not. According to the home side's skipper, the pace at which the game moved forward was due to the exceptional quality of the bowling and ineptitude of the batting.

His batting was far from inept, by all accounts. His partnership of 121 from 35 overs with wicketkeeper Phil Mustard alleviated the growing concerns of a pitch penalty and led his side to a potentially match-winning first innings lead of 129 runs with two wickets still remaining. This was exactly what we did not want to hear.

By the end of the first day, our deficit of 27.5 points behind leaders Durham had increased by a further four points, and our Championship hopes were growing as dismal as the weather. We were playing some good cricket, but not as good as our title rivals, and we would need a cricketing miracle to outdo the leaders with such little time remaining.

Despite a growing air of resignation at the advance of our rivals 90 miles away, there was still much to play for in this encounter. Namely the securing of second place in the Division One table – no mean feat for any side, let alone one just promoted, and with significant financial worth for the Club at an hour of need.

With Durham continuing to make headway at The Riverside, the cricket at Headingley was dominated by the seam bowlers. With every approach to the crease, each made dark and deepening marks in an outfield softened by the late-summer dew and frequent rain. Murtagh and Corey Collymore starred for the visitors, dismissing Yorkshire for 210 in our first innings, but then the ever-consistent Sidebottom and Patterson followed suit, leading us to a first innings lead of 82. Surely that would suffice on a pitch offering such assistance for the seamers?

Durham deliver their deathblow

On the third day, the inevitable was confirmed. Durham had extended their lead beyond the reach of us and our opponents at Headingley, and the Division One title was theirs. After Nottinghamshire's capitulation within the opening session of the game at The Riverside, most were talking of when – not if – the home side would cruise to the victory that would win them the Championship, and today it came. An eight wicket victory was the tenth of their campaign and just one away from a record haul in the top flight. No one could argue with that.

With the news filtering through, focus upon the game in hand at Headingley proved difficult for the players, but second place remained a desirable prize. The 'fairytale' had eluded us, we had fallen short of Geoffrey's exhortation to win the Championship in our anniversary year, but there was still much to play for, and standards to uphold.

Ballance certainly upheld such standards, bringing about a quick-paced half-century that dampened Middlesex's hopes of a second innings collapse. A lead of 212 runs with five second innings wickets still remaining was an encouraging position to enter the final day of this penultimate match of the season.

Gary's overnight unbeaten 53 became 90 from 114 balls – a fitting way for him to celebrate his achieving 1,000 runs the week before and sending a reminder of his quality to the England selectors. His near-century led us to a total of 194 and a lead of 276.

In a game so dominated by the seaming ball, that proved too much for the visitors. The removal of Rogers for 65 – caught at the wicket off the bowling of Plunkett – made the Middlesex chase all the more difficult and arguably put pay to their hopes of a victory chase. Figures of 7.5-0-33-4 were just reward for Brooks, whose contribution to our Championship challenge has more than justified his off-season signing.

So second place in Division One was ours, and with one game remaining in the season. En route to Scarborough a short while ago, the runners-up prize would have seemed a failure, but we had been beaten not only by some untimely showers, but an unavoidably impressive sprint to the finish by a Durham side playing some high quality cricket with bat and ball. Their title was just deserts for producing entertaining and match-winning performances when it mattered.

The season's finale at The Oval had been expected to be the Championship decider for many months, with the final round of fixtures producing the top flight's ultimate winner. But Durham's unstoppable progress had left it a rarity in domestic four-day cricket – a "dead rubber" – with no significant consequence of our performance upon the Championship table. The sesquicentennial season deserved a successful send-off, however, and there would be no better way to celebrate the distance run than with another four-day win against the "Brown Hatters".

The steel behind the smile

Joe Root is a young man in demand. When I meet him for a coffee one September afternoon in London, he is on his way to his latest engagement, an appearance in support of Graeme Swann's benefit dinner, at The Hurlingham Club. In his hand, 'Rooty' carries the standard attire for events of such standing: his tuxedo.

It is all a far cry from where this well-mannered Yorkshire lad found himself only 12 months ago. Going into the last match of the domestic season – a Division Two

Championship match at Chelmsford – Joe had no idea that the year ahead would be so eventful. His place on any representative tour, let alone the Test tour, was uncertain, and despite the whispers of his inclusion, he was making no assumptions.

Fast forward to the present day and Joe is reflecting upon a whirlwind of a cricketing year in which he became England cricket's "Golden Boy".

His successful summer for the Lions in 2012 rewarded him with a surprise inclusion on the Test tour of India, starting the busiest of winters finding his feet in England's middle order. There was talk of him achieving 1,000 runs before May after a bumper start to the Championship season with Yorkshire. A maiden Test hundred against New Zealand in front of a packed house at his home ground at Headingley - with his Yorkshire team mate Jonny Bairstow at the other end to share in his celebrations - was a fairytale confirmation of his ability to succeed in the international arena. With Nick Compton struggling for form in the opening slot, Joe was the natural successor, fulfilling the role in no less than a home Ashes series. Continued, if mostly moderate, success against Australia's new ball attack led to regular appearances in England's limited-overs sides where he showcased a batting versatility not to be underestimated. Not a bad year for a lad still shy of his 23rd birthday.

So why had the past 12 months been so successful?

In his instinctively modest way, Joe is quick to acknowledge his fortune. "I have been given some fantastic opportunities over the past couple of years", he says with an air of self-deprecation. "Being selected for the Lions match against Sri Lanka A at Scarborough in August, 2011, was key. I hadn't played that much for Yorkshire by that point, and hadn't even made a Championship hundred. But the 66 I made in the second innings gave me confidence and I went on from there."

Joe's words hold some truth, but there is no avoiding the fact that he has quite quickly begun to develop the reputation for making the slightest of opportunities count. "I suppose you're right," says Joe in reluctant agreement. "Recognising the key opportunities to perform well has been important. You know, if the pitch is flat or you've a chance to get on top of an attack, it's a chance to..." "Fill your boots?" I suggest. "Yeah, that's right - you know as well as I do, mate".

OK, so this is a Yorkshire batsman who has the wherewithal beyond his years to recognise his time to step up to the plate. But there is more to it than that, a characteristic tendency clear in his on-stage behaviour, particularly when the pressure is on.

"It might sound cheesy, but I've just been trying to enjoy it. I train really hard to be the best I can be so I don't see the point in ruining all that by not enjoying it. I'm here to have a good time."

It is easy to utter such words, and many do, but quite something else to put them into practice at the highest level of the professional game. And Joe has done exactly that, almost on a daily basis, with a cheeky playfulness and innocent smile. But do not be fooled by the choirboy looks, for there is plenty of steel behind the smile.

That steel has been vital in a year-long period of almost continuous international cricket in all three forms. And it was identified very early on in Joe's experience of the England squad dressing room.

"By the time I had arrived in India with the Test squad, it was clear how hard I was going to have to work. I had gone straight from the Champions League with Yorkshire to a training camp in Dubai, and was obviously feeling a bit tired already. But 'Goochy' had me in the nets shortly after I arrived [the England batting coach is renowned for his work ethic and intensity of training]. I would face three balls then run a six. Then he had me carrying bricks as I ran, doing all kinds of exercises between balls. He even had me 'running' a 'two' with my hands palm-down, touching the floor inside upturned Frisbees, sliding them along the floor. I suppose he was seeing what I was made of."

If his ahead-of-schedule selection was anything to go by, Joe was believed to be made of the right stuff. And from that "wake-up call" of a training session onwards, it seemed that he never looked back.

After a winter's cricket full of promise, Joe returned to the County circuit to help kick start Yorkshire's season. And that he did, with a series of match-winning contributions showcasing his accelerated development. He reflects on his time in a Yorkshire shirt as a vital part of his successful summer.

"The knock against Durham was just what I needed", he admitted, referencing his second innings 182 that steered Yorkshire to an improbable victory at The Riverside. "We were in a pickle in the first innings and I could feel things were not going our way. We dropped catches and I remember thinking we needed Jonny, 'Bres' or me to stand up."

His subsequent century was held in the highest regard, not only by the watching England selectors and his title-winning opponents, but by Joe himself. "It was probably my best knock in Championship cricket so far. For me, Jonny and Bres, there was a bigger picture, a goal beyond that game, but I wanted to win games for Yorkshire first and foremost."

Joe would return to the same ground later in the summer, batting in the same opening slot, but with Three Lions on his chest in the Fourth Ashes Test. And though he could not repeat his heroics with the bat, it would prove to be the most special of occasions for him, his first – and perhaps not last – experience of an Ashes series victory.

But opening the batting in Test cricket had proven the sternest of challenges in the preceding weeks, something Joe is quite ready to admit. "Batting in the middle order is noticeably different. Coming off the field after the opposition's final wicket, you can take a shower, have a cuppa, and relax for a while. It's quite refreshing. But going in first, particularly with over 100 overs of fielding in the legs, you've got to be right on your game from ball one."

That would have come as no surprise to Joe, for it had been his weekly routine with Yorkshire, quite often with me 22 yards away at the other end. But the Australian new-ball attack bowled well at him, making him earn every one of his series tally of runs. Again, Joe's reflection is as straight as his down-swinging blade.

"Australia bowled well at us with the new ball, particularly Ryan Harris. He hits the stickers at the top of the bat face hard and you're always mindful of that decent bouncer he's got in him."

Did he agree that the Australian bowlers adopted a clear plan to bowl gradually fuller at Joe as the series went on?

"Yeah, I reckon they did. It was pretty clear that I preferred to 'hang back' – you know I do – so they started to work that out after a while."

So how did that trend influence his preparation for the 'return leg' of the back-to-back Ashes series? After all, he would be back on a plane in a couple of weeks time, en route to the England team's pre-tour training camp. And was countering this mode of attack a key part of the future for Joe Root?

"Well, by all accounts, the wickets in 'Oz' are apparently going to be quick, so only time will tell whether they adopt the same methods. But yeah, I think you're right, playing well off both feet, forward and back, is going to be key. It is certainly something I'm working very hard on in training."

Despite his unquenchable thirst for further international success this winter, Joe remains very much connected to the ambitions of his County side.

"It's been a great year for Yorkshire. Since the disappointment of that opening Championship game against Sussex, we've turned it around quickly and been consistent in four-day cricket throughout the season. It's a shame we've not got over the line to win the Division One title but finishing second is an exciting step in the right direction. This Yorkshire team has more experience than the one that came close to silverware three years ago, and that bodes well for the future.

"It has been great to see the younger lads coming through in the first XI. Lads like Leesy, who has had a fantastic start to his first class career. Because of the pitches we've played

on favouring the bowlers, Gary Ballance has been at the crease earlier than we'd have hoped, but he's shown his ability to start against a newer ball and go on to big hundreds. Add to that Galey's success, coming through a lean patch with the bat to make 1,000 runs. It always helps when your captain does well."

After a year of such personal success, many would forgive this likeable Yorkshire lad for developing an unsavoury sense of self-importance. But the beauty of Joe, and one of the reasons why he will continue to find new levels in his performance, is that he remains grounded and yet ambitious, simultaneously modest and yet confident, generous with his time and yet clear on what he wants. This 22-year-old's qualities extend beyond the batting crease, and that is why I will always be a Joe Root fan.

The season's swan song

In this age of high stakes and fiercely competitive Championship cricket, a four-day match not significantly affecting the immediate future of either side, or "dead-rubber", is no less than a rarity. The majority of County cricket followers would agree that the high-incentive divisional system of Championship cricket, introducing promotion and relegation, has led to a greater quality and a more competitive nature of the game.

However, Durham had upped their game considerably when the bell rang for the final lap of the season, leaving us mathematically incapable of moving higher than second in the table. At the other end of the table, meanwhile, Surrey's torturous summer had resulted in their relegation from the top flight before the final round of fixtures.

So our last match of the season - for much of the summer tipped to be our fairytale finish to the campaign - had little consequence in relation to the final Division One table.

But there was still pride and personal records to play for and, besides that, much to celebrate. Our 150th anniversary season had been a successful one in the competition highest on our list of priorities. Having returned to Division One within a year of relegation, we had produced consistent four-day cricket with bat and ball, and our tally of outright victories may well have been sufficient for silverware in previous seasons. An anniversary year title had been prevented only by a timely surge in the performance of our rivals that had to be respected.

Further to the Club's upbeat reflections, there was news this week of the latest Yorkshire players to receive international recognition and of an overseas signing for the 2014 season.

To no surprise from his newly-made team mates, Kane Williamson agreed to sign a contract to become the Club's overseas player for next year's challenge for silverware. He had made light work of settling into the Yorkshire dressing room, contributing off the field as well as on it, as is so important for an overseas player. And though he had fallen short of scoring his first Yorkshire century in his temporary stay this summer, his average of just over 50 from nine Championship innings was indicative of a batsman making key contributions to our push for the title. Yorkshire followers can look forward to this 23-year-old Kiwi saluting their applause on many occasions next summer.

After a headline-grabbing start to his first class career, Alex Lees had cause for celebration after his inclusion in the England Performance Squad for the off-season to come. Meanwhile, and much to the satisfaction of his team mates and support staff, Gary Ballance was rewarded for his consistency across all formats with a seat on the plane to the winter's Ashes series. After their respective contributions to the Yorkshire cause this summer, both Alex and Gary were very deserving of their recognition.

Gary celebrated the news in sensational fashion with a first innings 148 at The Oval followed by an unbeaten 108 to make him the first Yorkshire batsman ever to score a century in each innings against Surrey. Admittedly, the pitch was flat, the opposition short of the strength they exhibited at Headingley, but the centuries – his fourth and fifth in the summer's Championship - were full of the qualities Gary has amply demonstrated on a regular basis throughout the season. As he saluted the applause of his parents, watching from the stands, talk of Gary's success leading him to a Test debut in the first Ashes Test at The Gabba was already starting to build. On the evidence of the past few months, few could argue with his selection.

Leesy was unable to celebrate in such style, but the team's 10th total in excess of 400 – 434 on this occasion - was a resolute and relieving way to begin the final fixture of the summer.

At 11.18am on the final day of the season, the Yorkshire opening pair of Lyth and Lees walked to the crease for the last time this summer. Little did they expect their second opportunity with the bat to come so late in this fixture, but they would certainly not have predicted the cricket that had gone before.

At the age of 18 years and 21 days, Dominic Sibley had become the youngest player ever to score a double century in the Championship, scoring 242 runs in a vigil lasting just a minute short of ten hours at the crease. He brought up his maiden first class century with a six over long-on, and then continued to make the most of an Oval surface offering negligible help for the ball.

With the placid pitch and the fast bowlers understandably nursing the aches and pains of a summer's toil, Captain Gale turned to an extreme version of a tactic he had previously used to good effect in the Championship. Known as "The Yorkshire Wall", Galey's field setting confronts a batsman with a line of evenly spaced fielders in his view as the bowler approaches. Pushing the theory to its limit on this occasion, Galey had positioned his fielders in a 'wall' extending from 10 o'clock to 2 o'clock in the striker's view. More moderate versions of the field setting had proven a valuable means of keeping catchers in play whilst restricting the run rate on the summer's more docile surfaces, but this was pushing the concept a little far. Whether motivated by curiosity, boredom or experiment, it made for an interesting view of this final fielding stint of the year.

Yorkshire were 67-3 at the lunch break on the final day, still 133 runs adrift after Surrey had declared on 636-5. But the slowness of the players' stroll from the field was indicative of a final match of the season petering out into a draw. For a while in the afternoon, Surrey looked capable of pulling off a shock win - until Ballance asserted his authority. Unsurprisingly, this cricketing week had become a process of counting down the summer's final hours, accepting the ups and downs that had gone before and considering how each side's respective finishing positions would influence their unknown futures.

Our opponents appeared to be on the verge of a threshold in their recent history, the moving on of an experienced and wealthy group of players, and the emergence of a new cooperative of talent, led by players like Dominic Sibley. The only regular Test ground they would be playing on in next summer's Championship may be their own, such is the difference between the two Divisions. But success is cultivated through cycles in professional sport, and this would simply be a phase in said cycle.

For us, our sesquicentennial anniversary season had been a success, at least in the longest form of the domestic game. After a sobering start, our Championship season had provided consistent proof of our standing in the top flight and fallen just short of the fairytale final chapter in the minds of many.

Developing players had graduated to make impressive progress in the early days of their first class careers, whilst familiar faces had contributed match-winning performances when it mattered most.

Meanwhile, whilst our red-ball cricket offered an increasing amount of promise, our limited –overs season continued as it had started, revealing a frustrating trend for team performances that showed encouraging signs but fell significantly short of our opposition's mark. The 2012 season had displayed this Yorkshire squad's ability to win one-day trophies through an effective combination of positive, carefree ambition and high levels of fitness and agility. But both were surprisingly lacking this season, perhaps partly due to our prioritising the Championship somewhat and blooding new talent, but this would be no excuse.

To see the cup half full, we could reflect upon a season of success that had at the same time revealed the lessons we must learn to fulfil our potential next time around. We had played well, very well on some occasions, but could play better, challenging for all trophies in the same year. The County game had become increasingly competitive, with a growing number of sides worthy of ambitions of silverware. Despite strong competition, this Yorkshire crop is able to – and should – win more trophies, and once the celebrations of our season's successes have subsided, this will be the focus of our efforts.

"The Yorkshire Wall"

Those were the days

A reflection by Editor David Warner

As you get swept along in the pages of this book, one thing above all others will strike you forcibly: that Joe Sayers, to misquote G.S. Gilbert, "is the very model of a modern professional cricketer".

His meticulous preparation for every Yorkshire game, his sharp analytical mind and his sincerity of purpose all tell you that here is a man who strives every inch of the way to do his utmost for his team and for himself.

Joe's diary of this special season which marks the 150th anniversary of Yorkshire County Cricket Club not only outlines the peaks and troughs of the summer of 2013 but it also marks him out as a true Yorkshireman and a true Yorkshire cricketer.

Since its formation in 1863, Yorkshire CCC has produced scores of cricketers who wear the White Rose cap with a burning zeal and a chest-bursting pride and Joe is among the foremost of this band of brothers.

Just as importantly he comes across as a very popular member of the first team squad, his colleagues happily accepting that an academic brain that brought him a BA Physics degree at Oxford University is no barrier at all to being simply one of the lads.

To misquote Gilbert again, Joe can say:

I'm very well acquainted too with matters mathematical,
I understand equations, both the simple and quadratical

To a large extent, Yorkshire's cricketers of the present day and age are all managed in very much the same way, reporting back for duty at the beginning of November and then placing themselves in the hands of the coaching and back-up staff until after the last ball has been bowled of the following season.

Personal fitness programmes, training schedules, dietary monitoring and hour upon hour of practising in the nets all lead up to the beginning of April and the battle to make it into the first team.

It's all a far cry from how Yorkshire cricketers would set about their business in the early years of the club's formation and it is fascinating to contemplate how Joe and his contemporaries would have shaped up had they been born in a bygone age and represented their county during the latter part of the 19th century.

In Joe's particular case it is difficult to be entirely sure which gate he would have stepped out of on to the field of play, such were the divisions of class structure in those days. Would it have been the gate used by the players (the professionals) or the one reserved for the gentlemen (the amateurs)?

Let us first assume that Joe would have been one of the early professionals, a man who played cricket to earn an honest crust rather than one who treated the game fondly as a pastime.

Were that the case and were Joe was starting out in Yorkshire CCC's earliest days, then his loyalties may not have been solely focussed on his native county. He could well have been a cricket mercenary, playing for whoever would pay him coin of the realm.

Roger Iddison, for example, was Yorkshire CCC's first official captain from 1863-1872 but during that time the butcher from Bedale also turned out in16 matches for the old enemy across the Pennines, Lancashire! Not only that he captained both sides on occasions but at least he had the decency to lead Yorkshire in all of the Roses encounters.

In August, 1865, Iddison played for Lancashire against Middlesex in Islington and a few weeks later he was back in Yorkshire colours for the fixture with Cambridgeshire at

Ashton-under-Lyne. He also represented both sides in the following season and against Surrey he opened the batting for Lancashire and notched his maiden century.

In addition, he played for England on three occasions and was also to be seen on the team sheet of an All England XI, as well as turning out for Married Men, North of England and the Players.

So, although Joe is an entirely committed Yorkshire cricketer in this day and age, he may well not have been had he been around in the 1860s.

Nor would his diet have been carefully monitored and a calorie-controlled lunch served to him on match days, as is currently the case. The professionals were expected to provide their own food and drink or, if they preferred, they could accept a hunk of bread and a glass or two of ale from hospitable spectators. Sometimes they could tuck in to such an extent that there was a good chance that sobriety would not be as marked after the interval as before it.

Indeed, excessive drink was one reason why Yorkshire were quite an ill-disciplined bunch until Lord Hawke began to sort out the wheat from the chaff – and sometimes the wheat went out with the chaff, as was the case with Bobby Peel, one of Yorkshire and England's greatest left-arm spin bowlers and a batsman good enough to register a double-century.

In 1897, Hawke reluctantly but firmly brought the axe down on Peel's career because of his excessive drinking habits. Ordered by Hawke to leave the field because of an unsteady gait on the final day of the match with Middlesex at Sheffield, Peel was not included in the team for the following day's game with Derbyshire at Bradford after George Hirst had reported to his captain that his friend and colleague was unwell and could not leave his hotel.

But Peel did turn up a bit later on and even took to the field with the chosen XI at which point he was observed by Hawke who instructed: "Leave the field at once, Peel," to which Peel replied: "Not at all, my Lord. I'm in fine form this morning" and proceeded to aim a cunning ball in the direction of the sightscreen, his very last delivery for Yorkshire.

As a pioneering professional, Joe would have just managed to make ends meet in the summer but he could have suffered real hardship in the winter until 1896 when, at the instigation of Hawke – captain from 1883 to 1910 and president from 1898 to 1938 – the Yorkshire committee decided to give winter pay to the professionals at the rate of £2 per week "on the express condition that they do not engage with any club or league during the summer."

Now, let us suppose for a moment, that Joe had not played for Yorkshire as a professional in those early days but as an amateur – which he would almost certainly have done had his Oxford University and Oxford cricket Blue days been 100 or so years earlier than they actually were.

To attend Oxford or Cambridge Universities or public school at Eton or Harrow was a sign of wealth and good breeding and had he gone on to exhibit his cricketing talents for Yorkshire then he would have been down on the scorecard as Mr. J.J. Sayers rather J.J. Sayers which is how the professionals appeared.

He would certainly not have been sharing a spectator's lunch or taking a draught or two of his ale, but who knows what his own lunch hamper might have contained?

Joe would have been addressed courteously by his professional team-mates and he would have been much respected for his obvious talent, without which he would not have remained in the side for very long.

Hawke himself, educated at Eton and Magdalene College, Cambridge University, was a very fine cricketer who played for England five times and organised his own tours abroad, while the Rt. Hon. F.S. Jackson, of Harrow and Trinity College, was brilliant by any yardstick and one of the greatest all-rounders in the golden era of amateurs.

Jackson became England captain in 1905, winning the toss five times out of five against Australia and plundering 144 not out in the Ashes match at Headingley to record the first

Test century on the ground. No wonder he was admired and envied by all when in his Yorkshire colours.

As an amateur, Joe would have taken seriously the responsibility of caring for his professional colleagues and making life more comfortable for them, in the same way that Hawke, Jackson and others of their class certainly did. By his very nature, such 'unwritten' duties would not have been burdensome to Joe.

But back to the present and Joe is very much a part of the recent history of this great Yorkshire club. His meticulous diary of the sesquicentennial season has ensured that the weeks and months of this special summer will never fade into obscurity.

Lord Hawke.

Joseph Sayers.

Fans of Yorkshire County Cricket Club

Derek Agar
Helen Ainsley
J C David Allan
Michael Allison
Chrisopher J Andrews
Andy and James
Peter R Arrand
Will Ash
John Askin
Andrew and Deirdre
Bailey
Matthew R Bailey
Jonny Bairstow
Alan Barber
Peter B Baren
Ian Barton
Olga Beardwood
John Beever
Keith M Bellwood
Roger H Benson
Dorothy Betts
Stuart Black
Richenda Blakelock
Thomas P Booth
Steve Boyde
Anthony Bradbury
Eleanor Bradley
Andrew P Bragg,
Lofthouse, Wakefield
John Bramman
P J Bridges
John Briggs
Matthew Briggs

Peter I Britton
John Broadhead
Roger Brooks
Rupert D E Brown
Peter Brownlow
Adrian J Burton
Stuart Butlin
David J Buttle
Pam Cadman
Richard Cadman
Ken Cant
Lee Cartwright
Phil Catchpole
Rob Champion
Professor J A Child
Paul and Alison Chubb
Howard Clayton
P R Clausen-Thue
Tom "T.C." Clements
Miranda Coates
B J Coates
David Ian Coldwell
Richard Colledge
Steven Common
John Conyers
James D B Cook
David Cooper
Paul F Cooper
John H Corney
Malcolm Coupe
Lawrence Craggs
Mick Croft
Jack Crowther

Ray Currie
Alistair Dales
Adrian Davies
Peter Deighton
Callum Dent
John H Dickinson
George Dixon
Mike Dods
Michael M Dossor
Brian Douglas
Ben Duckworth
Dr Philip E Dunn
Stephen Dunning
Paul Dyson
F Edgeworth
Mr J R Ellis
Betty Fairhurst
Robert Fawthrop
Paul Firth
Paul Fletcher (Fletch)
Carl Foxton
Tony Gale
Tony & Susan Gardner
Mick Gibson
Robert Gilbert
Thomas Robert Giles
Tim Gilfoy
Alan Gill
H Glover
Ian M Goddard
Paul R W Goddard
James Goldthorp
Craig Greensmith

(Greeno)

Steve Grindley (Grinders)

Andrew Guest & Holly Horridge

Terry Hague

John and Billy Haigh (Denby CC)

Rob Hampstead

Arthur Hanley

David Hardisty

Kevin Hardisty

Janet Harker

John Harley

Graham 'bomber' Harris

Peter Haslam

Brian Heald

Jack Leonard Hebden

Denis Heeley

Colin Hickford

William Hickson

David Hills

Jacob Hill

Andrew Hinchliffe

Paul Hindle

Grant Hinks

David Hirst

John Hoather

Jeremy Hockin

Martin Hodgson

Les Hopkin

Peter, Tom and Nick Horsman

John Howe

Martin Howe

Peter Hoyle

David William Hoyle

Roy Humbles

Ian Hunter "The Best Father Ever"

John V Hutchinson

Geoff Illingworth

Jim Illingworth

Peter Ingham

Mark Inman

Haydon Jackson

Scott Jackson

Finley Jarvis

Tony Jenkins

Philip Jennings

Tom Jennings

Robin Jepson

Andrew A Johnson

Ruth Johnson

Trevor Jones

Josh Hope

Andy Kaye

Martin Kettle

Peter Kiddle

Robert Kilby

Iain Kimberley

Michael Knight

Slawomir Michal Kucharek

Joe Lambton

Lane Ends

Douglas H Laurie

Sachin Lavender

Mark David Lawlor

Peter Leather

Janet Leighton

Huw "Scorch" Lloyd

Alastair Mackinnon

George Mallender

Peter Mason

Robert Mawson

Kenneth Merchant

Simon Middleton

Trevor Middleton

Peter Miller

Mary Mills

Derek Milner

Stella & Howard Milner

Peter Mirfield

Gill Moody

John Moorhouse

Jim Moore

Michael Stewart Edward Nevin

Samuel Newton

Craig Farnol Nicholls

John Nilen

Tony Ogley

Edwin J O'Sullivan

Matthew Parker

Keith Parkin

Richard Parkin

Max Perry

Ryan-Joe & Adam Phillips

John Pickering

Don Poulton

Mark Powley

Tony Ptak

Simon Quarrell

John Rawnsley

Gordon Read

Malcolm Reed

Geoff & Sheila Relton

Keith Rhodes

Dennis Richards

Daryl M M Richardson

James Richardson
John Ridge
Andrew Ripley
Christopher Ripley
Adrian Roberts
David and Chris Robbins
William Roberts
Phillip Robinson
David Rogers
Joe Root
W G Rounding
Anthony Ryder
Edward Sadofsky
Melvyn Sadofsky
David Scally
Kevin Scotter
Martin Scott
Tony Scotter
Graham Seabrook
Professor Paul Senior
Dave Shack
James Shaw
Jonathan M Shaw
of Bradford
Andy Sheldon
Joan Sherwood
Peter Shires
Malcolm Short
Gary Alan Skillington
Mick Smalley
Andrew Smith
Barrie Smith
David Smith
Dennis Smith

John & Brenda Smith
John C Smith
Jonathan C Smith
Martyn Smith
Michael Smith
W C Smith
Tim Soutar
Mike Speddy
Robert Speight
Patrick W Spencer
Geoff Stalker
James Stanfield
Colin W Stansfield
The Stathams
David Stead
John Stevens
Robin Johnston Stewart
John Stoney, my Papa
John B W Summerskill
Stephen Suttle
Stuart Sykes
John Neville Tattersall
Darren Taylor
Luke Taylor
Sarah Taylor
Adam Ternent
David N Theaker
Jennifer and Wilfred
Theakstone
Garth Thistlethwaite
Susan Thistlethwaite
Chris Thompson
Don Thompson
Peamen CC
Tara Thompson

Colin Thompson
Don Thompson
Anthony Thornton
Peter Thorp
Tony Thorp
Geoffrey A Tiffney
Chris Timewell
Chris Topping
Robert M Town
Dave Townend
Bill Tunnicliffe
Ken Tunstall
Peter Turner
Andrew Walker
David Ward
John Ward
Stephen Ward
Adrian Wardle
John Watmough
Gordon Webster
Mr & Mrs J H Welbourn
Colin Wickham
Andrew Wigglesworth
Eric W Wild
Peter Wildsmith
Andrew Michael Wilson
Carole Wood
Howard Woodbridge
Richard Worthy
Alice Rebecca Worsley
Gerry Wright
N J Wright
Robin A F Wight
Jillian Young